CATASTROPHIC INCENTIVES

JEFF SCHLEGELMILCH
AND ELLEN CARLIN

CATASTROPHIC INCENTIVES

Why Our Approaches to Disasters Keep Falling Short

COLUMBIA UNIVERSITY PRESS

NEW YORK

Columbia University Press
Publishers Since 1893
New York   Chichester, West Sussex
cup.columbia.edu
Copyright © 2023 Columbia University Press

Library of Congress Cataloging-in-Publication Data
Names: Schlegelmilch, Jeffrey, author. | Carlin, Ellen P., author.
Title: Catastrophic Incentives : Why Our Approaches to Disasters Keep
Falling Short / Jeff Schlegelmilch and Ellen Carlin.
Description: New York : Columbia University Press, [2023] | Includes
bibliographical references and index.
Identifiers: LCCN 2023004573 (print) | LCCN 2023004574 (ebook) |
ISBN 9780231204224 (hardback) | ISBN 9780231204231 (trade paperback) |
ISBN 9780231555432 (ebook)
Subjects: LCSH: Emergency management—Political aspects. |
Disaster relief—Political aspects.
Classification: LCC HV551.2 .S384 2023 (print) | LCC HV551.2 (ebook) |
DDC 363.34/8—dc23/eng/20230501
LC record available at https://lccn.loc.gov/2023004573
LC ebook record available at https://lccn.loc.gov/2023004574

Cover design: Milenda Nan Ok Lee
Cover image: Mega Pixel / Shutterstock

For the disaster professionals throughout government, the private sector, nonprofits, and academia. Your tireless efforts for a more resilient tomorrow should continue to be celebrated as the work of heroes amid the search for ways to place organizational winds more squarely at your backs and further extend the reach and affect of your efforts.

CONTENTS

ACKNOWLEDGMENTS

OUR WRITING of this book and our evolution of understanding the incentives and disincentives that govern disaster prevention and preparedness would not have been possible without the intellectual contributions of many individuals. Ryan Remmel provided exceptionally diligent research support on federal disaster appropriations. Jennifer Alton, William Painter, and Erin Sorrell provided especially helpful perspective and feedback as we researched and wrote many complex sections of the book. Curtis Brown, Stuart Firestein, Jason Friesen, Andrew Weis, and Greg Witkowski agreed to be interviewed and provide feedback on the manuscript. We are deeply appreciative of the time and expertise that all these individuals graciously provided and their contributions to our understanding. We also very much appreciate the enthusiastic support of Caelyn Cobb and Monique Laban, our editorial team at Columbia University Press, in developing this work from idea to book.

ACRONYMS AND ABBREVIATIONS

ASEAN	Association of Southeast Asian Nations
ASPR	assistant secretary for preparedness and response
BARDA	Biomedical Advanced Research and Development Authority
BCG	Boston Consulting Group
BIPOC	Black, indigenous, and people of color
BOLD	Business Opportunities for Leadership Diversity
CCC	Commodity Credit Corporation
CDC	Centers for Disease Control and Prevention
CEPI	Coalition for Epidemic Preparedness Innovations
CSR	corporate social responsibility
DHS	Department of Homeland Security
DRF	Disaster Relief Fund
EID	emerging infectious diseases
ESG	environmental, social, and governance
EU	European Union
FAR	Federal Acquisition Regulations
FEMA	Federal Emergency Management Agency
GADRI	Global Alliance of Disaster Research Institutes
GDP	gross domestic product
HHS	Health and Human Services

IHR	International Health Regulations
ILI	influenza-like illness
INGO	international nongovernmental organization
ISAC	United Nations Interagency Standing Committee
NAAHDRI	North American Alliance of Hazard and Disaster Research Institutes
NFIP	National Flood Insurance Program
NGO	nongovernmental organization
NIH	National Institutes of Health
NRC	Nuclear Regulatory Commission
OCHA	Office for the Coordination of Humanitarian Affairs
OMB	Office of Management and Budget
OTA	Office of Technology Assessment
PAHPA	Pandemic and All-Hazards Preparedness Act
PEF	Pandemic Emergency Financing Facility
PG&E	Pacific Gas and Electric
PKEMRA	Post-Katrina Emergency Management Reform Act
PPE	personal protective equipment
SARS	Severe Acute Respiratory Syndrome
TEPCO	Tokyo Electric and Power Company
TMC	Texas Medical Center
UNSC	United Nations Security Council
USAID	United States Agency for International Development
USDA	United States Department of Agriculture
WHA	World Health Assembly
WHO	World Health Organization
WMD	weapons of mass destruction

CATASTROPHIC INCENTIVES

INTRODUCTION

IN THE first twenty years of this century, disasters affected more than 4 billion people, were responsible for nearly 1.23 million deaths, and cost the global economy more than $2.97 trillion.[1] These staggering figures do not account for COVID-19, a pandemic whose impacts on lives and economies would far exceed, in just a couple of years, these collective two decades of disasters. No global denizen has been left untouched.

Even without the influence of the pandemic, disasters are so common that many people experience them in multiples over the course of their lives. Those left directly unscathed must at a minimum bear witness to the myriad news reports about the destruction disasters have caused. In these ways, disasters come to feel a part of the very fabric of the time in which we live, their impacts exacerbated by the built environment and unequal social structures in which we reside.

The occurrence of disasters is not a modern phenomenon. These events have defined and punctuated history since the beginning of time. Catastrophic natural events battered the planet before humans inhabited it, wiping out early life forms and kick-starting evolutionary processes anew. They continued to do so long after human evolution was underway, with many reminders found in biblical narratives, historical accounts, archaeological sites, and the geological record. Today's human populations continue to experience disasters and catastrophes from natural hazards while also confronting others of our own making, whether through intentional acts of destruction or accidental trips of technological vulnerabilities.

The study of disasters is much more recent than disasters themselves. Samuel Prince's analysis in 1920 of a devastating explosion on a munitions ship in the inner harbor of Halifax three years earlier is often considered the first systematic study of disaster.[2] His work was followed by that of pioneers in the field such as Russell Dynes and Enrico Quarantelli, who wrote some of the most influential treatises on disasters, framing the theory and sociological constructs of disasters within civil society.[3]

In the United States, the operational management of disasters came to fall within the purview of first-responder agencies, as well as some specialized government agencies. It was usually driven as an extension of an existing mission associated with the fire service, the military, or civil defense. There was occasional crossover of academia and the practice community through collaborations among researchers and disaster practitioners. Some complex disasters brought forward challenges significant enough to prompt government reorganization around disaster management.

Disaster management developed and matured intellectually and materially over the course of the twentieth century. In this time the field grew toward greater professionalization and eventually into a career track in its own right.[4] Across this same era, disaster science as a research discipline began to grow and take shape, once again with some cross-pollination between academic pursuits and the operations of the practice community.

Planning took on an increasingly important role as disaster management and science matured. Standards and codes for the built environment for earthquakes, fires, hurricanes, and other natural hazards increasingly became the norm. California's Sylmar earthquake in 1971 took sixty-four lives and resulted in $505 million in damage; it also triggered the development of hundreds of new safety standards and programs across the state for public and private buildings, hospitals, dams, and freeways.[5] Diverse professional communities,

including architecture, urban planning, and federal standards setting, were brought into the fold. The National Institute of Standards
and Technology, in existence since 1906, notably began to advance
the science of standards setting for fire hazards in the 1970s, supported by congressional legislation and an increased political sensi-
tivity to fire hazards in the built environment.[6]

As we write this during a pandemic, a special category of disasters
is at the forefront of our minds: infectious diseases. Outbreaks have
plagued humankind throughout recorded history and undoubtedly
since long before. Historical records show that microbes were among
the primary causes of death in ancient populations, particularly
among infants and children.[7] Infections in ancient people include
many familiar to modern populations—tuberculosis, cholera, malaria,
influenza, yellow fever.

Standing on the marshy shores of the southern reaches of the Hud-
son River in New York City, one would probably be unaware that, in
another time, these beaches would have been a hotspot for contracting malaria. The "malarious" area of the United States was in fact
most of the United States—it cut a wide swath up and down most of
the Eastern seaboard, attacked the center of the country from North
Dakota to the tip of Texas and almost as wide an area from East to
West, and spread across a section of central California hundreds of
miles long. But targeted and persistent public health efforts led by the
National Malaria Eradication Program had eliminated stateside
malaria by 1949.[8] Yellow fever, another mosquito-borne disease, had
terrorized early American colonists. An outbreak in Philadelphia in
1793 caused the federal government to temporarily remove itself to
Maryland, as half the city's inhabitants, including George Washington, fled.[9] The disease was finally eliminated from the United States
in 1905; Europe's trajectory was similar. While both of these infections
are still prevalent in many equatorial parts of the world, their aboli-
tion from huge geographic regions was proof of concept that infectious diseases could be purged.

By the twentieth century, remarkable advances were forcing pathogens further into retreat. The advent of antibiotics, the global distribution of effective vaccines, and the advancement of basic public
health and sanitation improvements created highly effective barriers

between us and the microbes. Humanity had proven that it could take on infectious disease and win.

But just as our biomedical progress was thwarting some of the most serious infectious diseases, other human activity was foiling this headway. New infections were appearing at an increasing frequency, and scientists were coalescing around the idea that what was driving this uptick were our own behaviors—socioeconomic, environmental, and ecological dynamics driven by human activity that were in turn pressuring these pathogens out of their natural reservoirs and into us.[10]

New dynamics of disasters amplified by anthropogenic climate change and other artifacts of human activity are now demanding a sense of urgency in how we look at disasters and the world around us. We live in a modern world that has the illusion of stability and the reality of fragility. We have a tendency to ignore signs of instability as we move through the routines of the world we have created.

As humanity endeavors to identify solutions, we must pay increasing attention to human development and how human activity contributes to disasters.[11] What is nature's versus humanity's role in disasters, in creating the threats and vulnerabilities that can enable and define disasters? Some critics argue that there is in fact no such thing as a "natural" disaster.[12] The lens we use to understand disasters, our vulnerability to them, and their causes influence how we approach prevention and mitigation. The understanding of disasters is being increasingly achieved through a lens of vulnerability, one that identifies the layering of physical hazards on social inequalities as characteristic of the vulnerability problem. This definition of vulnerability comprises sociopolitical elements such as the ability to participate in and experience the benefits of broader development policies.[13]

Most approaches have merit in helping to illuminate different aspects of the disaster landscape. But they also fall short of fully enabling a comprehensive understanding of what motivates disaster-related decision-making (whether before or after disasters), and therefore identifying weaknesses or dysfunction in that decision-making that make us ever more vulnerable to the disasters we seek to avoid. To further understand these dynamics, it becomes necessary to identify the underlying motivators that drive behaviors among sectors involved in dealing with disasters, and the "business models" on which these sectors run. Doing so can help us understand why mission statements, goals, and stated objectives don't always seem to reflect levels of investment in resilience or outcomes after a catastrophe.

A RECIPE FOR DISASTER

The chapters of this book tell a story about disasters and institutional responses to them. This story can help reveal patterns about what does and does not matter to these institutions, on which much of the responsibility for dealing with disasters lies. Time and, in some cases, human activity are driving us into eras when disasters will become more frequent, more intense, or both. Reflexive responses and the one-off patching of holes without correcting underlying pathologies will at best remain inefficient and at worst become a recipe for excess morbidity, mortality, and economic calamity. Identifying the dysfunctions is the first way out of the status quo.

One challenge in the disaster planning space is that risk is often insufficiently or differentially defined. In academia, the hazard faced is explored by the field of study from which it is originating. For the geosciences, the physical hazard becomes the lens of understanding risk, and solutions come in the form of the built environment and early detection. A sociology-based lens may look more at inequalities in representation and access to political capital to reduce vulnerabilities. Governments, like academia, take a compartmented approach across sprawling bureaucracies to manage risk and prepare for disasters. A more holistic approach to understanding risk is lacking when the analysis is overly compartmented, and when perceived certainty is prized over more accurate framing of uncertainty. Financial risk assessment is good at looking at historical losses but does not tolerate uncertainty well; companies and markets create increasingly sophisticated methods built on faulty premises to measure risk, seeking to alleviate the burden of uncertainty at the heart of risk management in a changing world. These methods become standard and undervalue investments that could actually build resilience and alleviate losses downstream. For their part, nonprofits specialize in operations for a certain kind of response, and this specialization challenges them to adapt to new settings unplanned for.

No matter the lens, the data on the risks and vulnerabilities are right there. The warnings are imprinted in reports, in testimony, and in speeches. But there is a lack of action (or proportional action) that leads to a kind of ill-preparedness for disasters. This reality is driven by signals incongruent with overall resilience building. Through voter behaviors that value response over preparedness, and politicians' existential need to keep voters happy, preparedness often gives way to acute needs, which are in fact exacerbated by chronic underfunding of preparedness. Globally this is compounded by national interests and competition among nation-states that lead to positioning for strategic influence within international organizations and in limiting agreements to the lowest common denominator on which they all already agree.

Even when action is taken, and trumpeted as progress, it is often anything but. Nonprofits herald response statistics, and governments hail the speed with which they made emergency dollars available, but these data points do not speak to the root causes of our vulnerability, and how focusing on them at the expense of those vulnerabilities may contribute to increasing hazards. Humanitarian responses are quick to highlight the short-term benefits of their actions, but this obscures the relative absence of value in preventing harm again in the future. Universities that create new degree programs in fields like homeland security when the ink on the legislation has barely dried may seem forward thinking, but with many areas of disaster science still being developed, the actual value of such programs is difficult to measure or predict. Corporate communications teams may highlight corporate climate initiatives, when in fact some of these efforts may have no real impact on climate mitigation.

We tend to be insufficiently receptive to risk before a disaster, then react to the last disaster by seeking to fix the vulnerability most recently exposed. We do this through a patchwork of legislation or new initiatives, and through disbursement of corporate checks to large nonprofits. Beneath these well-intentioned responses lies a failure to ask the tough questions—the ones that require answers we are not prepared to give. Such answers would call into question whether our emergency management structures are properly designed to meet twenty-first-century disasters; whether the private sector should own more of our disaster readiness as part of its cost of doing business; and whether we are just assuming that nonprofits are a net benefit because of their good intentions and adherence to charitable financial practices, instead of asking if we are overreliant on them and over-donating to the wrong end of the disaster cycle. Universities and other educational institutions are not sufficiently questioning if the way we have been teaching and funding science for centuries is not up to the task ahead of us. Governments are not asking if their priorities, whether driven by elections or budgets or by other incentives and disincentives, are the right ones.

The world of today looks little like the world of yesterday. As a result, the institutions we have built across many different sectors are operating on business models that are increasingly obsolete. Through our faith in their historical outcomes, we are sleepwalking into danger instead of consciously steering ourselves toward greater resilience.

UNDERSTANDING THE DISASTER BUSINESS MODEL

This book explores why organizations behave the way that they do in relation to disasters. Its goal is not to criticize the way human institutions respond to disasters, although that is an inevitable by-product of any such inquiry. Rather, it is to better understand the motivations, incentives, and levers of influence that drive our movement toward and away from preparedness, effective response, and equitable recovery.

We approach this first by examining what we define as the "modern era of disaster management." This time period begins with major events of 2001 followed by two decades of seminal events, which we argue have collectively and iteratively driven and defined today's approach to disasters. While some key events—9/11, Hurricane Katrina—are uniquely U.S. disasters, many of the others we have included affected other parts of the globe. We discuss key actions taken by the United States and by international bodies with respect to disasters, while aiming to contextualize the role of the United States vis-à-vis the larger world. While additional events certainly could have been included, we have captured those key events that can reasonably be grouped into "eras" that have continued to reshape and reframe how the world, particularly the United States, is looking at disasters, and how key sectors have adapted to these shifts. We introduce these sectors broadly as government, the private sector (for-profit), the philanthropic sector (including nongovernmental aid organizations), and academia.

We include these sectors as broad categories of actors and influencers that we have seen most directly involved in the disaster cycle domestically and internationally, and with which we have direct experience collaborating. Government most often refers to national governments, but we also discuss state and local governments, as well as intergovernmental organizations such as the United Nations. Private sector refers to for-profit companies, large or small, national or multinational. The nonprofit sector is in some ways the most complex to group into a single term; we approach it as one that comprises nongovernmental organizations that provide funding, those that receive funding for services, hybrids of these two, and nonprofit arms of companies. Collectively we sometimes refer to this as the "philanthropy" sector but urge readers to understand we do not use this term solely in the most common sense of purely fiscal donors. Our focus is primarily on the interface between disaster survivors and the nonprofit assistance community that supports them. By academia, we refer to institutions of higher education that support research, acknowledging that research also occurs in each of the other sectors.

In the second half of this book, we take a closer look at each sector to understand the business model by which it engages in the disaster space. We do this predominantly through a U.S. lens, but with purposeful acknowledgment of key global institutions and dynamics that relate to the issues under consideration more globally. We examine the incentive structures in place that drive decisions on the part of actors in each sector, identifying areas where incentives are missing, or indeed where disincentives are present. The purpose of this analysis is to develop a baseline understanding of each of these sectors that can help foster improvements in the business model that enable more optimal disaster engagement. It is also to advocate for changes in incentives where change is warranted.

These chosen subdivisions are imperfect artifices; there are never clean lines between sectors, and subdivisions within each sector can behave very differently. This book does not purport to be the exhaustive or final word on the ways that they function, but it offers a furtherance of our understanding that can hopefully contribute to more effective disaster programs, whether in research, policy, or practice. There are certainly other sectors not included here that are worthy of exploration, and there is more nuance among the subdivisions of the sectors presented. Ultimately, we seek a more honest relationship between these actors and disaster stakeholders—the people and the communities whose lives and livelihoods are on the line—that is transparent about capabilities and limitations. In doing so, we believe we can build more just and effective systems that truly benefit all.

PART I

A RECENT HISTORY OF DISASTERS

Events, Trends, and Organizational Responses

1

THE BIRTH OF THE MODERN ERA OF U.S. DISASTER MANAGEMENT AND ITS GLOBAL IMPLICATIONS (2001)

I N THE 1970s, complex disasters were bringing forward challenges significant enough to prompt bureaucratic reorganization within the U.S. government that largely created the structures that would remain through the upcoming turn of the millennium. Perhaps the most significant was the creation of the Federal Emergency Management Agency by President Carter in 1979. FEMA was established in recognition that there was a need to consolidate disparate entities and provide a stronger federal approach to disasters, focused on more than merely the "response." It moved the field further into an "all-hazards" approach to emergency management.[1] Still, a problematic complexity and rigidity of federal approaches to disasters remained, particularly for large catastrophes. The response to Hurricane Andrew in 1992, which resulted in legal action and reparations to approximately twenty-one thousand survivors, led to significant rethinking of how we respond as a nation to catastrophic disasters and spurred additional changes to FEMA's policies and procedures.[2]

The next major shift occurred as the century drew to a close, when a new hazard garnered the attention of policy makers. The central moment for the United States in understanding that terror groups based thousands of miles away could successfully target the U.S. homeland and cause their own disasters occurred in 1993. On

February 26 terrorists detonated a 1,500-pound truck bomb on a garage ramp beneath the World Trade Center, killing six people and injuring about a thousand.[3] Six radical jihadists were ultimately arrested for the crime. According to the U.S. State Department, the bombing was the first indication for the Diplomatic Security Service that "terrorism was evolving from a regional phenomenon outside of the United States to a transnational phenomenon."[4]

In 1995 it was home-grown terrorism that caught the nation off guard. Timothy McVeigh and Terry Nichols detonated a truck bomb in front of the Alfred P. Murrah federal building in Oklahoma City. This act resulted in so much carnage—168 lives lost, more than 300 buildings damaged or destroyed, and an estimated of $650 million in total fiscal losses—that in an instant it became the largest terrorist attack in American history.[5]

As the new millennium drew closer, new vulnerabilities seemed to hint at what the coming era was to bring. Attacks on U.S. interests overseas were raising concern in the national security community about a growing threat from Islamic extremism. Bombings of the U.S. embassies in Kenya and Tanzania in 1998 were perpetrated by an Egyptian Islamic jihadist group and linked to al-Qaeda and Osama bin Laden. Two years later, as the navy ship U.S.S. *Cole* refueled in Yemen's Aden Harbor, al-Qaeda launched a suicide bombing on her flank, killing seventeen sailors.

These events were pivotal to the evolution of national security thinking and decision making of the time. The warning signs were heeded—to some extent. The 1993 bombings resulted in modifications to emergency and fire preparedness at the World Trade Center, efforts that involved the Port Authority, the Fire Department of New York, and the buildings' management. Department of Justice grants were issued to help augment security in Oklahoma, a foreshadowing of the major emphasis on homeland security grants that was to come.

But it was the events of September 11, 2001, and the anthrax attacks on its heels that ushered in what we refer to as the Modern Era of Disaster Management. Oklahoma City and the first World Trade Center attacks were jarring locally and nationally, but not to the point of enabling era-defining shifts in the priorities of federal agencies. The modern era of disaster management is rooted in the attack that came next, the worst terrorist attack and one of the worst disasters in American history.

THE 9/11 TERRORIST ATTACKS

Shortly after the turn of the millennium, the growing threat from terrorism and nonstate actors culminated in the largest terrorist attack on U.S. soil. The morning of 9/11 witnessed the crashing of commercial airliners into New York City's iconic World Trade Center towers, in short order leading to their collapse. A third plane was crashed into the Pentagon in northern Virginia, destroying several sections of the building. Owing to a delayed take-off and the heroism of passengers and crew, a fourth flight crashed into a Pennsylvania field rather than a likely intended target in Washington, D.C., killing all aboard but sparing lives on the ground. In the end, 2,977 people were killed that day, with many more succumbing later to environmental and psychological impacts.[6]

The failure of the federal intelligence and security apparatus to foresee the threat—both in an immediate sense and in a larger, strategic sense—made it the burden of emergency responders to deal with once it had manifested. As the National Commission on Terrorist Attacks Upon the United States (known as the 9/11 Commission) report would later reflect, "Emergency response is a product of preparedness. On the morning of September 11, 2001, the last best hope for the community of people working in or visiting the World Trade Center rested not with national policymakers but with private firms and local public servants, especially the first responders: fire, police, emergency medical service, and building safety professionals."[7]

The moniker of responders as "the last best hope" is at once a truthful representation and an undue burden. We hear often that all disasters are local, and this is accurate. But what officials finally began to understand from September 11 and ensuing disasters was that the world was changing so dramatically there was no way responders alone could shoulder the responsibility. On September 11 national policy and planning had failed us, and it was overwhelmingly the responsibility of local actors to deal with the problem. This, of course, was not optimally effective for a disaster of such a massive scale and proved unsustainable under existing disaster management structures.

Readiness couldn't be just about response—it had to be about preparedness and prevention, too. Achieving this would require a "whole of community" apparatus that could work all the elements needed to establish and keep such a system in motion.

But of course, the experience of September 11 was not as neatly defined as it is in concise summaries like this. The day itself and the years that followed it were chaotic and jarring. The existential jolt of September 11, 2001, was perhaps the most dramatic the nation had experienced since December 7, 1941. The Pearl Harbor tragedy woke U.S. political leadership and military brass to the realities of a global war from which they could no longer escape involvement. In a few short years, the military assets of the United States had expanded intensely to meet that challenge, and by 1947 a new department—the Department of Defense—had come into existence.

September 11 woke the political and security communities to the realities of a global terrorism threat that had been knocking at the door for some time. The 9/11 Commission found that the institutions of authority "did not understand how grave this threat could be, and did not adjust their policies, plans, and practices to deter or defeat it."[8] After 9/11, that is precisely what they did. Arguably every intelligence, security, and defense apparatus at all levels of government was drafted into the new service of protecting the homeland from any future insult that could look anything like 9/11. By 2003 a new department—the Department of Homeland Security—had been established for this purpose.

THE AMERITHRAX CRISIS

The shifts that occurred as a result of that single day in September were unavoidable in the aftermath of the attacks. There was no way to circumvent the dramatic turns in priorities, focus, and funding the attacks had set in motion. But we weren't done. Another attack in the weeks that followed again terrorized America and triggered its leaders into actions that would further redefine the era that was to come.

The anthrax attacks that occurred on the heels of 9/11 were quiet and insidious. As Americans went about their post-9/11 response and recovery activities—everything from digging through the rubble for human remains to reopening bridges, tunnels, and businesses in an effort to restore some semblance of normalcy—an infection was breaching the fragile veneer. Reports began surfacing of an individual in Florida who had died of inhalation anthrax—an exceptionally uncommon event, especially in the United States—and of threatening letters delivered to reporters in New York and policy makers in Washington, D.C. While the story unfolded in the coming weeks with more details, more deaths, and more paralysis, Americans were yet struggling to understand the events of September 11, which were still reverberating in their daily lives and in the decisions occurring in the nation's capital, as they would for many years.

Someone had taken anthrax spores, spun them into a fine powder, and mailed them. This person or persons not only used *Bacillus anthracis* as a weapon but turned the unwitting United States Postal Service against the United States. This act in its way was akin to the terrorists who had transformed a peaceful engine of commerce—commercial jetliners—into a weapon. The fabric of the world we had built to serve our needs and wants was being used against us.

The U.S. government never made an arrest in what came to be known as the Amerithrax case. Its primary suspect—Bruce Ivins, a U.S. Army scientist—committed suicide. The case played out over weeks, which turned into months and years, without a firm conclusion. While the Federal Bureau of Investigation's official position is that Ivins was the culprit, this is not a unanimously accepted conclusion.[9] It does appear, however, that most if not all lines of investigation led to strong evidence for a domestic perpetrator, not a foreign terrorist.

Amerithrax forced America into an even more dramatic reimagination of the existential threats to its security. It added a new layer to the now clear-and-present danger from al-Qaeda and other terror groups. Not just that, this one appeared to have come from an insider—an American. At once we were dealing with transnational terrorists and domestic terrorists. And their weapons ranged from microscopic life forms to jetliners and skyscrapers.

It is difficult to imagine a time more disruptive to national security. It was a one-two punch that forced decision makers to reassess their priorities, their processes, and their level of risk acceptance. Anthrax took the lives of 5 individuals, compared to the 2,997 who died on September 11. But it instilled a kind of terror in people that is historically unique to infectious disease, to the way we process an unseeable enemy.[10] Amerithrax required officials to dramatically reconsider their assumptions about biological threats and how the federal government, with partners at all levels from within and outside the government, needed to handle them.

A GOVERNMENT REORGANIZED

On October 8, 2001, President George W. Bush created the Office of Homeland Security, with the mission to coordinate a national strategy to secure the nation from terrorism, to "coordinate the executive branch's efforts to detect, prepare for, prevent, protect against, respond to, and recover from terrorist attacks within the United States."[11] This was just one of many executive actions designed to pivot and reimagine the security apparatus of the nation toward the threat of terrorism.[12]

The USA PATRIOT Act was among the first legislative volleys to reorganize the way the government would now attempt to prevent and respond to disasters, particularly terrorist-driven disasters and other incidents. This bill became law on October 26, 2001—six weeks after 9/11—passing the House by a wide margin (357–66) and the Senate by a nearly unanimous vote (98–1).[13] The law was heavily focused on the detection and prevention of acts of terrorism. It set up new mechanisms for collaboration among law enforcement and removed barriers for investigation and detainment of suspected terrorists and their supporters. It revised and bolstered state and local terrorism preparedness programs funded by the Department of Justice, programs that would later become part of the yet-to-be-established Department of Homeland Security. It also set the stage for subsequent homeland security legislation. It included, for instance, a section titled "Expressing the Sense of the Senate Concerning the Provision of Funding for Bioterrorism Preparedness and Response."[14] The anthrax attacks were still unfolding as this bill was written and moving through the legislative process, but the authors did not miss the opportunity to set down a marker. Through these expressed concerns, the requirements for future bioterrorism preparedness monies were beginning to take shape.

Passage of the Homeland Security Act of 2002 paved the way for the creation of the Department of Homeland Security (DHS).[15] This consolidation of twenty-two federal agencies and offices into a new cabinet-level department is widely considered the largest reorganization in American government since the Goldwater-Nichols Act reorganized the Defense Department in 1986.[16] The agencies absorbed included the Coast Guard, the Secret Service, FEMA, and numerous Department of Justice programs.[17] These were long-standing agencies and programs—the Coast Guard was born in 1790—and well-rooted and well-established bureaucracies that in short order were forced to work as part of a new unit. The act also prompted a total reimagination of border security with the dissolution of existing structures and the creation of new immigration, transportation, and border security agencies.

While the reorganization had bipartisan support, the trauma it caused was occurring within administrative and political structures unready to accommodate such a massive restructuring of bureaucracy. The creation of DHS after 9/11 was a very big, very public way to demonstrate action in the face of adversity. It wasn't just messaging—it certainly was meant to solve a problem—but there was a lot of debate over whether it was the right way to solve that problem. Andrew Weis, a homeland security expert and former Capitol Hill staffer interviewed for this book, said, "You know, they created the Department of Homeland Security by moving boxes around, whether it was the right move or not," noting that a lot of effort did go into trying to make the department work once it was established.

But fashioning partnerships often took precedence over actual security concerns. For years after DHS's creation, according to Weis,

"You had departments and agencies wanting to get back their old pro-grams and funding," many of which didn't like being a part of DHS. Further, the government was increasingly moving into the role of stan-dard setter, but not necessarily of fiscal sponsor of local efforts. The decentralized approach of managing a federalist democracy had to give way to more centralized leadership—but to what extent, and with what degree of fiscal support, was cause for confusion. It was 2003 before federal funding to defray the costs of new security require-ments began to emerge through more formalized programs, and the Homeland Security Council (later integrated into the National Secu-rity Council) began to provide planning guidance.[18]

Funds were initially distributed through grant programs in the absence of a grounding in a national plan for homeland security. The PATRIOT Act required at least 0.75 percent of the total grant funds available annually to be appropriated to each state. It sounds like a small amount, and, while the idea was to ensure a measure of broad distribution across the states, in practice it meant that the funds were often disproportionately allocated to states with very small popula-tions. In fiscal year 2005 Wyoming received $18.23 per capita under the State Homeland Security Grant Program, while larger and arguably higher-risk states like New York received less than $3 per capita. The Urban Area Security Initiative was, at the time, the only risk-based grant and was exempt from the minimum threshold for states set in the act.[19]

Often the funds received did not adequately cover the costs for which local governments were most in need of support. There were restrictions against use for police overtime, and states (which received and managed the federal funds) steered locals to buy certain equip-ment that was not always considered vital at the local level. As policy makers began to evaluate the various funding programs to assess how well they were and weren't working, they also began to consolidate some of the disparate funding programs, the beginning of a trend toward increasing consolidation.[20] Over the coming years many smaller grant programs would be consolidated into the larger State Homeland Security Grant Program and the Urban Area Security Initiative.

Congress also reorganized itself to some extent around the terrorism problem. It established a dedicated Committee on Homeland Security in the House and added responsibility to the standing Committee on Governmental Affairs in the Senate. This process was characterized by an unwillingness on the part of many other committees to cede their jurisdiction. As a result, the new Department of Homeland Security ended up having to report to more than a hundred committees and subcommittees (compare that to the Defense Department's thirty-six).[21] In addition to the enormous administrative pressure this placed on the department (in 2009, DHS reported that it spent sixty-six work years and $10 million responding to congressional inquiries[22]), this kind of fractured jurisdiction meant and continues to mean that some things simply don't get done because committees cannot agree on jurisdiction.

The legislative deluge didn't stop with antiterrorism laws and grant programs. The passage of the Public Health Security and Bioterrorism Preparedness and Response Act of 2002 ushered in a new era in biodefense and public health preparedness programs. Its initial five-year authorization called for $2.4 billion in the first year, $2 billion in the second, and as-needed appropriations in the following years to, among other activities, upgrade facilities at the Centers for Disease Control and Prevention (CDC), purchase smallpox vaccine, expand the national stockpile of medical supplies and other countermeasures, and provide grants to state and local governments to improve healthcare sector readiness, specifically among hospitals for preparing for "bioterrorism and other emergencies." It also created new mechanisms for regulating and tracking facilities working with biological agents with the potential for misuse and outsized harm. It included provisions to protect the nation's food supply through new import restriction powers for the Food and Drug Administration and required vulnerability assessments for public water systems.[23]

The passage of the Intelligence Reform and Terrorism Prevention Act in 2004 dramatically reimagined and realigned the community of disparate intelligence agencies. The position of director of national intelligence was created to directly serve the president and to oversee sixteen agencies defined as part of the broader intelligence community. The act also created the National Counterterrorism Center as a central inter-agency hub focused on threats to U.S. interests domestically and abroad. This law, along with a variety of executive orders, transformed the intelligence community in the hopes of enabling greater coordination across agencies and creating new tools in the fight against terrorism.[24] It was big, but it stopped short of the full cabinet reorganization and hierarchical shift that had occurred under the Homeland Security Act.

Globally, new regulations in the interests of security and transnational cooperation to prevent and prosecute terrorism began to emerge. With the specter of bioterrorism and the emergence of diseases like severe acute respiratory syndrome (SARS) that had pandemic potential, the World Health Organization developed and adopted revisions to the International Health Regulations in 2005 that became binding in 2007. This creation of clearer obligations for member states for disease reporting and response has been hailed as a new era in health governance, although it has not always lived up to expectations. Global shipping came under international frameworks through the World Customs Organization, bilateral and multilateral agreements, and mutual recognition among countries of new security programs.[25] New efforts also emerged to combat terrorism, such as by going after financing through a variety of supranational vehicles, with mixed success. One critique of the European Union (EU) noted that while the much of the conversation was taking place among European Union (EU) countries, the union lacked much of the executive decision making authority needed to regulate its members, thus requiring much of the actual implementation to be left to its member states.[26] For its part, the U.S.-led coalition worked with and without international institutions like the United Nations, ultimately sidestepping the U.N. Security Council when its perceived national security interests were not going to be accommodated by the member states.

ECONOMIC AND PRIVATE-SECTOR IMPACTS

The private sector was, of course, not immune from the rippling effects of September 11. Most directly, the attack resulted in a significant if temporary loss of productivity in the directly affected areas. One analysis of New York City found that the number of jobs available in the city was as much as seventy-one thousand lower than it would have been without the attacks, with positions in financial services, air transportation, hotels, and restaurants making up the largest proportion of this deficit. Lifetime earnings losses of those killed reached approximately $7.8 billion. This, in addition to the damage, cleanup, and rebuilding costs, led to an estimate in 2002 of between $33 and $36 billion in economic losses in New York City alone.[27]

Direct impacts, however, were relatively short-lived. Initially it was believed that nationally, the attacks pushed the already-weak economy into a recession. A retrospective analysis finds otherwise, in part because of the myriad federal actions taken to mitigate impacts. The Federal Reserve took steps to ensure liquidity, and support from foreign central banks helped to stabilize the dollar and further limit global economic impacts. There was some trade disruption due to border closures, and spikes in oil prices. But on the whole, these were limited and temporary.[28] The U.S. government also responded swiftly to stabilize certain industries, such as with the Air Transportation Safety and System Stabilization Act, which passed only eleven days after 9/11 and authorized loans and other means of assistance to the airline industry.[29] With these and other economic stabilization efforts, the private sector found itself thrust into the front line as both potential target of terrorism and partner in response.

Homeland security is about keeping people safe and secure, which can be achieved only through the protection of critical infrastructure. With 85 percent of the national critical infrastructure owned or operated by the private sector, it became even more incumbent on industry, not just government, to invest in security across a wide range of industries, from transportation to banking, agriculture, food, water, public health, emergency service, and postal services, among others.[30] The private sector found itself at once responsible for helping to secure critical infrastructure while being on the receiving end of the massive influx of dollars needed to do so. Companies that could develop processes, services, and technologies to support those security goals found a major new market opening up.

Like any major government reorganization, this one created entirely new industries in its wake. *Forbes* reported in 2004 that a security-industrial complex was rapidly emerging, witnessed through a new security tech boom and more than eight hundred companies packing exhibit aisles at the American Society for Industrial Security in Dallas that year.[31] A revolving door of early DHS and other biodefense officials were scooped up by consulting firms, contractors, lobbying groups, and other organizations seeking to inherit the knowledge and have an edge in emerging opportunities in a post-9/11 world.[32]

NEW ROLES AND OPPORTUNITIES FOR NONPROFITS

With most of the nation struggling to cope with what had just happened, bearing witness to this tragedy in twenty-four-hour news cycles and interrupted media programming, the donations poured in. It is estimated that as many as two-thirds of American households donated to a charity in the wake of 9/11, as much as $2.7 billion. Much of the money was intended to be used for cash assistance, services to families of those killed, and other support for those who lost livelihoods as a result of the attacks, with some planned for long-term support such as mental health services, scholarships, and employment assistance. The money passed through a narrow spigot: of the billions raised, about 70 percent went to just thirty-five charities.[33]

In many ways, the American Red Cross, perhaps the most visible and well-known charity in the United States, became emblematic of the windfall and the perils of nonprofits in the new millennium. Some estimates purport that as much as half of the 9/11 donations went to this single nonprofit. What's more, the Red Cross was presented with a major opportunity to replenish the national blood supply—one of its core functions being blood banking—because so many Americans were donating blood in response to the attacks. But with the influx of generosity came challenges in managing this new reality. The Red Cross became involved in one of the largest scandals to date involving nonprofits: less than a third of the approximately $543 million raised to help survivors and families of those killed had been distributed by the time of the chief executive officer's resignation by the end of 2001.[34]

In addition to the new funding and assistance dynamics within which charities began operating, charities themselves came under scrutiny as part of efforts to combat the global financing of terrorism. As scrutiny of charities grew during the war on terrorism, many changed their portfolios of services, eliminating some that could potentially bring them into conflict with new or anticipated regulations.[35] This included a notable decrease in giving and opening of new Muslim charities, and reductions in activities in areas in close proximity to terrorism hotspots in the Middle East. Many charities complied with new laws and regulations through revising due diligence procedures, reviewing terrorist lists regularly, and including antiterrorism language in their contracts. As they sought to comply, a tension between compliance and allowing increased intrusion by government officials into charitable giving grew. This tension was not new but was heightened in the post-9/11 antiterrorism climate.[36]

KNOWLEDGE GAPS AND THE ROLE OF ACADEMIA

Academia's response to 9/11 was overwhelming and immediate. While the sector had always had a role in understanding disasters, the post-9/11 environment thrust many institutions into the field with dedicated programs and a level of engagement and influence on policy that persists to this day. Academia became a much larger and more present actor in the disaster space in an unprecedented way. Large numbers of new courses were introduced. The University of California at Los Angeles posted fifty new courses on terrorism in the 2001–2002 academic year. George Mason University saw enrollment in courses on the history and psychology of terrorism increase from thirty-five to five hundred students. Subjects related to weapons of mass destruction (WMD) and to studies of Islam dominated new offerings among academic institutions. In the ensuing years, new courses led to new programs and degrees. The Naval Post-Graduate School launched a master's degree in homeland security in 2003, and American Public University established a bachelor of arts major in the same subject. All told, there were suddenly dozens of programs across twenty-nine colleges and universities, ranging from awarded diplomas to undergraduate and graduate degrees.[37] There was a new appetite to learn about terrorism and homeland security, and academia responded to meet this demand.

Accompanied by the surge in courses was a surge in research funding. Research efforts increased in academia (and industry) in the fields of forensics, biodefense, cybersecurity, infrastructure, energy, WMD, and the study of terrorism itself. The science and technology budget of the newly created DHS hit its peak in 2006 at $1.3 billion, with billions more contributed by agencies such as the National Science Foundation, the National Institutes of Health, the Department of Health and Human Services, the Department of Energy, and the Department of Defense.[38] Much of this money supported research at academic institutions.

A twenty-fold increase in biodefense spending in the coming years led some, years later, to consider whether there was an emerging biodefense industrial complex. In just a few years there were at least six new scientific advisory boards focused on biological research related to national security, new journals dedicated to the topic, and special biodefense sections in existing journals. The National Institute of Allergy and Infectious Diseases "Strategic Plan for Biodefense Research" in 2002 committed $1.7 billion for the construction of research laboratories at regional Centers of Excellence.[39]

Initial research specific to terrorism was focused on relatively narrow goals of understanding terrorists' motivations and behaviors and gradually grew more sophisticated. The early years were tainted with an influx of newcomers into the field, who, at least initially, took part in a discourse that became filled with self-proclaimed "experts" who were not truly scholars but rather advocates and pundits.[40] The academic interest in terrorism by many was relatively short-lived, with as many as 83 percent of articles published after 9/11 being by one-time contributors to the subject, and 80 percent by single authors, suggesting (although not necessarily guaranteeing) a lack of collaborative expertise and depth in research outputs. Some of this may owe to the difficulty in collecting primary data and other methodological challenges.[41]

While funding declined with time, academic institutions remained dependent on federal awards for homeland security research. Some have argued that the alliance that grew between institutions of higher education and national security eroded the ability to provide objective criticism of national security policy and institutions or otherwise created an environment that was not conducive to what were perceived as unpatriotic views.[42]

———————

National security professor Erik Dahl argued that the real problem with 9/11 was that "in the years leading up to 9/11, national-level decision makers were insufficiently receptive to the warnings they received about the threat from bin Laden. This suggests that even if tactical intelligence on the threat had been available, it is unlikely that policy makers would have been prepared to listen and take the actions necessary to stop the attacks."[43] The same is arguably true of all the sectors that suddenly responded in its aftermath, awakening to the challenges of the new century.

The beginning of the twenty-first century ushered in a new era of disaster management intentioned both to respond to revealed vulnerabilities and to get ahead of perceived future threats. This era would bring with it a flood of new resources and an urgency of action prompted by the realization of how vulnerable we were to adversaries looking to do us harm. But in our rush to build new paradigms for managing disasters and our obsession with acts of terrorism, a growing vulnerability to natural hazards and the trauma of reorganization led to the next phase in our realization: that responding to the most recent disasters would leave us ill prepared for the disasters to come. Most of the disasters described in the coming chapters tell a story similar to 9/11. They demonstrate a receptivity that is often post-hoc and that misses opportunities to address underlying vulnerabilities in the very way we govern.

2

A PANDEMIC WARNING, EARTHQUAKES, TSUNAMIS, HURRICANE KATRINA, AND A BIRD FLU (2002–2007)

THE SEMINAL events of the early 2000s created fundamental shifts in the disaster preparedness and response culture. From 2002 through 2007, a series of catastrophes and near-misses spurred new thinking on what the threats were and how they might be better addressed. The government reorganized itself against what it viewed as the most pressing hazard of the day. This affected political priorities, the writing of laws, where the money went, and how disaster management agencies from top to bottom were oriented toward the threat.

The events of that brief but pivotal period also embroiled the United States in a War on Terror in the Middle East and South Asia from which it is still struggling to emerge. The war was, and is, an effort to interrupt adversary-driven disasters at their source. And for the most part, the nation has avoided the stateside Islamic jihadist-driven terrorism that those wars were designed to avert. But it has been at significant costs to lives and livelihoods within and beyond the United States, with questionable long-term achievement of the objectives and the creation of new vulnerabilities in their wake.[1]

While our focus shifted to acts of terror and adversaries, the threat of natural hazards nurtured itself unabated. New disasters were lurking. Our population continued to grow, and our infrastructure continued to crumble, combining to make us more vulnerable. While the United States engaged in battling terror overseas and, from stateside, securing the homeland, nature was preparing an onslaught of earthquakes, tsunamis, catastrophic hurricanes, and a deadly avian flu. But first, even before these disasters and just as the new paradigms for antiterrorism were shifting into gear in 2002, a pandemic coronavirus was readying itself for its own entrance. It was not the COVID-19 pandemic that would emerge nearly twenty years later but an earlier coronavirus that public health professionals in a post-COVID-19 world now refer to colloquially as "SARS-1."

SARS: A BULLET DODGED

In November 2002 an unusual respiratory syndrome began appearing in Guangdong Province, China.[2] By February 2003 the infectious pneumonia had reached Hong Kong, Vietnam, and Canada. Clinical features were severe in some patients and included fever, pneumonia, cough, pneumomediastinum (air in the space between the lungs), and pneumothorax (air leakage out of the lungs and into the chest cavity). In one study in Hong Kong, the average hospital length of stay was twenty-one days.[3] From November 1, 2002, until July 11, 2003, what came to be known as severe acute respiratory syndrome, or SARS, spread to thirty-two countries and caused 8,437 reported cases, among which 831 died.[4] The apparent 10 percent case fatality rate was shocking.

The pathogen was fast moving, exploiting global commerce routes to reach beyond Asia to island nations of Australia and New Zealand, and then to Europe, Africa, North America, and South America. It was the first pandemic of the twenty-first century. It tested how well prepared the global community was to confront a high-consequence respiratory pathogen as health officials scrambled to contain it. And that's what they did: SARS disappeared, almost as quickly as it emerged. By July 2003 the outbreak was over.

A review by the U.S. Institute of Medicine found that the medical community was taken by surprise that a coronavirus like this had emerged in healthy adults.[5] Human coronavirus infection to that point had been limited to strains that caused variants of the common cold. It was worrisome, and experts came to perceive it as a bullet dodged, a warning.

SARS turned out to be the first in a line of emerging outbreaks that would redefine the paramount threats of the new century. Global governance bodies heightened their focus on infectious disease. In May 2003—the outbreak still happening—the World Health Assembly of the World Health Organization (WHO) issued a draft of revised regulations. These had already been under development, but SARS prompted a new urgency, a sense of concern that "experiences following the emergence and rapid international spread of severe acute respiratory syndrome (SARS) have given concrete expression to the magnitude of these challenges, the inadequacy of the current Regulations, and the urgent need for WHO and its international partners to undertake specific actions not addressed by the Regulations."[6] The assembly adopted the revised regulations in 2005. The many changes addressed a range of weaknesses in the prior regulations, from their extremely narrow disease scope (only cholera, plague, and yellow fever outbreaks required notification to WHO) to the lack of formal mechanisms for coordinated global response. They marked a milestone of enhanced global focus on emerging infectious disease.

THE INDIAN OCEAN EARTHQUAKES AND TSUNAMI

On December 26, 2004, the seafloor 250 kilometers south-southeast of Banda Aceh, Indonesia slipped. Thirty kilometers down, a 1,200 kilometer stretch of the Indian plate thrust up beneath the Burma plate, raising the seafloor by several meters.[7] This seismic event released energy equivalent to approximately twenty-three thousand times that of the atomic bomb dropped on Hiroshima.

Waves began spreading across the ocean. When the resulting tsunami hit Sumatra, it was ten meters high. It continued to travel as far as Thailand, Sri Lanka, and Somalia, reaching a height of four meters. As the waves moved inland, more than 200,000 people died. The world launched a colossal relief effort, historic in its proportions, donating more than $6.25 billion to a centralized United Nations fund for the response.[8] Indonesia received more money than other nations, being the hardest hit given its proximity to the origin event.

A representative from the London-based Overseas Development Institute, a think tank, was quoted as saying that the distribution of the funds to Indonesia only added to national inequities: many people there were already suffering from poverty and conflict, but the aid went only to the areas specifically affected by the tsunami.[9] The dynamics of individual donorism enabled both relief and problems: tens of millions of individuals throughout the world gave personal donations to nonprofits and response organizations. In some cases, the private donations (individual and corporate) surpassed aid commitments from donor governments such as those of the United Kingdom, the United States, Italy, and Germany. This, along with the wide geographic area of impact, created new stressors and exacerbated old ones in international aid in areas of operational duplication, ensuring pledges turned into actual aid, and overwhelming areas recovering from the tsunami with a cacophony of aid organizations looking to help.[10]

The areas affected by the tsunami were large commerce centers, particularly with regard to tourism, and most prominently in Thailand, Sri Lanka, and the Maldives. Phuket, Thailand, alone boasted 119 hotels, including those from well-known international chains. Only 20 percent of the hotels in Phuket sustained damage, but a mass exodus of tourists and cancellations led to an 85 percent decline in tourists by January 2005. This translated into 10 percent occupancy in hotels, rebounding only to 40 percent by that August. As part of a growing trend of "corporate social responsibility," the global hotel industry responded by allocating donations to support hotel employees and families. Hilton pledged an initial $354,000, Accor staff collected $840,000, and Best Western committed $1,000,000 to relief efforts, among others in the industry. With all this aid, it is not clear how much finally reached those in need; there were reports of bureaucratic, political, and other barriers to money actually getting to those for whom it was intended.[11]

The Indian Ocean tsunami was the deadliest in recorded history. Another of that magnitude is not expected to occur for six hundred years. The scale of the event nevertheless prompted the development

of efforts in the region to reduce the risk from future disasters, including improvements to early warning systems, evacuation planning,
and public education. Earthquakes have continued to hound the
region, and some have produced tsunamis. Results have been mixed.
Early warnings were sounded, and some evacuation efforts were successful, while others were characterized by panicked traffic jams of
the kind that resulted in fatalities in 2004.[12]

HURRICANE KATRINA:
THE NEXT BIG U.S. INFLECTION POINT

The first few years following the terrorist attacks of 2001 in the United
States were fairly quiet with respect to disasters from natural hazards.
There had been a tremendously damaging storm in June 2001—Tropical
Storm Allison, which deluged the Texas Gulf coastline but resulted in
little change at the national level. What it did result in were in twenty-
two fatalities, seventy-three thousand damaged residences, and
more than $5 billion in property damage, $2 billion of which was
incurred by the Texas Medical Center.[13] It caused catastrophic flooding at TMC institutions, including the Baylor College of Medicine, the
Texas Heart Institute, and the University of Texas Health Science Center at Houston. The flash flooding killed roughly thirty-five thousand
laboratory animals—rodents, primates, rabbits, dogs—as their care-
takers risked their lives wading in waist-deep water to try to save
them.[14] Housing research animals in basements, it turned out, was not
good disaster planning.

But as tragic as Tropical Storm Allison was, things didn't really
start to shift until 2004. The hurricane season that year saw four major
hurricanes in the span of only six weeks. All hit Florida, affecting
nearly every part of the state. This brief but impactful series of events
led to many eye-opening moments for policy makers and the public.
Commentators used these events to note how government and the
public interact with regard to preparedness and response, and whether
that relationship was optimal. Although many emergency management systems were significantly stressed, in truth they would not
reach their breaking point until the following year.[15]

Hurricane Katrina in 2005 quickly became one of the costliest and among the five deadliest hurricanes ever to hit the United States. Initially crossing over southern Florida as a Category 1 hurricane, it later grew to a Category 5 in the Gulf of Mexico, before weakening to a Category 3 as it made landfall in Louisiana and Mississippi. The death count varies and may never be fully known, but estimates from state reports put the toll at around 1,833 people. The majority of the deaths were caused by the storm surge, levy breaches, and utter destruction in parts of New Orleans. The number of deaths elsewhere was not insignificant.[16] As radar images of the monstrous storm gave way to images of widespread destruction and people clinging to their roofs amid floodwaters while awaiting rescue, a new disaster was unfolding: the response itself.

A report from the Select Bipartisan Committee to Investigate the Preparation for and Response to Hurricane Katrina, titled *A Failure of Initiative*, was damning in its conclusions about federal, state, and local officials. It faulted then-Louisiana governor Kathleen Blanco and New Orleans mayor Ray Nagin for delaying the ordering of an evacuation until nineteen hours before landfall, when there was adequate warning a full fifty-six hours prior to landfall. The review also found that a failure to anticipate conditions after landfall delayed evacuations and support. This likely "led to preventable deaths, great suffering and delays in relief." Communication issues arose at all levels owing to downed communication infrastructure without planned alternatives, as well as confusion from lack of information, planning, and coordination. The report also found that key elements of the national response plan were not executed, were executed poorly, or were not executed in a timely manner. In short, our national, state, and local response systems were not ready for a catastrophic event of this magnitude.[17]

Charitable organizations were able to help many in need but were also overwhelmed by the size of the response and by logistical and organizational limitations. The Select Committee's report noted that the American Red Cross received substantial criticism, probably owing in part to it being the only charity that had specific responsibilities enumerated under the National Response Plan, and in particular its designated role as leader of the Mass Care Emergency

Support Function (the group responsible for providing shelter, among other services, in a disaster). The implementation of sheltering was uneven and, at times, disorganized. Many criticized the intense bureaucracy for establishing and managing shelters as part of the problem, while some acknowledged that many shelters were difficult or dangerous to reach. The report went on to recognize that "Katrina was bigger than the Red Cross" and noted how its enormity overwhelmed the available resources and was comparatively unprecedented in U.S. modern history. To put it in perspective, the recent series of four hurricanes in Florida were attended by 35,000 volunteers; for Katrina, approximately 220,000 were needed. Of course, the Red Cross was not the only game in town. Important assistance was provided by other charities, including the Salvation Army, Catholic Charities, the United Way, and the National Voluntary Organizations Active in Disaster. And similar to the Red Cross, there were plenty of failures and lessons learned.[18]

In the shadow of so many government and humanitarian response failures, the role of the private sector in whole community response became clearer. Some organizations, particularly companies like Walmart and Home Depot, were lauded for their ability to get supplies to affected areas within hours of the storm passing, reaching evacuees outside of the affected area, and getting businesses reopened quickly both to aid local disaster recovery and to get people back to work. McDonald's closed more than five hundred restaurants and had 80 percent operating again within a week. Walmart closed 2 distribution centers and 126 stores, yet both centers and all but 10 stores reopened within 10 days. These kinds of successes led the way toward increased private sector involvement in disasters from natural hazards in the future.[19]

What came later from the failed response to Hurricane Katrina was a look at the trauma of the absorption of FEMA into the recently created DHS. Prior to the existence of DHS, FEMA had been an independent agency responsible for managing the federal response to disasters in the United States since its creation in 1979. What Katrina began to expose was an agency weakened by infighting within DHS, with various departments jockeying for power and authority, all the while with a FEMA administrator who was arguably unqualified due to a lack of experience as a leader in emergency management, but who was also fighting the erosion of disaster preparedness responsibilities within the agency.[20]

The notion of preparedness in its latest terrorism-focused iteration was also becoming overly myopic, while broader disaster recovery was becoming too complex for existing paradigms. A report from the National Academies of Science, Engineering and Medicine observed in examining Louisiana State University Health Sciences Center's recovery efforts that "LSUHSC's experience suggests that FEMA was more accustomed to relatively simple mitigation proposals, such as elevating a damaged piece of equipment above the flood water level, and installing storm shutters over broken windows." The report also said that in the experience of LSUHSC, "the greatest delays in securing FEMA-approval [sic] were in the two largest projects that proposed the most complex and sophisticated mitigation measures—taking approximately eight years to secure FEMA-approval [sic] and funding of these permanent repairs and hazard mitigation measures."[21] Those directly affected by these disasters bore the brunt of the missteps. Many households exposed to Hurricane Katrina and subsequent Gulf Coast disasters continue to suffer physically, mentally, and financially years and even decades later.[22]

Hurricane Katrina also further exposed the uneven distribution of vulnerability and the disproportionate impacts of and access to resources in a disaster. Many factors influenced decisions not to evacuate, including perceived racism and inequities, as well as financial and neighborhood crime factors that also have roots in systemic inequalities.[23] The resources available for evacuation were insensitive to these dynamics, leading to delays in evacuating communities of color.[24] The appalling conditions that those left behind faced were front and center in the media and persist to this day through the long-term damage and diaspora driven by this disaster but rooted in generations of social and economic policies that contributed to these underlying vulnerabilities.[25]

There would be other hurricanes and weather-related disasters after Katrina. About a month after it made landfall, another monster of a storm, Hurricane Rita, struck many areas still recovering from Katrina. Its impacts were similarly severe and punctuated the point that Katrina had so dramatically made: that catastrophes brought on by natural hazards made more extreme from our constructed underlying vulnerabilities could not be managed by a predominantly terrorism-focused preparedness posture.[26]

AVIAN INFLUENZA:
A THREAT STILL IN THE MAKING

While SARS, tsunamis, and hurricanes were posing global threats, another infectious disease threat was percolating: avian influenza. As its name implies, this is a disease of wild birds and poultry, but under the right circumstances, it can make the jump to people. While its impacts began before 9/11, we place it here in the mid-2000s timeline because it was at that point that the United States and World Health Assembly, among other governing bodies, began to signal major redirection toward addressing this threat.

In 1997 a three-year-old boy died in the hospital of acute pneumonia, respiratory distress, Reyes syndrome, multiorgan failure, and disseminated intravascular coagulation.[27] Scientists had isolated a virus from the boy's trachea that they identified as influenza A H5N1, the first documented isolation of an H5 influenza from a human being.[28] This was not your average flu—it was a severe systemic infection that went well beyond causing upper or even lower respiratory system symptoms.

This particular virus was previously known to exist only in wild birds and poultry (and, indeed, there had been a recent outbreak in poultry in Hong Kong). It had never been isolated from a person with a respiratory infection. Somehow, it seemed it had crossed the chicken-human species barrier directly, with no intermediary animal involved.

Six months after that first case, seventeen more occurred in Hong Kong. Of the eighteen patients to that point, six had died, a 33 percent case fatality rate. The viruses in these new cases were very similar to the first case but had some genetic distinctions. All the genes were of avian origin, which suggested that most or all cases were the result of independent transmissions from bird to person—not a chain reaction of person-to-person transmission.[29] But if the virus could develop the ability to do that, it would have everything it needed to become a pandemic.

With domestic poultry identified as the source of transmission to people, Hong Kong culled its 1.2 million chickens. The country's poultry industry reeled; the rest of the world watched and waited.

No pandemic followed. In the ensuing years, the virus would be repeatedly isolated in poultry and occasionally cause disease in people in southern China.[30] It wasn't until late 2003 that it expanded its range beyond southern China into Southeast Asia, entering poultry and repeatedly jumping the species barrier.[31] It reached Vietnam, Thailand, and then Cambodia and Indonesia. By 2006 it was in people in Turkey, Iraq, and Egypt. The first reported case in the Americas occurred in Canada in 2014; in all, nearly nine hundred human infections have been reported to the WHO, primarily from countries in the Eastern Hemisphere.[32]

It was spreading, probably via wild birds who contracted it from domestic flocks and then carried it along their flyways, and then incidentally back into domestic poultry. Like other infectious outbreaks, the global diaspora of influenza A H5N1 leaned heavily on human activity. While wild birds contributed to the spread of the virus, human commercial activities, particularly those associated with poultry, may have been the major factors determining its global dispersal.[33] The H5N1 subtype that caused the outbreaks likely originated in 1996 as a triple reassortant of three strains in geese, quail, and teal, animals housed together in Hong Kong poultry markets.[34] From there it spread through commercial channels to poultry, and then on to people.

The central problem with avian flu was the specter of its potential: the possibility of person-to-person transmission that would result in a cascade of infections across a community, a country, a continent, and finally, all continents, at the mercy of a highly pathogenic virus that could lead to systemic infection and high case fatality rates. The spread of H5N1 influenza starting in 2003 prompted extraordinary attention and distribution of resources not only from China but from across the globe. SARS had prompted concern among the human medical community, but it was avian flu that became a pivot point for even wider uptake across medical, agricultural, and homeland security interests.

The spike in U.S. congressional activity was striking. Congress doubled the number of its committee hearings on epidemic and pandemic topics in 2005 compared to the years immediately prior.[35] In 2005 more than half of committee hearings on emergent infectious disease were held in response to the H5N1 situation. Appropriations, Energy and Commerce, Agriculture, Homeland Security, Foreign Affairs, Veterans Affairs—each took to the dais. At the same time, in November 2005 the U.S. Homeland Security Council issued a first-ever U.S. *National Strategy for Pandemic Influenza.*

The flurry of activity wasn't limited to the United States. Other countries were looking hard at pandemic preparedness. On May 23, 2005, the World Health Assembly passed two resolutions: one urging member states to develop and implement influenza preparedness plans, and another overhauling the International Health Regulations, revisions begun post-SARS and adopted during the avian influenza scare.[36] Eventually the WHO developed a Pandemic Influenza Preparedness Framework designed to guide influenza efforts, particularly with respect to sharing of viral samples and vaccines.[37]

H5N1 has never become the pandemic experts feared it might. We don't really know whether this is because the actions taken against it have been effective, or because it simply didn't develop the wherewithal to easily transmit from person to person, or has not yet done so. According to influenza expert and Georgetown University professor Erin Sorrell, who provided input into the authors' research of this book, "It cannot easily transmit human-to-human—that is the rate-limiting step for what could be an exceptionally lethal pandemic if current countermeasures are ineffective."

A GOVERNMENT REORGANIZED, AGAIN

In comparison to extreme weather—floods, hurricanes, tornadoes—tsunamis have been the cause of comparatively few fatalities in the United States, fewer than eight hundred lives in two hundred years.[38] Still, Congress, loath to let a disaster go by without a piece of legislation, introduced the Tsunami Warning and Education Act, Public Law 109-424, which became law on December 20, 2006. The law directed the National Weather Service to operate a tsunami detection, forecasting, and warning program for the Pacific and Arctic Ocean regions and for the Atlantic Ocean, Caribbean Sea, and Gulf of Mexico. It directed the service to maintain a Pacific Tsunami Warning Center in Hawaii, a West Coast and Alaska Tsunami Warning Center in Alaska, and additional centers as it determined necessary. In the spirit of preparedness that was moving Congress at the time, it required a tsunami hazard mitigation program to improve tsunami preparedness of at-risk areas in the United States and its territories, and a research program to develop detection, forecast, communication, and mitigation science and technology for tracking and numerical forecast modeling.

The relentless disasters and near-misses in this short period prompted much legislative productivity among lawmakers. Over a brief but unusually productive period, the U.S. Congress passed three laws that became foundational reforms for dealing with disasters and platforms for future statutory change. This triad of new laws—a natural disaster reform act, an all-hazards preparedness act, and a homeland security overhaul act—created a scaffolding that would define a decade of activity and remains in place and highly influential over disaster planning in the United States today.

THE POST-KATRINA EMERGENCY MANAGEMENT REFORM ACT

Congress had no escape from legislating on the failures of government exposed by Katrina and other response failures to disasters caused by natural hazards. The Post-Katrina Emergency Management Reform Act of 2006 (PKEMRA), became law on October 4, 2006.[39] This law elevated the status of the FEMA administrator to the deputy secretary level; enhanced the agency's autonomy, classifying it as a distinct entity within DHS; insulated it from the DHS secretary's reorganization authority; and created a direct-reporting function to Congress. The act also returned to FEMA many of the functions of which it had been stripped over the course of its absorption into DHS,

including numerous preparedness, alerting, and continuity of government functions. It also created a stronger regional presence throughout the country and required key positions in the agency, such as a
disability coordinator, a small state and rural advocate, and a National
Advisory Council. For response efforts, it allowed greater flexibility for
the predeployment of resources and further elaborated the development of response teams and the categorization schema for resources
in support of response.[40] FEMA was essentially restored as the principal emergency management agency for the United States. It was pro-
pelled toward taking what would later be defined as a "whole community" approach to disaster management.

Although PKEMRA became a kind of legislative touchstone for
disaster reform, and the most consequential in terms of changing federal authorities, it was not alone among successful attempts at legislative reform for disasters. Additional laws passed at about this time
that would have repercussions for years to come included sections of
the Security and Accountability for Every Port Act of 2005 (SAFE Port
Act), the Pets Evacuation and Transportation Standards Act of 2006
(PETS Act), the Federal Judiciary Emergency Special Sessions Act of
2005, the Student Grant Hurricane and Disaster Relief Act, and sections of the John Warner National Defense Authorization Act for Fiscal Year 2007. Congress had an appetite for passing laws, and, with a
single party (in this case, Republicans) controlling both chambers and
the White House from 2005 to 2006, moving sweeping agendas was
possible.

THE PANDEMIC AND ALL-HAZARDS
PREPAREDNESS ACT

As the homeland security committees were busy drafting Katrina
reform, the health committees were at work creating a public health
preparedness law. While PKEMRA was distinctly reactionary to a single event, the Pandemic and All-Hazards Preparedness Act, or PAHPA,
was different.[41] It drew inspiration from the anthrax attacks half a
decade earlier, from the near-misses of SARS and avian influenza, and
certainly from the Katrina and Rita catastrophes. Congress cited
"uncoordinated and inadequate" federal, state, and local responses

to Katrina in its rationale for the bill, as well as federal and independent reports that evidenced an inability of states and localities to deal with large health incidents. It noted the confluence of Katrina with the growing threat from H5N1 overseas. "The threat of an avian flu pandemic and the inadequate response to the hurricanes that hit the Gulf Coast were reminders that the public health and medical infrastructure plays a critical role in national security."[42]

This law was not just about pandemics, but about the public health responsibilities of the federal government for any threat or disaster that could negatively affect human health. It was less prompted by a single event than other bills, and as it took shape it looked toward the future in anticipation of a rising frequency of those very kinds of events that would necessitate its authorities.

Passage of the law on December 19, 2006, elevated the leadership of the HHS Office of Public Health Preparedness, which had been established one month after the anthrax attacks, to the assistant secretary level. Someone needed to be in charge of the national responsibility for preparing for and responding to public health security threats, and a Senate-confirmed position at a higher level within the department who was accountable to Congress fit the bill. PAHPA consolidated federal public health and response programs and authority under this position; mandated the development of a National Health Security Strategy; required that a tracking system be put in place for vaccines to maximize their availability and delivery; and addressed hospital preparedness, medical surge capacity, and coordination of disaster health volunteerism.

IMPLEMENTING RECOMMENDATIONS
OF THE 9/11 COMMISSION ACT OF 2007

As the early post-9/11 years developed, terrorism remained a considerable concern for policy makers. It punctuated Congress's work in any number of other areas, including domestic preparedness, public health emergencies, border protection, transportation safety, information security, food safety, and natural disasters.[43] A flurry of legislation followed in those months and years. The 9/11 Commission produced its monumental work in 2004, but it would be three years before

Congress would turn the panel's many recommendations into new laws.

The 9/11 Act became law on August 3, 2007, enacting sweeping new mandates and authorities.[44] The bill's twenty-four titles covered just about every domestic security flaw and potential solution identified by the commission. It covered intelligence and information sharing, prevention of terrorist travel, transportation security (planes, trains, busses, hazmat, and more), cargo security, critical infrastructure security, weapons of mass destruction defense, emergency communications, and state and local grants. Other provisions had an international reach: creating educational opportunities in Muslim countries, promoting democratic values abroad, and other efforts to prevent radicalization and improve our relationships with foreign governments. It seemed there was nothing the bill did not touch.

The flurry of legislating was followed by the hard work of implementation and oversight. Much of the execution of the laws happened rather invisibly to the public eye, with notable exceptions—Americans were, for instance, quite aware of the new aviation security measures. In a less tangible but still paradigm-shifting way, the beginnings of a new kind of governance were emerging. The nation began to experience a move to whole-of-community planning, and, remarkably, the beginnings of a de-emphasis on terrorism and concomitant increased emphasis on natural hazards and all hazards.

The 9/11 Act was born from the worst terrorist incident America had ever experienced. Its provisions aimed to prevent any event like that from ever recurring. A close read reveals provision after provision focused on terrorism. And yet so much of what was in there actually supported all-hazards preparedness. From emergency communications to state and local grants to nationally coordinated biosurveillance, the act was supporting capacity building that would benefit response not only to terrorism but to almost any other variety of disaster. Interoperable communications would mean that police and fire responding to a terror attack could talk to each other, but those same platforms could be critical to any mass emergency response. State and local grants would support traditional security upgrades, but they would also be put to work helping cities and states plan dispensing sites for vaccines and medicines for any outbreak, terrorist-borne or not. Biosurveillance system integration would support early detection of bioterrorism, but those same systems could also detect other pathogens of less criminal origin.

Notwithstanding the burst of legislative activity, government priorities began to witness a shift from an era of homeland security—one that was characterized by a "failure of imagination" paradigm of 9/11 and harbored few immediate limits to what the United States would spend to keep Americans safe—to one where government budgetary and resource realities were setting in. Funding was by no means drying up, but political will for boundless financing of antiterror programs had its limits. There were also observable shifts in the ways in which society was willing to keep Americans safe, seen, for instance, in rising critiques of what were perceived as unchecked intelligence collection programs and calls for more targeted intelligence gathering and information sharing. This was, still, the tenure of the George W. Bush presidency; 9/11 was not yet a memory but an event with visible scars in lower Manhattan and the Pentagon. And yet there were attempts to collapse grants and programs, either because the value of the programs was being reconsidered, or because the pockets of the federal government just weren't quite so deep anymore. Yet for a while longer, constituent pressure on members of Congress to sustain these programs often did just that.[45]

GLOBAL GOVERNANCE SHIFTS

Globally, response paradigms were experiencing their own growing pains during this period. In response to the increasingly complex array of organizations involved in humanitarian disasters, the United Nations Interagency Standing Committee (ISAC) under the Office for the Coordination of Humanitarian Affairs (OCHA) initiated the Humanitarian Reform Process. From this emerged the Cluster Approach to humanitarian response. These clusters sought to better organize humanitarian and disaster response processes by grouping organizations into sectors of humanitarian action as defined by the ISAC.[46] Prompted in part by the Asian tsunami, the creation of the cluster system reflected a growing concern about the difficulty in coordinating the various stakeholders in a response and was an attempt to coordinate across entities operating with varying degrees of independence.

The cluster system was first used Pakistan in 2005 after a major earthquake, and by its first evaluation in 2007 it had been operationalized in fourteen emergencies, both sudden-onset and chronic humanitarian crises. And while the initial roll-out had significant problems, the use of the system was beginning to improve sectoral programming, foster stronger and more predictable leadership across sectors, and enhance preparedness and surge capacity. There were reported efficiencies and lower transactional costs. It was noted, however, that partnerships with international nongovernmental organizations (INGOs) only marginally improved overall, with no significant gains reported among local NGOs. Monitoring and evaluation continued to be problematic, even under the cluster system, and host nation engagement and overall cluster performance was mixed. This early initial evaluation provided some early signs of improvement in some areas but not a total success, with more iterations of the cluster system to come.[47]

NEW ROLES AND OLD CONCERNS FROM THE PRIVATE SECTOR

The multinational private sector organizations, nonprofits, and academia welcomed the boon in U.S. federal funding that was still coming from the post-9/11, postanthrax era federal bank accounts. The spike in support for biotechnology was particularly notable. Companies and nonprofits were becoming heavily engaged in public-private partnerships to support stockpiling of influenza antivirals and development of the next generation of vaccines and other medical countermeasures. But while the influx of funding in some areas was a boon to industry, engaging the major players in vaccine development was still a challenge, with pharmaceutical companies concerned about long-term federal commitment to these programs, and liability they might incur from adverse events associated with their products. This paved the way for less-proven start-ups to carve a niche in the biodefense countermeasures mission space.

Some may attribute the increased engagement on the part of the business sector to good corporate citizenship. Indeed, such motives should be recognized. Companies are run by people, and people are often driven by a desire simply to help in times of tragedy. Yet there are also more fundamental reasons for private sector involvement in preparedness and response that speak to the underlying incentive structure that drives such behavior. For companies to survive, they need to provide goods and services to those who want, need, or otherwise value them. Companies in a position to make money off of preparedness or response are therefore incentivized to do so. In addition, a certain degree of decision-making is often decentralized from headquarters to regional and local extensions of the larger corporation. This enhances the understanding and integration of local knowledge and nuances into business operations. This at once makes for good business sense, while it also seems to facilitate more rapid and efficient response and recovery to disasters.[48] It suggests a role for corporations where altruism and capitalism are compatible, a Venn diagram with some, if not total, overlap.

While corporate social responsibility was making headlines, behind the scenes disaster management was increasingly becoming a private enterprise. In the United States the move toward privatization of government services had taken on an accelerated pace in the 1980s as more and more essential services were moved from the public into the private and not-for-profit sectors. The Homeland Security Act of 2002 carried on this tradition by furthering the role of agencies as contract managers and eroding many direct service capabilities. In response to Hurricane Katrina, this transformation manifested in a heavy reliance on contractors and outsourcing, and significant use of no-bid contracting. Four multinational corporations were awarded more than $2.7 billion of the $3.3 billion in contracts for individual assistance alone. (Individual assistance, which supports the basic needs of individuals and households, is one kind of aid provided under Stafford Act emergencies, along with public assistance and mitigation assistance.) As a result of loosely defined contracting terms, costs spiraled but effectiveness waned.[49]

FEMA officials lamented this and the lack of contracting staff, even having to hire contractors to manage the contractors. This decentralization of response further led to extended wait times for key resources and poor-quality resources, such as the infamous trailers with toxic levels of formaldehyde, and the implementing of disaster policy was pushed further into vast supply networks that were designed to maximize shareholder value.[50]

FAILURES AND GROWTH AMONG NONPROFITS

The for-profit business sector was not alone in benefitting from the rise in public funding during this era. Nonprofits also saw an enormous influx of federal funds. Meanwhile, high-profile NGO failures were making headlines. The tension of these two realities led to questions about what the role of major NGOs in disasters was and should be; meanwhile, local groups began to shine in their agility and capacities to meet urgent community needs. A shift toward private donations also suggested a growing frustration and disillusionment with government and international aid organizations and with the flow of funds through the governments to the countries receiving aid.[51] Direct support to direct relief operations was becoming a preference for many private donors, and charitable organizations were taking note.

The response to Hurricane Katrina was seen as both a success and failure for nonprofits and other charitable organizations. It was among the first time in generations that there was substantial international assistance flowing to the United States, with more than a dozen international NGOs providing some sort of humanitarian aid. Across domestic and international NGOs, more than $3.3 billion was raised in private donations (the American Red Cross benefitting the most, with about $2.1 billion raised).[52] But this influx of resources hindered efficacy by adding complexity across the myriad of actors coming in to provide assistance.[53] It often occurred against a backdrop of local nuance and social structures for which outside organizations were not adequately prepared.[54]

One analysis of local nonprofits in New Orleans found that those that adapted in response to the needs and dynamics of Hurricane

Katrina were the most effective and the most sustainable as conditions continued to evolve in the decade after the storm. Among some of the most vital were nonprofits that provided essential social services but which were not necessarily defined as acting in the disaster space. Local nonprofits were found to contribute more to preparedness and mitigation than the private sector and other groups with more resources. But despite this demonstration of value, the study found a policy disconnect whereby national responses worked through larger nonprofits with specified responsibilities, generally leaving these local groups out of national policy and program formulation. As such, their potential value was not fully realized and remained unlikely to be unless directly integrated in these national preparedness deliberations.[55]

An emerging theme during this time was growth among nonprofits that continued to operate within old structures of responding but were unable to keep pace with needs on the ground and disbursement. A study of international NGOs responding to the Asian tsunami suggested that the sheer volume of humanitarian aid vastly exceeded the ability to absorb and coordinate it and did not allow for critical organizational development in areas such as human resources and human resource management, among other organizational capacities.[56] The importance of nonprofits was increasingly being recognized and resourced, but despite near constant reenvisioning of the nonprofit sector, our understanding of the needs of their mission continued to outpace the evolution of operational models, coordination approaches, and national and international policies for managing it.

ACADEMIC EFFORT VERSUS ACTUAL NEED

This era saw a deluge of new research and empirical analyses of disasters, driven in part by the opportunities created by active disasters globally, and also from increased interest and institutional shifts toward disaster studies that had begun in the preceding years. But much as with other sectors, the need and opportunity often exceeded the maturity of the field. Researchers produced studies in large numbers, but the work reflected biases in geographical and topical focus

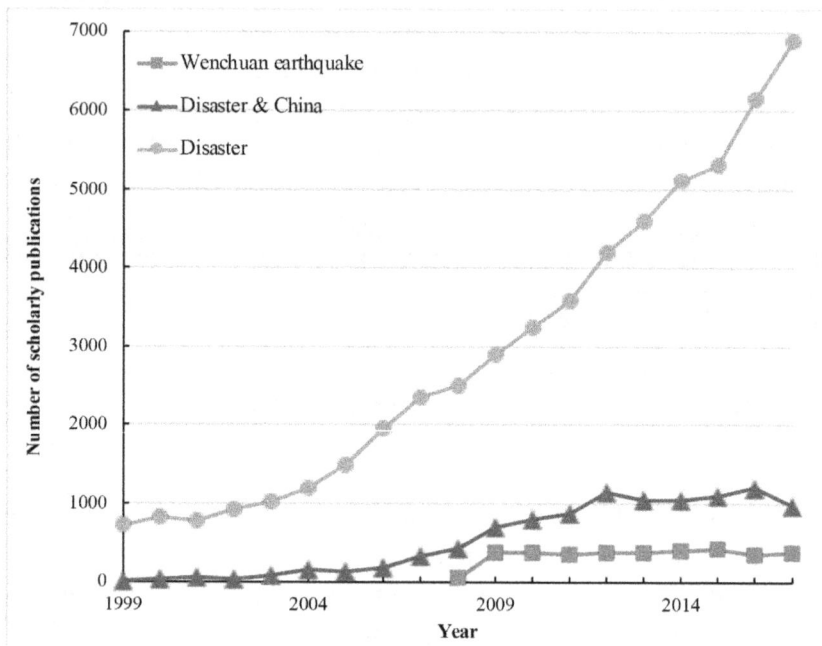

FIGURE 2.1 Disaster research articles published from 1999 to 2017.

Source: Cailin Wang et al., "Emerging Trends and New Developments in Disaster Research After the 2008 Wenchuan Earthquake," *International Journal of Environmental Research and Public Health* 16, no. 1 (2019): 1–19, https://www.mdpi.com/1660-4601/16/1/29.

areas based on where disasters were happening or the particular interests of the researchers conducting the studies.

Figure 2.1 is from an analysis that examined disaster research publications from 1999 to 2017.[57] A severe earthquake in Wenchuan, China, in 2008 prompted about 350 articles per year for years thereafter. During this time, with catastrophic events stirring up a "massive wave of disaster research," the authors noted the sizable influence of the earthquake on publication activity. The chart also reveals the dramatic rise in scholarly publications on disasters in general. The authors also assessed that after 2008, the focus of the literature shifted from examining response-oriented questions about disaster victims and medical treatment toward one emphasizing disaster risk management. In another analysis, disaster researchers Shi Shen and colleagues reviewed twenty thousand disaster research articles spanning more than a century of disaster research from 1900 to 2015. The United States, China, and Italy topped the global list of major contributors. One of the important findings was that "the frequency and citation of emerging disaster events grow rapidly after it occurs, which reflects the great influence of catastrophes on academia."[58]

A literature review from research team Adriana Leiras and colleagues found that in the humanitarian disaster logistics literature from 1998 to 2003, studies emphasized the mitigation stage of preparedness, and then, beginning in 2006, this shifted to the response phase.[59] Overall, preparedness and response were the most addressed phases, with mitigation less well represented, and recovery least of all. The paper, which reviewed studies from across the world, did not analyze whether Katrina or other contemporaneous disasters contributed to this change, but the finding is consistent with the palpable shift toward response in the policy and operational communities at the time.

Although the Leiras study was fairly narrow in its scope—humanitarian disaster logistics is but a subset of all disaster research areas—its findings raise some alarms if indeed the results are more broadly applicable. The authors cited an "imbalance in academic efforts and actual needs." Papers linking theory and practice were rarely explored. The authors commented on the necessity of closer collaboration between academia and nonprofit humanitarian organizations and other stakeholders toward more tactical, applied research.

In the United States, much of the research funding emerging was either event-specific or focused on previously defined objectives. The Homeland Security Act of 2002 mandated DHS to establish "a university-based center or centers for homeland security. The purpose of this center or centers shall be to establish a coordinated, university-based system to enhance the nation's homeland security."[60] These centers tended to be focused on different domains of response with a security focus, such as the study of terrorism, food protection and defense, and zoonotic and animal disease defense.[61] The National

Science Foundation offered flexibility for researchers whose work was adversely affected by disaster events and created targeted funding opportunities to study the disaster.[62]

Many of the studies that followed ranged from direct assessments of interventions to critical analyses of coordination structures, to deep partnerships with communities and quasi-ethnographic studies. In some ways, researchers "rediscovered" communities, the importance of the connections within communities, and the ways they are connected to regional and national institutions. These complex and dynamic interdependencies were further illuminated as factors that determined resilience in the aftermath of Katrina.[63] The frames of social capital—the bonds between people and among communities— were also rediscovered as key drivers of resilience for Katrina and subsequent disasters.[64] In short, academia was following an awakening similar to the U.S. government, finding that a broader focus on natural hazards was needed, and that the available data to understand and support decisions were woefully inadequate.

———————

This era was characterized by yet another round of reimagining disaster management. Affected by natural hazards, the terrorist paradigm began to shift more significantly to an all-hazards approach. While government was codifying these shifts into policies and operations, external actors were reacting to the framework being constructed, and to the opportunities that were being created. But while vulnerabilities to natural hazards had come to the forefront of our thinking, the documentation of lessons did not necessarily correlate with the needs in future disasters. And the cost of disasters increasingly could not be ignored.

3

AN INFLUENZA PANDEMIC, EARTHQUAKE IN HAITI, FUKUSHIMA DISASTER, AND SUPERSTORM SANDY (2008–2012)

THIS ERA in our disaster timeline, covering the brief but impactful period of 2008–2012, was immediately preceded by a global economic shock that cascaded across financial institutions, economies, and livelihoods. The 2008 global financial crisis, although not quite like the other crises discussed in this book, was a disaster of its own kind and had ripple effects on political decision-making in the years that followed. Some people termed it a "once-in-a-century credit tsunami."[1] Years of cheap and easy access to credit, along with increasing complexity of methods for repackaging and transferring debts across different financial instruments, led to a massive bubble of debt for assets that were of questionable value relative to the level of financing. Improper regulatory oversight, predatory lending, and greed were given their share of blame. It was a systemic failure. When the bubble burst, international trade collapsed to levels not seen since the 1930s, and global financial institutions had to be buoyed through unprecedented state action, gobbled up by competitors, or simply left to fail.[2]

In the end, millions of people lost their homes and their jobs. Economies, from individual households to global markets, would take years to fully recover. The public and political reaction to increased government spending, austerity measures, and the existential crisis that these economic shockwaves created would have indirect repercussions on underlying vulnerability and on the political landscape as calls mounted to reduce deficits and for governments to "live within their means."

While the financial crisis was still unfolding, many more calamities would follow. A pandemic, an earthquake, a tsunami, and a superstorm became severe insults in their own right. These were experienced during and in the immediate aftermath of the economic reality created by the financial meltdown. In this era we began to see stronger signs, particularly among certain policy makers in the U.S. government, of an aversion to excessive government spending, including on disasters.

2009 H1N1: AN ANTICLIMACTIC PANDEMIC FLU

In March 2009 Mexico began experiencing outbreaks of respiratory and "influenza-like-illness," or ILI. ILI is a descriptor for the common kinds of symptoms that present like influenza: cough, sore throat, fever. Any number of conditions can mimic flu, making patients difficult to diagnose based on their symptoms alone. On April 12 of that year, officials reported an outbreak of ILI in Veracruz to the Pan American Health Organization. A case in Oaxaca followed on April 17, prompting enhanced surveillance.[3]

It would become clear a few weeks later that similar cases had begun occurring in the United States at that same time. On March 30 a ten-year-old boy in San Diego County, California, presented at an urgent care clinic with flu-like illness; samples taken from nasal passages couldn't be diagnosed using an experimental diagnostic test, so they were sent to a reference lab, and then on to the CDC where, on April 15, the virus was identified as a novel influenza A (H1N1) of swine origin. This stopped the CDC in its tracks: this was a new flu virus, previously unknown to science.[4]

The CDC also received a sample from a nine-year-old girl in Imperial County, California, who had presented with cough and fever to an out-patient clinic on March 28. The clinic was participating in an influenza surveillance study, and her sample transited through a U.S.

naval laboratory and on to the CDC, where on April 17 it became the second laboratory-confirmed case of the novel influenza virus.[5]

Neither of these U.S. patients had been exposed to swine, a well-known intermediate host for avian and human influenzas, nor to each other. This raised a red flag that human-to-human transmission was occurring, and that there were almost certainly more cases out there. Meanwhile, on April 23, laboratory diagnosis in Mexico confirmed the cause of the outbreaks there: a triple-reassortant swine influenza A virus, with human, avian, and swine genes, of the H1N1 variety—the same virus as in the children in California.[6]

By May 4 the United States had counted 394 confirmed and 414 suspected cases.[7] Numbers skyrocketed from there: by April 2010, just a year later, the CDC estimates that the United States had endured *sixty million* cases and more than twelve thousand deaths from the virus.[8]

The virus, of course, did not remain in North America. The World Health Organization declared H1N1 a "public health emergency of international concern" on April 25, 2009, raised several alert levels in the coming weeks, and declared it an influenza pandemic—the first since 1968—on June 11.[9] By one estimate, nearly a quarter of the world's population became infected within a year.[10] Children and young adults were bearing the brunt of the virus.[11] This was a departure compared to seasonal flu trends, but consistent with other pandemic outbreaks like the 1918 influenza. Mortality rates appeared to be relatively low, but infection rates were high.

The development of a safe and effective vaccine became a global priority. The CDC had begun working on a vaccine on April 21, 2009, just six days after the discovery of the first U.S. case in California.[12] Existing vaccine platforms for seasonal flu and prior investment in research and development for pandemic vaccines allowed development and distribution to progress relatively quickly. The Food and Drug Administration had approved four vaccines by September, and the CDC began a national immunization campaign the following month.

Because the U.S. government had no bank account available to finance an emergent public health situation, the Obama administration issued an emergency supplemental appropriations request to Congress. President Obama requested $2 billion in new money and nearly $7 billion in transfer authority from existing accounts; Congress ultimately funded $1.9 billion to be available immediately, with an additional $5.8 billion authorized and contingent on a documented need for the additional funds to be made available if needed.[13] The use of emergency supplemental funding for this outbreak was noteworthy in the context of other disaster trends. Congress routinely provides funding for disasters via emergency supplemental appropriations, as it did for Hurricane Katrina, for instance, but does so as a follow-up to the immediate funds made available for disasters under the Stafford Act and the Disaster Relief Fund. Public health disasters have no such fund, necessitating the primary use of emergency appropriations as the method for funding outbreak response.[14]

The emergence of a pandemic influenza from swine from Mexico had come as "a total surprise."[15] It wasn't that governments and the WHO hadn't been surveilling or preparing. It was that what they were expecting was an avian-origin pandemic from Asia. The strains circulating and causing rare but serious human cases in East and Southeast Asia were viewed as a harbinger. So when three strains of flu—one from a person, one from a bird, and one from a pig—merged their RNA inside a pig in Mexico, where they reassorted once again with yet another pig flu virus that had been imported from Eurasia, resulting in a novel H1N1 variant that then jumped from that pig to a farmworker—well, nobody saw that coming.

The actual origins of the novel virus became the subject of speculation and debate for some time. While there remains no definitive answer, a study in 2016 posited that the virus most likely evolved in central Mexico, but with the help of an Asian-lineage strain that had arrived via the international swine trade and the sharing of viruses that goes with it.[16] The new virus likely jumped from a pig to a person in Mexico, at which point person-to-person transmission began.

The U.S. investment portfolio in pandemic influenza over the preceding years helped foster some of the readiness witnessed during H1N1. Resources that had gone into pandemic flu prior to 2009—even under the assumption of a different strain from a different hemisphere—may have bought some success. Nancy Cox of the CDC explained to the Institute of Medicine that investments in avian flu helped with swine flu: one of the California patients was diagnosed via an assay undergoing clinical trials for avian flu detection, and the other was identified through an influenza surveillance project.[17] According to Georgetown professor Erin Sorrell, "Strong collaboration between laboratories in Mexico, Canada, and the United States allowed for detailed reporting and collaboration on testing. That network was key, surveillance and lab capacity were key. I'd argue had this popped up in a part of the globe with weaker health systems, particularly laboratory diagnostics, we would have had much greater spread and caseloads before viral characterization."

In the end, the 2009 H1N1 pandemic had a high infection rate but low case fatality rate. It is often referred to as a mild pandemic, as a bullet dodged—as a chance to hone our preparedness for when a crueler respiratory pandemic might come along.

AN EARTHQUAKE CATASTROPHE STRIKES HAITI

A 7.0 earthquake can mean different things in different contexts. For communities built to rigorous standards, it can be alarming, and even prompt warnings for follow-on disasters like tsunamis, but ultimately cause only minor disruptions, such as a 7.0 earthquake that struck Japan in March 2021.[18] For communities blended of old and new infrastructure, it can be a disaster of significant but not devastating proportion, as was seen in the Loma Prieta earthquake in the San Francisco Bay Area in 1989 (7.1 magnitude), with some damage, including to a section of freeway, but with newer infrastructure performing well.[19] But for Haiti, a nation with weak infrastructure at the center of postcolonial politics marred by civil war, weak governance, and extreme poverty, a 7.0 proved truly catastrophic.

On January 12, 2010, a 7.0 earthquake struck about 25 kilometers from the capital, Port au Prince. Widespread poverty was a preexisting vulnerability in Haiti, where more than half the population subsisted on less than US$1.25 per day. The child mortality rate was double the average for the region, and nearly a third of people were considered food insecure. These liabilities were compounded by increased and poorly planned urbanization that led to substandard building practices, among other systemic vulnerabilities.

The earthquake event—a single intersection between a natural hazard and the built environment—is believed to have killed 220,000 people; an additional 300,000 are believed to have been injured, and 2,000,000 were suddenly homeless.[20]

The international community responded. Haiti became heavily reliant on international assistance overnight. Yet with significant damage and loss of life to both the Haitian seat of government and the country's UN headquarters, any domestic capacity to coordinate those international efforts was largely destroyed with the earthquake. All told, as many as sixty-seven international search and rescue teams deployed, twenty-two nations provided military assistance, and an estimated two thousand nongovernmental organizations (having raised more than $1.4 billion) responded. The UN Cluster System's Health Cluster coordination calls had more than four hundred organizations attending (fifteen to twenty had been the prior census). Much of the massive influx of resources simply piled up due to lack of domestic coordination capabilities or logistical infrastructure. International disaster response is designed to be coordinated by the affected nation, theoretically equipped to prioritize response, but Haiti was a class of disaster where the very models of response broke.[21]

It is difficult to evaluate the impact that the international aid may have had. An attempt to ascertain the effectiveness of the forty-four foreign field hospitals sent to Haiti was unable to draw definitive conclusions. Despite the large presence of "hospital" beds (peaking at 3,300) and 8,700 major surgeries in the month after the earthquake, there are little data about them, and attempts to gather data failed to draw conclusions as to the effectiveness of the foreign field hospital interventions.[22]

Of the resources that came in after the earthquake, only 1 percent actually went to the Haitian government, with the rest primarily going to NGOs, donor nations' own deployment expenses, contractors, and other nonstate actors.[23] In many cases, and in line with historical interventions, donations made by governments and nongovernmental partners were driven by agendas other than those of the Haitian government. In some cases, donor pledges greatly exceeded Haiti's request, such as for transportation infrastructure (510 percent greater than requested), while other areas, such as strengthening democratic institutions, were pledged only 20 percent of the requested funding. These kinds of donor-recipient disconnects were nothing new for Haiti. Chronic political and economic instability driven by colonialism and relentless postcolonial foreign interventions created a vulnerability torn wide open by the earthquake and recovery efforts.

JAPAN'S 3/11 TRIPLE DISASTERS

Japan's 3/11 disaster trifecta began on March 11, 2011, with a magnitude 9.0 earthquake off the northeastern shore of the main island, Honshu, approximately eighty miles east of the city of Sendai in Miyagi prefecture. The movement along the fault lifted the seafloor fifteen feet over nine thousand square miles and created some of the largest geological displacements ever recorded for an earthquake. Within an hour, the first tsunami began to reach the shore. The resulting waves achieved heights of as much as thirty-three feet and reached as far as six miles inland in some areas, devastating prefectures along the Pacific coastline. The flooding that resulted from the tsunami is estimated to have killed as many as twenty thousand people and displaced up to half a million.[24]

The nuclear power plants in the area responded by shutting down their reactors. The Fukushima Daiichi plant was operated by the Tokyo Electric and Power Company (TEPCO). After the earthquake, TEPCO shut down each of the plant's three operating reactors. But in the days and weeks that followed, the damage and loss of power to the plant's cooling systems led to the overheating of the nuclear cores and a partial meltdown of some of the nuclear fuel rods.[25] The tsunami waves had damaged backup generators, leading to a failure of cooling systems and a partial meltdown of all three reactors. A fourth reactor that was not in use other than for storing spent fuel rods also began to overheat. The meltdown caused nuclear fuel to breach containment vessels, and there were several explosions resulting from buildups of hydrogen gas. By April 12, officials raised the nuclear alert to the highest level, not seen since the Chernobyl accident of 1986.[26]

The response can be characterized as confused, especially to the general public. Evacuation zones were at first limited, then expanded as the scope of the damage became more apparent. The availability and instructions for use of potassium iodide (used to prevent thyroid cancer in nuclear accidents) were similarly inconsistent, with limited distribution to the public outside of a few local areas. Communicating the risks of radiation exposure to a broader population is an imprecise operation to begin with. There are general senses on what lethal doses are for most people, and more precise regulatory thresholds. But health effects can vary by isotope, type of exposure, duration of exposure, and the biology of the individual exposed, among other factors. The long-term impacts from exposures are even less clear scientifically. There are guidelines based on what information is known, but knowledge of overall cancer risk and other adverse outcomes of lower-dose exposures over longer durations is generally insufficient to answer more precise operational risk questions. While the nature of radiation exposure and its consequences on health is frustratingly opaque to disaster planners, frameworks do exist. And while risk communication can be complex, messaging can be developed and socialized with communities prior to a disaster. This, along with improved planning for evacuation zones, exposure assessments, and prophylaxis strategies, was among the shortfalls identified in meeting the challenges of the Fukushima meltdown.[27]

The coziness of the Daichii operators with TEPCO came under intense scrutiny in investigations of failures to address vulnerabilities before the accident, and for shortcomings in the response afterward.[28] An analysis of press releases during the crisis shows TEPCO framing most of its communications in four ways. The vast majority were *official updates* along with a small number of *announcements*. The others are *attribution*, communications that typically sought to attribute blame for radioactive releases to the earthquake, and finally *apology*, which expressed remorse and sympathy for the effects of the meltdown and loss of lives of the workers at the plant. In the analysis, it appears that the attribution frames sought to reinforce the root cause of the impacts as a natural event, whereas with the apology frame TEPCO assumed full responsibility for the subject of those releases.[29] This oscillation between attribution and apology provides some insight into the complex interplay among government, the private sector, and naturally occurring events.

Another study, by Daniel Aldrich, evaluated the social and political structures that came into play. Normal justifications for investments in large seawalls to prevent tsunami damage proved a less reliable predictor of survival than social capital, a measure of communities' connectedness. There are countless stories of individuals bucking instruction and returning to aid the elderly and disabled to escape the coming waves that overtopped existing seawalls. Communities with greater cohesion also fared better in recovery. What is also striking is that those who were well connected with representatives from all levels of government have been better able to capitalize on recovery funding and other resources. In many ways, while much focus on disaster resilience is seemingly obsessed with the built environment, these social and political dynamics may be more of a driver of disaster resilience and recovery than physical investments. Yet in the aftermath of the disaster, the built environment continued to be the primary focus of national policy and investments.[30]

SANDY: AN EPIC NONHURRICANE

"Superstorm" Sandy—referred to as such because it was technically no longer a hurricane when it made landfall in the U.S. Northeast—did not easily match the traditional Saffir-Simpson categories for measuring hurricane strength. This scale, and scientists' communication of hurricane risk, is largely based on wind speed. What made Sandy so devastating was not its wind speed but rather its size, the storm surge it produced, and its path across the Long Island Sound during an astronomically high tide.[31]

When mid-autumn 2012 arrived, the idea that catastrophic hurricanes could devastate both coastal and inland areas of the East Coast from south to north with storm surges and flooding rains was not new. Still, Sandy was a gut punch to the mid-Atlantic. She had ebbed to tropical storm status before landing in Brigantine, New Jersey, on October 29 but was, according to the National Hurricane Center, "an extraordinarily large hurricane."[32] She grew and grew from the Bahamas until making U.S. landfall, becoming the largest Atlantic tropical cyclone on record. Water levels rose from Florida to Maine, with

New York taking the brunt of the surge—12.65 feet above normal tide levels at Kings Point, Long Island, immediately outside of New York City.

Sandy caused seventy-two deaths in the United States, most due to the storm surge, and the rest to wind hazards, near-shore waves, and related dangers; eighty-seven additional deaths resulted from extended power outages and their sequelae, such as hypothermia and carbon monoxide poisoning. An estimated 8.5 million customers lost power, and 650,000 houses were destroyed.[33]

By one count, economic losses totaled approximately $50 billion. Of that, an estimated $30 billion was from direct damage to property and infrastructure; $19.9 billion was in lost economic output, the New York City metropolitan area accounting for more than half of that.[34]

The storm had made landfall on the New Jersey coast just to the south of the city and then headed northwest. This is the worst-case scenario, a conformation that directs a storm and its surge straight into the New York Bight, the right angle formed by New Jersey and Long Island.[35] Sandy was a colossal storm whose impacts could never have been completely mitigated no matter how thorough the planning, although certainly, more could have been done. Understanding the particular tragedy of Sandy requires placing the storm's impact in the context of lessons from prior storms.

For decades, storm after storm had pounded rains, flooding, and hard lessons along the 3,700 miles that make up the U.S. Atlantic and Gulf coastlines. Time and again, storms had destroyed or put out of commission hospitals and biomedical research laboratories, particularly in the South: in Texas by Tropical Storm Allison (2001); in Louisiana by Katrina and Rita (2005); in Texas again by Hurricane Ike (2008). These storms wiped out entire programs at academic research centers, taking careers and tens of thousands of animal lives with them. In many cases the research animals had been housed in basements. Yet it all essentially came as a surprise to New York in 2012. As the East River rose catastrophically, it flooded the basement of NYU Langone's medical center, including the animal section of the Smilow Research Center. Animal rooms were spread throughout the building, including on low floors that became flooded, along with fuel tanks for generators. The center, which had opened in 2006, had been designed to withstand a storm surge that was 20 percent greater than New York City's largest recorded surge to that point.[36] NYU reported that it was prepared for 12 feet of surge; it got 14.5.[37] Damage took an estimated thirty-five thousand animal lives. NYU's preliminary estimate of its total economic losses, animal and otherwise, was almost $1.5 billion.[38]

Response challenges were everywhere. To find and access city residents unable to descend multiple flights of stairs from their high-rise apartments required a level of heroism from volunteer groups for this need that was unplanned but well predicted from past storms.[39] Perhaps most alarming was the lengthy and inequitable recovery, leaving some in limbo for years living in houses that were partially damaged, with measurable health impacts, including on children.[40] Some recovery efforts were codified in new plans, while others were force fed via citizen lawsuits that argued that planning had failed to accommodate the needs of people with disabilities.[41]

THE GOVERNMENT RESPONDS

In the United States, the federal government had spent the decade preceding this era transforming the legislative foundation for disasters. From terrorism to infectious disease to natural hazards to all-hazards, sweeping authorities and reforms were put in place to help organize the U.S. approach to preparedness and response for some of the precise kinds of disasters described in this chapter. Even Haiti and Fukushima, while outside the direct purview of the United States, put U.S. funding, foreign aid, and nuclear accident readiness to the test.

This era witnessed a rising reliance on funding disaster response via emergency funding. The routine funding of the federal government is designed to undergo a standardized annual process by which the president submits to Congress a budget request around February of each year for the coming fiscal year, over which Congress deliberates and ultimately funds across twelve spending bills (or, more recently, one large bill). Annual appropriations are the long-standing, customary way that Congress appropriates money to the federal departments and agencies.

Emergency requests, on the other hand, can come at any time. This kind of spending exists outside the annual appropriations cycle. Emergency funding bills are, by definition, used for emergencies, for times when new money is needed to address a crisis. Emergency dollars can supplement the primary mechanism by which the government funds disasters, a standing FEMA account known as the Disaster Relief Fund (DRF). This fund is used to support response to emergencies and major disaster declarations under the Stafford Act.[42] Emergency supplemental bills are often introduced in amounts that far exceed typical disbursements from the DRF, allowing for much larger response activity.

The House put forward an emergency funding bill for Sandy that contained $17 billion to meet immediate needs and $33 billion for longer-term recovery and resilience.[43] The bill passed nearly three months after the disaster, and while this was fairly quick compared to normal legislative processes, a greater uneasiness over spending on disaster response began to creep in, along with an introduction of more overt politicization of disaster recovery. Another issue was that, as had been the case for some time, emergency funding was not always going to emergency needs, but to longer-term mitigation and resilience building spent over years. A measure of flexibility regarding when and on what the dollars are spent may help agencies as they respond to a disaster whose dynamics may still be unfolding and affecting communities for years; yet it runs contrary to the foundational idea of emergency spending as being for immediate needs. It also sidesteps well-established appropriations processes.

The granting of emergency funding is a process that operates outside of annual funding protocols and the various control mechanisms embedded within them, subverting some of the benefits of thoughtful and ritualized spending debates and decisions. Nevertheless, presidents and Congresses would continue to rely on supplementals in the coming decade in response to disasters.

Additional political dynamics related to congressional spending began to characterize this era. These were fiscally conservative moves driven in part by some conservatives' concern over runaway spending. The financial meltdown, the trending increases in emergency spending, and, importantly, shifts in control of legislatures toward more conservative blocs in the United States (as well as glob-ally) may have together created an environment that supported their advancement.

A budget move known as sequestration was an effort by congres-sional Republicans to rein in spending. The Budget Control Act of 2011 imposed caps on the congressional appropriation of new discretion-ary budget authority, beginning at $1.043 trillion in 2012 and reach-ing $1.234 trillion in 2021.[44] If the caps were exceeded, funds from other programs would be cut—sequestered—across the board to make up the difference. Additionally, in 2011 House and Senate Republicans banned their caucuses from requesting earmarks.[45] Democrats even-tually followed suit. What became known as the "earmark ban" would last for a decade. The ethos of the ban was to limit pork-barrel spend-ing. Taken together with sequestration, it was another way in which Congress was squeezing expenditures. At the same time, though, a parallel ethos was that the money for much of disaster response still needed to come from the federal government.

GLOBAL GOVERNANCE REACTS

Beyond the United States, global systems were also struggling with the complexity of disasters in this era. An evaluation of the response of the United Nations Office for the Coordination of Humanitarian Affairs to the Haiti earthquake reiterated that a cacophony of assis-tance overwhelmed the cluster system and government-led coordina-tion processes at all levels. The report cited OCHA's many statistics on tangible outputs like the number of latrines built but faulted OCHA for its failure to conduct a "needs assessment"—that is, a real-time identification of what Haiti actually needed in terms of latrines or any-thing else, citing it as a "serious handicap in the entire response."[46] An overwhelming literature before and after the earthquake links excessive foreign interventions throughout Haiti's existence as an independent nation as a core vulnerability for the country. But much of this literature also measures success as the number of things built rather than the ability to address these underlying vulnerabilities in a more holistic way. Reform recommendations continue to be focused on coordination of interventions rather than ameliorating the cycle of intervention dependence.

Following the tragedy of Fukushima, Japan immediately placed a moratorium on construction of new nuclear power plants. The government put additional safety requirements in place for restarting reactors. An aggressive construction effort for building seawalls moved forward, despite a lack of evidence that they prevented tsunami deaths, and often despite the objections of local communities who did not want their access to the sea, vital to their livelihoods and quality of life, to be cut off. There was a concern that mitigation spending was mechanical, reactive. Some areas more connected to the purse strings of government were able to get outsized mitigation spending: one town's entire downtown area was elevated in the reconstruction efforts. This illuminated an increasingly understood tenet in disaster recovery: that those with significant access to government attention before a disaster benefit from it after a disaster.[47]

The repercussions of Fukushima were felt worldwide. In Europe, countries that were opposed to nuclear energy reinforced their opposition, while those that supported nuclear energy doubled down on their own views. Those less certain or newer in their nuclear investments had more mixed reactions. Some countries imposed moratoriums on new power plants; others reiterated their commitments to construction, or to timelines for retiring plants at the end of their lifecycle.[48] In the Association of Southeast Asian Nations (ASEAN) region, the Fukushima accident seemed to have blunted a growing nuclear renaissance that was previously seen as a way to meet increasing energy needs with negligible greenhouse gas emissions. The rhetoric, however, was not matched with action, and many countries saw an increase in nuclear power production with new construction continuing in the absence of suitable renewable energy sources at the scale needed for the region's energy needs.[49]

BUSINESS RISKS—AND OPPORTUNITIES

The world's coasts, river deltas, forest regions, and fault lines are increasingly home to a growing share of the world's business interests.[50] As a result, disasters that occur there can have outsized economic impacts. If it hadn't already been understood, this became increasingly clear to the private sector in the wake of the disasters described in this chapter.

In 2011 alone, Japan suffered the nuclear/tsunami calamity; Thailand, a severe monsoon season; New Zealand, an earthquake; Australia and China, floods; and the United States, the usual order of hurricanes, tornadoes, wildfires, and floods. According to the *Economist*, reinsurer Munich Re estimated its economic costs in 2011 at $378 billion, a record-breaking year for the company.[51] Direct costs of major disasters can be significant, but the ripple effect of interruption to businesses because of power outages, transportation system disruptions, and other obstacles can lead to cascading effects whereby the cessation of outputs from one sector prevents inputs for another. One study calculated Sandy's direct economic costs at up to $97 billion, indirect at $16.3 billion, and business interruption at $10.8–15.5 billion.[52] With a combination of increasing payouts for disasters and storms like Sandy directly affecting financial powerhouses where they are headquartered, these industries seemed to be getting more involved in promoting disaster resilience and better defining the role of insurance in building resilience. The role of insurance and other financial institutions also became a focus of federal planning efforts, eventually becoming formalized in FEMA's strategic plan, which highlighted closing the insurance gap as one of its major components.[53]

But disasters can also be good for business. The private sector benefitted from the billions the government was spending on pandemic influenza preparedness. The nearly $7.7 billion H1N1 emergency bill allowed some of its funds to be used for renovation of private vaccine facilities and vaccine purchases for the Strategic National Stockpile.[54] By November 2009 the FDA had approved vaccines from five pharmaceutical companies. Other nations also bought up supply. According to one analysis, H1N1 vaccine manufacturers reported $3.3 billion in sales in 2009.[55]

Some commentators raised concerns about conflicts of interest with respect to the private sector and governments. The Fukushima disaster brought to light a concern about the closeness of the industry being regulated with the regulating authorities. Often this is a fine line: the expertise and cooperation of industry are needed for effective regulation, and government officials find jobs after public service in the industries they previously regulated. In Japan there were additional nuances. A single agency was responsible both for regulating and for promoting the nuclear power industry. Cultural norms, such as for deference to authorities, may have also contributed. This issue is by no means unique to Japan. The United States proposed a divorce of agencies after the BP oil spill in the Gulf of Mexico in 2010, recognizing potential conflict of interests between oil companies and the agencies that regulate them that also may benefit from industry profit.[56]

Companies also increasingly saw opportunities for good-will spending through corporate social responsibility accounts. After a sharp decrease in 2009, the years 2010 and 2011 saw an increase in the total gifts made by corporations.[57]

THE CONTINUED RISE OF NONPROFITS

As the twentieth century transitioned into its second decade, the disaster landscape invited the ever-increasing participation of the nonprofit and philanthropic sectors. NGOs ratcheted up fundraising campaigns through telethons and other means, raising hundreds of millions of dollars. With new technologies to enable giving easily, and an increasing availability of social and traditional media tools, the disaster telethon began to take on new dimensions, incorporating these technologies with unprecedented fundraising results. But as fundraising is often based on emotional appeal, it can have the effect of exploiting and even normalizing the hardships of survivors in the process. With many musical artists coming forward to help raise funds, scholar Elizabeth McAlister analyzed these "soundscapes of disaster humanities," with particular attention paid to the *Hope for Haiti* telethon. Building on the analysis of other scholars, she described the aesthetic and impacts of "naturalizing suffering" and highlighting the voices of the performing artists juxtaposed against the disaster survivors who have been relegated to backdrops for the performance.[58] The fundraising was becoming more connected and more lucrative but at the same time making it easier for givers to contribute from a distance, literally and metaphorically.

Many of these organizations became embedded in the new missions they had taken on, with mixed results. Haiti saw a windfall in disaster donations, but with few results worth noting on the ground. The more than $1.4 billion raised for earthquake relief overwhelmed systems for managing relief efforts.[59] Many charities that were recipients of the massive donations had trouble demonstrating success and showing where the money had gone. Philanthropic powerhouses were criticized for accepting large sums that did not achieve their purpose. The Red Cross famously raised a reported half a billion dollars for homes to be built after the earthquake; it built six new structures.[60] In other cases, the blurring of philanthropic and government spending led to aggressive, but ultimately failed, development projects. The Caracol port investment championed by former president Bill Clinton and the Clinton Foundation is a prime example: it promised massive foreign investments in Haiti, only to fall far short of promised goals, with donors quietly walking away after tens of millions in investments in the project.[61] Not all projects were failures, but Haiti proved that often the desire to do good, especially when uncoordinated or driven by competing agendas, can have minimal and even negative effects on disaster recovery.

In the midst of chaos, this period also witnessed some attempts to create a more cohesive and coordinated philanthropic catalyst to building resilience. Among the most ambitious were those that came in response to Superstorm Sandy. In her book *The Resilience Dividend: Being Strong in a World Where Things Go Wrong*, then-president of the Rockefeller Foundation Judith Rodin reflects on her work in disaster philanthropy and how it drew close to home as Sandy inundated Manhattan. This, in part, led to the launching of the ambitious 100 Resilient Cities Initiative. A global network of cities networked and supported by the foundation, the initiative was the largest coordinated resilience effort ever undertaken. An initial commitment of $100 million from the Rockefeller Foundation (later increased to $164 million), along with support from other partners, led to the hiring of chief resilience officers in ninety cities and establishment of a global network of peer support and technical assistance. Ultimately disbanded in

2019, the initiative was not without criticism, but it serves as another milestone among philanthropic initiatives and donors seeking to advance resilience in civil society.[62] Some elements continued under other programs across foundations and other organizations in the network. Rockefeller also continued supporting the resilience officers that had been part of the network, but one study found that the overall number of cities with a chief resilience officer has fallen since 2019.[63]

ACADEMIA RECEIVES MORE SUPPORT FOR DISASTER R&D

Federal post-Sandy recovery research grants created a first-of-their-kind research mechanism that required researchers to provide contributions to the postdisaster communities they were studying. The assistant secretary for preparedness and response (ASPR) at Health and Human Services, CDC, and National Institute of Environmental Health Sciences each funded disaster recovery research projects under the Sandy emergency appropriation. ASPR supported two-year research grants looking at long-term recovery of health systems and communities in affected areas. It described these grants as providing an "evidence base for community members and leaders as they make decisions about recovery and about their future preparedness and response efforts." This work was designed to pull community members into the research process. The CDC also used some of its funds to support preparedness and response research, covering areas such as fungal exposure, mold mitigation, morbidity and mortality of at-risk populations, mental health, and overall evaluation of the public health system response.[64] For its part, NIEHS supported research and development of programs related to dealing with hazardous materials. Together, these agencies put more than $20 million into more than forty grants of this kind.[65]

Many universities, primarily from the U.S. Northeast, took part in this research. Columbia University studied Sandy's impacts on local health systems; Rowan University evaluated the hurricane's impacts on older individuals and the nature of their resilience; Queens College looked at ways to reduce hazards to immigrant day-laborers who were helping communities to rebuild. Other kinds of organizations also implemented some of these projects, including the RAND Corporation and the United Steelworkers of America.[66] Outputs of this research produced a number of publications and findings that directly led to improving operational and policy outcomes.[67] This series of grants provided an important new model for integrating research into post-disaster environments, but like many investments, it lacked a sustainable funding vehicle for replication in future disasters and, as of this writing, has not been replicated.

Academic activity is measured not only by inputs of funds but by outputs of papers. Academic publications on "postdisaster reconstruction" spiked between 2009 and 2011; the authors of one study speculated that this may have resulted from the severe earthquake in Wenchuan, China, in mid-2008 and the Japanese tsunami in early 2011.[68] (They also noted that most of the researchers who produced these works were from the United States, the United Kingdom, and Australia, with Asia, Africa, and South America lagging.) Humanitarian logistics, another discipline within disaster science, began to emerge in the literature around the turn of the century. Adriana Leiras and colleagues noted that this subdiscipline was characterized by a sharp increase in the number of papers in general beginning in 2009.[69] The trends cited in this study were particularly concerning, in that they reflected a lack of research into recovery and an overall imbalance between academic lines of effort and actual need.

Other disasters occurred during this period. The BP oil spill in the Gulf of Mexico in 2010 was a devastating technological disaster that battered the U.S. Gulf coast at a time when it was still recovering from Hurricane Katrina. As the years progressed, it became harder to identify milestone events, particularly as record-breaking storms and seasons increasingly become the norm. These disasters continued to outpace our ability to plan, respond to, and recover from disruptions.

While they faced difficulty keeping up with individual disasters, governments, nonprofits, the private sector, and academia each experienced new opportunities, demands, and expectations in a rapidly changing world. The financial shock of 2008 preceded a coming political hesitancy for spending that would begin to reveal itself in the American response to disasters of this era. It also helped create political polarization nationally and internationally, as seen in the rise of the Tea Party in the United States and a resurgence of nationalism in America and elsewhere. It should come as no surprise, then, that political polarization of disaster response began to deepen.

4

EBOLA, HURRICANES, WILDFIRES, AND A PANDEMIC FOR THE AGES (2013–2021)

A S THE prevalence of disasters increased and consumed more of our attention, the individual disaster events in the next era, 2013–2021 and beyond, began to blur. Like the prior era, this era was defined by a series of devastating events, but also by an experience of clusters of domestic disasters that offered no breathing room, and a global pandemic that redefined the infectious disease threat. It became harder to talk about one hurricane or one wildfire, as some disasters begin to cluster in memorable disaster "seasons." Across the domains that respond to disasters, it became increasingly clear that existing models of managing disasters were breaking under the stress of overlapping and compounding events, but the reigning narrative persisted: adjust programs, rather than look holistically at changes to governance and business models toward better alignment for the growing threats and underlying vulnerabilities to them. One thing was certain amid the uncertainty: disasters were getting worse faster than we were transitioning the approaches of government, philanthropy, the private sector, and academia to deal with them. And along with this, issues of equity in disaster management and response were starting to get more attention in the mainstream discourse about disasters.

EBOLA EMERGES IN WEST AFRICA

To the surprise of many, West Africa became home to the largest Ebola virus disease outbreak ever recorded. Since the discovery of the virus Ebola Zaire (later renamed Zaire ebolavirus) in 1976, Ebola outbreaks had mostly been limited to the Democratic Republic of Congo, with occasional occurrences in the nearby countries of Republic of the Congo, Uganda, Sudan, and Gabon. The Zaire, Sudan, and Bundibugyo strains were implicated in these human outbreaks.

A strain that came to be called Taï Forest ebolavirus had also been discovered in chimpanzees in Cote d'Ivoire in 1994, when a scientist studying them became infected.[1] A fifth strain, Reston, circulates in nonhuman primates in the Philippines. Other countries, including the United States, had experienced laboratory-based cases of some strains or detected them in primate facilities due to importation of infected research animals.[2] (Reston ebolavirus was named for the Virginia location in which it caused an outbreak in animals at a primate quarantine facility in 1989.) For some time, the United States had also been concerned that malicious actors might weaponize Ebola and had made some investments in addressing that threat. But as naturally occurring outbreaks went, the Ebola family of viruses was considered a heart of darkness kind of problem.

By 2014 the days of consigning Ebola to the ranks of exotic diseases of remote jungle communities were over. In March of that year, health officials from the Forest Region of Guinea alerted the central government about clusters of fever, severe diarrhea, and vomiting associated with a high fatality rate (as much as 86 percent of early cases).[3] Further investigation revealed that the first case had likely occurred three months prior, in December 2013, as a single introduction into the human population. This case and those that succeeded it would go undiagnosed for months.

Guinea is located on the western African coast, thousands of miles from the Zaire ebolavirus cases that had plagued communities in central Africa. It wasn't on doctors' radar there, and the United States, the WHO, and medical NGOs had not worked to build detection or treatment capacity in countries outside those that had historically suffered outbreaks. Ebola viruses are believed to be harbored by bats, which are widespread geographically. But without a history of human cases in West Africa, nobody was looking for the bats, or the virus.

Our inattention did not prevent an outbreak. The introduction of Ebola into a person in Guinea is believed to have been a local event, almost certainly a spillover from a bat to a person. This focal event in a very remote part of Guinea soon erupted into the largest Ebola outbreak in history. As the virus transmitted from one person to another, cases soon spread to Conakry, Guinea's populous capital, and to neighboring Liberia and Sierra Leone.

It would be June 2016 before the outbreak finally ended. Over those two and a half years, Ebola in West Africa took more than eleven thousand lives of the more than twenty-eight thousand individuals we know were infected. Tallies were the worst in Liberia and Sierra Leone. These are some of the poorest countries in the world, with the fewest resources available to detect and respond to an epidemic. The outbreak may not have been predicted, but the outcome was predictable.

Scientists from the U.S. CDC would later write that many factors led to the "unprecedented scale of this epidemic, including the wide geographic spread of cases, slow response by the international community, population intermixing and mobility, disease transmission in densely populated urban areas, poor public health and societal infrastructure, local unfamiliarity with the disease, and distrust of government authorities and health care workers."[4]

The Ebola crisis brought about significant criticism of the WHO, which was faulted for delaying to take action and for an anemic operational response. It also exposed a key misunderstanding about what the WHO's mandate is versus what people seem to *think* it is. All the same, without a major international organization stepping in with a big assist, the countries at the center of the outbreak were left largely to fend for themselves until aid trickled in piecemeal through well-meaning NGOs and allies.

For its part, the U.S. government once again was faced with dealing with a disaster, albeit one beyond its borders, that necessitated emergency supplemental spending. The humanitarian disaster unfolding abroad, layered on a fear of imported disease at home, had

Americans glued to the news and lawmakers arguing over how to prevent introduction and spread of the virus into the United States. The first known U.S. case occurred in Texas in a man who had contracted the virus in Liberia before flying to Dallas; he died while hospitalized there. Two nurses who cared for him were infected and recovered. Eight additional individuals, most of whom were healthcare workers assisting with the response abroad, either came back or were put on a specially chartered flight back from West Africa; one died.[5]

The crisis in West Africa and the gut fear of such a disaster occurring stateside prompted officials to invest in Ebola treatments and vaccines, in personal protective equipment for hospitals, and in aid to quell the spread abroad. In November 2014 President Obama requested $6.18 billion—$4.64 billion for immediate response and $1.54 billion for a contingency fund to be available as the crisis unfolded.[6] The request was quickly granted: Congress appropriated $5.4 billion the following month.

Yet even the fearsome and drawn-out Ebola outbreak could hold our attention only for so long. Before it was over, an outbreak of another terrifying virus, Zika, was spreading globally with a major locus in South America. Zika, too, got an emergency supplemental. This one, however, was for much less money and took much longer to get through—seven months of wrangling between the president and the Congress, as some policy makers began to question the need for yet more funding for an emerging infection that seemed only a minimal threat to the United States.

Ebola would be the last big emergency spend for an infectious disease until March 2020.

HURRICANES: HARVEY, IRMA, MARIA, FLORENCE, AND MICHAEL

The U.S. hurricane seasons in 2017 and 2018 proved a turning point. While hurricanes like Katrina and Sandy showed the devastation that could occur in a single event, the back-to-back and seemingly nonstop billion-dollar disasters over this two-year period began to tear the very fabric of the response and recovery system.

The first in this series of devastating storms was Hurricane Harvey. Harvey garnered a lot of attention, as the first major hurricane of a season to threaten a big city often does. But this one received added attention, as it was the first major hurricane faced by the recently elected Trump administration, testing new leadership from the White House and throughout the federal agencies.[7]

Hurricane Harvey reached the United States on August 25, 2017, as a Category 4 storm at the Port of Aransas, Texas. As its forward motion slowed, Harvey battered the Texas coast and parts of Louisiana for four days, making landfall three times as it swept back and forth between land and the Gulf of Mexico. Its slow movement and heavy rainfall meant that some areas experienced in excess of forty-five inches of rain.[8] Widespread flooding ensued in Houston and along Texas's Gulf coast, reaching as far south as Corpus Christi and into parts of Louisiana. But as devastating and long-lasting as the impacts of this storm would be, our national attention quickly had to absorb another major storm, Hurricane Irma.

Irma tread so closely on the heels of Harvey that the media found itself covering two major hurricanes at once. Irma reached "major hurricane status" only two days after its genesis over the Atlantic Ocean, a rare feat.[9] It made landfall on island after island in the Caribbean as a Category 5 during the first week of September. The storm produced significant coastal and inland flooding on many islands, up to eight feet in inland parts of Barbuda, and as much as ten feet in Cuba, a surge that pushed 1.2 miles inland. The hurricane hit the U.S. mainland in southwest Florida as a weakened storm on September 10 and affected much of the state and up into Georgia. Six million people evacuated from Florida. Irma led to forty-seven direct deaths, mostly in the Caribbean, where winds were the most aggressive. The United States experienced ten of these deaths.

As bad as Irma was for the islands and the southeastern United States, Maria was worse. Maria made landfall in Dominica on September 19, devastating the island as a Category 5 storm. The island was all but destroyed—both its built environment and natural areas. According to a U.S. report, "The once-lush tropical island was effectively reduced to an immense field of debris."[10] Puerto Rico was next. Maria hit the island as a high-end Category 4 with sustained winds of

155 miles per hour on September 20; wind speeds had actually decreased from peaks of 175 mph near St. Croix.[11] But the storm had increased in size, cutting a swath across the island from the southeast to the northwest. Sensors recorded inundations ranging from one to nine feet across the island, but frequently the sensors went offline and the peak levels in some cases went unrecorded.[12] Rains were torrential: nearly thirty-eight inches in one location of the island. The federally reported death toll in Puerto Rico from Maria is officially sixty-five, but the debate that followed the storm cast significant doubt on that figure. The Puerto Rican government, whose figure initially aligned with that number, dramatically raised the toll to 2,975 a year later based on a George Washington University study.[13] The Trump administration disputed that study.[14]

While all disasters amplify underlying inequalities, Hurricane Maria brought inequity to the forefront. There were significant questions as to whether Puerto Rico received the same level of response attention that other disaster areas did, with accusations of colonialism and racism abundant. The U.S. government response was also largely overextended at this stage, responding to the prior disasters of that year and preceding years. There is evidence that it responded unequally and less effectively.[15] Some argue that this was not merely an issue of inadequate response in the moment but resulted from an extended history of neglect leading to systemic vulnerabilities.[16] These issues and controversies persist to this day, in Puerto Rico and elsewhere.

Hurricane difficulties picked up again the next summer. Florence was the first major hurricane of the 2018 season, arriving after transit across the Atlantic as a weakened Category 1 at the southern end of North Carolina on September 14. But this large and slow-moving storm dropped record-breaking rainfall. One location in North Carolina measured thirty inches of rain, a historic first, and record flooding destroyed roads and damaged thousands of residences and businesses.[17] South Carolina also experienced fatalities, dam breaches, and thousands of damaged homes. The storm resulted in twenty-two direct deaths, thirty indirect deaths, and estimated wind and water damage worth $24 billion.[18] The Trump administration's response to Florence was closely watched after the disastrous Maria response the prior year.[19]

Hurricane Michael struck land with far more force than Florence had. Michael "made a catastrophic landfall" in the United States as a Category 5 storm near Tyndall Airforce Base in the Florida panhandle on October 10.[20] In that instant, Michael became tied for the fourth-strongest hurricane to make landfall in the contiguous United States and the strongest on record in the Florida panhandle. The storm produced surges causing inundations of dry areas into as much as fourteen feet of water. Flooding occurred as far north as the Chesapeake Bay in Virginia. The storm resulted in sixteen direct and forty-three indirect deaths, along with an estimated $25 billion in damage.

These hurricanes punctuated a broader trend of increasing frequency and impact of disasters, particularly billion-dollar weather events in the United States and globally.[21]

WILDFIRES RAGE

Between 1997 and 2008 the United States spent more than $11.5 billion on fire suppression. Total fire-related expenditures during that time are believed to be in the hundreds of billions of dollars. Extreme figures like these are not restricted to the United States: losses from wildfires in South America during the 1990s totaled $1.6 billion annually. Southern Europe between 2000 and 2007 experienced an annual average of sixty thousand fires, burning 476,000 hectares of land.[22]

While hurricanes and severe weather events tended to dominate the billion-dollar weather events in this era closing out the 2010s, chronic droughts, prolonged summers, higher temperatures, and other factors, including those related to climate change, have meant that wildfires continued to increase in both size, scope, and cost. The year 2018 broke records for wildfires in the United States, amounting to $26.4 billion in damage, with 2017 close behind at $20.3 billion.[23] In 2020 wildfires burned more than 10.2 million U.S. acres, a record.[24] Some of the globe's most devastating fires were Australia's "bushfires" in 2019 (and again in 2021). The fires that year scorched more than 30 million hectares (over 74 million acres), destroying more than three thousand homes in the process. The fires were so intense that they created thunderstorms at least seventeen times.[25] Many people were exposed to pollution in excess of national air quality standards for up to five months. This led to hundreds of excess deaths and thousands of hospital admissions.[26] The impact to wildlife was far-reaching: one report stated that more than three billion animals were estimated to have been killed or displaced.[27]

Relentless fires in California dominated the U.S. fire landscape during this time. The infamous Camp Fire of November 2018 wasn't nearly the largest fire at just over 153,000 acres, but it burned more than 18,000 structures and killed 85 people.[28] In 2020 more than 4.1 million acres burned in California, more than doubling the record set in 2018.[29]

Several of California's deadly wildfires, and many more smaller-scale fires, are believed to have been triggered from electrical equipment.[30] As a result of this revelation, and to prevent further damage from the electrical infrastructure, the utility Pacific Gas and Electric (PG&E) implemented public safety power shutoffs during periods of high fire danger. This helped to alleviate some risk but also created impacts of its own on those forced to go without electricity for businesses and for personal needs.[31]

Partisan politics also quickly became a central theme to the wildfires, with then-president Trump publicly blaming California for poor forest management policies and other missteps that he said resulted in its wildfire problems. While these social media communications were littered with largely incorrect assertions, they brought disaster response further into the partisan political warfare. The conflict led to threats to pull federal aid for wildfires, although this was nothing more than rhetoric, and the agencies responsible for relief continued to carry out their functions.[32]

SEVERE ACUTE RESPIRATORY SYNDROME, THE SEQUEL

Most readers will require no primer on the pandemic that came to be known as COVID-19. They lived through the early news reports about a respiratory infection spreading in Wuhan, China; affirmations from the American government that community spread in the United States was not a risk; and the unstoppable rise in cases that belied those proclamations.

Readers became familiar with terms previously confined to epidemiology textbooks: zoonotic disease; case fatality rate; flattening the curve. Never had the lay public so much as heard of mRNA, no less dropped the term in casual conversation. COVID-19 changed all that.

Like most of the disasters already described, the central tragedy of the COVID-19 catastrophe seems to live in its sheer predictability. The singularity—in this case, the emergence of the pathogen itself—was something of which scientists and others who had been paying attention had warned for decades. Equally predictable were the ways in which country after country proved ill-equipped to respond.

Many efforts are published or underway to understand the series of events that led the outbreak to become a pandemic and to quarterback national and global failures. Here, we look briefly at the outbreak timeline to identify areas of dysfunction in the United States that were based less on momentary errors of judgment and more on an endemic dysfunction that had plagued public health security and preparedness for decades.

While the origins of the virus called SARS-CoV-2 are unknown, a dominant school of thought is that it emerged from a natural animal reservoir, most likely a bat, and may have transited through an intermediate host animal before making its way into a person.[33] Theories of a leak from a nearby infectious disease laboratory are mostly predicated on the assumption of an accidental leak during research to understand this very risk—i.e., whether and how this family of viruses could spill over from animals to people. The U.S. government had understood this risk quite well. NIH research into coronavirus transmission risk, U.S. Agency for International Development (USAID) missions abroad to discover unknown viruses living in tropical forests, Defense Department research into pathogen risk levels in key countries—these programs were hard at work to assess the risk of a natural emergence of a pandemic strain. The government understood what such an emergence, whether of animal origin or otherwise, could mean.

Unclassified threat assessments from the director of national intelligence had warned of the national security threat of infectious disease almost every year since 2006.[34] Each report was delivered, via written and verbal testimony, to both chambers of Congress.

The issue was not one of ignorance but of a relative inaction of the kind needed to address the concerns the experts were articulating. It would take substantial and sustained resources to do that adequately. More funds would be needed for local public health and for hospitals. Once the cases arrived, it was well understood that a respiratory pandemic would overwhelm hospital and public health capacity. Advocates had been arguing for years that the single source of federal funding for hospital preparedness—known as the Hospital Preparedness Program—was underfunded to begin with and on a steep decline for over a decade.[35] This grant program—the only federal program for hospital readiness for disasters—was arguably never the sole answer to hospital preparedness: physician and preparedness expert David Marcozzi has said, "We simply can't grant our way to preparedness."[36] A kind of sister program for public health preparedness—the Public Health Emergency Preparedness cooperative agreement—was equally understood to be insufficient and relentlessly undersupported. The declines in appropriations for these programs did not start during the Trump administration: they actually began almost as soon as the programs had been created during the Bush administration in 2002, and the declines continued under President Obama and the various Congresses doing the appropriating.

We also knew that we would have no vaccines or treatments. How could you have a vaccine for an unknown virus? Experts had been recommending for years that the government make much bigger investments in the very technologies that could shorten the timeline from index case to vaccine.[37] The production of a vaccine made available inside of a year for public immunization campaigns was indeed a remarkable achievement made possible in part by previous NIH funding of mRNA "platform" technologies. But there had been little coherent federal effort to build a program for emerging infectious disease, to be more ready for unknowns, to be ready in weeks or a few months instead of a year. And activities designed to create dedicated facilities for surging production capacity for such countermeasures were plagued with problems for a decade; by the time we needed them, only one such facility out of three that Health and Human Services had created was fully operational and available for COVID-19 vaccine surge, and its failures were such that it was less an asset and more a drain on hundreds of millions of dollars in valuable resources.[38] So, for that first year, Americans were told essentially to wash their hands, wear a mask, and keep their distance from one another—the same tools available during the great influenza pandemic of 1918. One hundred years had passed, but the interventions were the same.

The unavailability of personal protective equipment (PPE) was also predicted. The federal government had understood for well over a decade that PPE shortages were not only a risk but a certain outcome of a respiratory pandemic unless drastic measures were taken. The influenza pandemic in 2009 strained availability of N95 respirators and masks as healthcare facilities placed orders that exceeded available supply.[39] Gaming a hypothetical influenza pandemic, CDC scientists estimated in 2015 that as many as 400 million surgical masks could be required for *patients alone*—a number that did not include those needed for healthcare providers or the public.[40] During COVID, each of these three demographics (patients, providers, and the public) needed masks and other PPE that was simply unavailable. But no administration nor Congress had been willing to appropriately fund the federal stockpile or create contracts to secure supply when the time came—nor make the case that states, localities, and hospitals should be taking this on themselves.

The coronavirus crisis launched the greatest emergency supplemental spending series of events in history. From March 2020 to March 2021, Congress approved six funding bills to deal with the emergency. The first, passed on March 6, 2020, before the idea of "lockdown" came into the public consciousness, approached a mere $8 billion in budget authority.[41] This was more than the president had asked for ($1.8 billion) but amounted to little more than Congress had put toward the Ebola emergency. It was a signal that decision makers recognized a threat but perceived it as containable. The vast majority of the money was for health and public health: CDC activities, vaccine and other countermeasure development, purchase of PPE for healthcare providers. About $1 billion was for small business loans.

Just three weeks later, the ground shifted. On March 27, 2020, Congress passed a $1.7 trillion spending package.[42] This was the largest emergency check the nation had ever cut. Unlike its predecessor, the CARES Act reflected the full scope of the crisis—its dollars went not only to public health and healthcare but to addressing the now clear-and-present danger of second-order effects of the unfolding disaster. The law contained provisions governing small business loans ("Paycheck Protection Program"—nearly $1 trillion), emergency food assistance, continuity of food inspection and safety, distance learning, telehealth. An entire section was devoted to "Economic Stabilization and Assistance to Severely Distressed Sectors of the United States Economy."

Globally, governments were responding with a range of lockdown measures aimed at reducing the spread of the virus among populations. They introduced vaccination requirements as vaccines become available, although vaccine equity and nationalism were in constant tension and remain so as of this writing.[43] Governments with resources to provide financial assistance and reduce macroeconomic shock attempted to do so, such as the European Union Central Bank's pandemic emergency purchase program.[44] The WHO has worked during the pandemic to create standardized approaches to evaluating, approving, and buying medical countermeasures for poorer nations as part of its COVAX initiative, which has shown potential as a model for this kind of response.[45] However, international bodies like the WHO have been criticized for delays in declaring a global emergency and for donor favoritism and as such have become flashpoints for geopolitical tensions among countries, most notably the United States and China.[46]

Despite calls for equity, early testing and vaccination strategies left out communities of color, even though these communities experienced higher rates of infection and mortality, were more likely to be categorized as essential workers, requiring them to report to work in person, and were more likely to have hourly jobs and limited savings, among other risk factors.[47]

States were told to include equity in vaccine planning and were specifically pointed toward resources such as the CDC's Social Vulnerability Index. Indeed, some states moved in this direction, although with more attention to it after the initial pushes of vaccines. Traditional planning processes and muscle memory of response systems do not reflexively respond to inequities. Our rhetoric is growing in its outrage at inequity; our performance is generally not. There are signs of improvement—reductions in vaccine hesitancy in communities of color have been noteworthy—but real and perceived barriers to access and consequences of side effects from having to miss work hinder vaccine uptake, among other challenges.[48]

GOVERNMENT RESPONSE: AUTHORITIES, MONEY, AND POLITICS

The U.S. government responded to every one of these disasters with emergency supplemental funding. Federal money was clearly necessary in each of these situations—there was simply no way to mount an adequate response without it. But the frequency and magnitude of expenditures were unprecedented. The boiling point of COVID-19 necessitated tremendous spending in part because of the sheer scope of the problem, but also because so much of what had been warned about pandemics—the high cost of response, the social and economic second-order effects—had not been planned for. Little had gone into preparing for these effects, and there was no savings account on which to draw. The only option, then, was to fund through increasingly partisan supplemental battles, reaching a pinnacle in March 2021 when the sixth supplemental—President Biden's American Rescue Plan— passed after prolonged effort on the part of the Democrats, squarely along party lines.

The funding battles became part of the fabric of a politicized response that was now regularly characterizing disasters. The injection of politics into disasters was not, of course, a new phenomenon: Katrina pitted Republican against Democrat as issues of inequality were raised; H1N1 reared the perennially popular and divisive issue of whether to close national borders. But more and more signs of polarization along party lines had appeared. Many of these lines were fiscal. Congress was quick to provide money for Ebola, but with Zika nipping at its heels, a reticence to write yet another check for another infectious disease (and one that seemed a fairly distant threat to the United States at that) began to materialize. The check that Congress finally did write was nine months late and hundreds of millions of dollars short of the request; some blamed that delay for operational difficulties encountered during the Zika response with regard to release of diagnostic tests and development of vaccines.[49]

Federal aid for Puerto Rico became a pitched battle, too. It pushed beyond the immediate crisis and well into the years that followed as the island was still struggling to recover. Still, response politics wasn't only about spending. The political reaction to the devastation in Puerto Rico became a sign of the political times as the death toll itself became a point of enormous contention along party lines. Similarly, the rampant debate about the virtue of shutting down the U.S. border to incoming travel during COVID-19—a question that should on its merits be answerable based on evidence alone—was a touchstone for a kind of "with us or against us" approach to the impending infectious disease disaster.

Beyond specific disaster spending, broader disaster funding programs were similarly showing signs of trouble achieving any kind of funding coherence. With increased spending in flood recovery and underinvestment in flood prevention that would reduce postdisaster costs, programs like the National Flood Insurance Program (NFIP) in the United States have teetered on insolvency for years. The NFIP had nearly $16 billion in debt written off as part of emergency appropriations to cover claims for Hurricanes Harvey, Irma, and Maria. Most agree that the program artificially depresses insurance premiums, creating a circumstance where market forces are not preventing development in hazard-prone areas. The last long-term reauthorization authorized the program through 2017; while this bill created more flexibility for FEMA to set rates and to seek more private sector involvement, the program remains in need of reform. But no one can agree on how to fix it. Between 2017 and 2021 there were sixteen short-term reauthorizations to extend the NFIP as Congress struggled to reinvent the program in a way that could address growing flood costs, the depression of the true cost of flood insurance, and the need to not price people out of existing homes in risk-prone areas.[50]

Finally, the rather central question of what authorities the government could or would actually use to respond to certain disasters was in question. Major disaster declarations were fine for hurricanes and tornadoes, but were they legal for a health crisis? COVID-19 brought this question to the fore. The only time the Stafford Act had been invoked for an infectious disease was to address West Nile virus in New York and New Jersey in 1999. And this emergency declaration involved a smaller and more limited scope and resources than the larger *major disaster* declaration.[51] While the language of the law allows it to be applied to "public health and safety" needs, officials simply never felt compelled to draw on it for an infectious disease outside of West Nile. Other legal authorities, most notably the long-standing ability of the HHS secretary to issue a "public health emergency declaration," have instead been used and deemed sufficient for infectious disease health threats. But when the massive emergency of COVID-19 created almost overnight tremendous pressures to mobilize fiscal and other resources, President Trump invoked the Stafford Act to declare a disaster emergency on March 13, 2020. While this move went largely undebated, the use of the Defense Production Act, a Cold War–era law that helped the nation mobilize civil defenses, became a political hotbed as dispute over whether the federal government could or should use it to impel private sector actors to work on behalf of the federal government began to permeate narratives about government overreach.

As more people experienced the impacts of disasters, new global energy was going into advancing frameworks like the Sendai framework for disaster risk reduction led by the United Nations. Other efforts included the development of the global sustainable development goals and more aggressive attention to climate change, all of which helped to center and drive discussions of disasters. Yet geopolitical tensions continued to influence or inhibit action. The emergency of the COVID-19 pandemic exacerbated these tensions and global disparities as international institutions struggled to keep up with need amid growing criticism in increasingly unprecedented times.

PRIVATE SECTOR SHIFTS

The economic impacts of disasters during this period were large enough that they should have been forcing a reckoning with the reality that massive disasters could have massive second-order financial effects. The World Bank estimated that Ebola cost the three primarily affected countries $2.8 billion, slowed GDP growth, and resulted in high unemployment.[52] Confined to West Africa, Ebola had little economic impact internationally, but Zika affected countries with tourism sectors, and COVID-19 of course was felt economically the world over.

The United States was enduring elevated economic pain during this time with the high cost of the hurricanes, wildfires, and COVID-19. Direct economic effects aside, an emerging central fiscal issue concerned the viability and sustainability of the insurance and reinsurance markets for these kinds of disasters. Debate was growing on costs and risks, but only nominal progress was being made.

The Biggers-Waters Flood Insurance Reform Act of 2012 and the Homeowner Flood Insurance Affordability Act of 2014 authorized FEMA to utilize private reinsurance products as part of the NFIP, expanding the financial mechanisms beyond direct insurance premiums to underwrite the program. Efforts to operationalize this strategy began in earnest around 2016. As of 2020 there were twenty-seven carriers engaged to reinsure approximately $1.3 billion from the NFIP.[53] But while there were new entrants into the flood insurance markets, insurers were beginning to exit the wildfire insurance markets in increasingly risky areas.

As the scope and frequency of wildfires worsened with climate change, insurers were finding it harder to find viable markets in wildfire-prone areas. In California, insurers would not have renewed tens of thousands of policies if the state had not introduced a moratorium on cancelling policies. This was as the industry was reeling from wildfires that caused $24 billion in damages, of which it covered $18 billion, in the 2017/2018 wildfires alone.[54] The Rand Corporation found that wildfire risk varies based on different greenhouse gas emissions scenarios, creating enormous uncertainty for insurers who may use such scenarios to raise rates or stop insuring all together. Without significant changes to the insurance and hazard paradigm, researchers forecasted increases in premiums and deductibles, increases in the underinsured and uninsured, and decreases in the availability of insurance providers.[55]

Utilities also found themselves on the front lines of responsibility for wildfires caused by faulty equipment. PG&E admitted fault in the California Camp Fire that killed eighty-four people in 2018. Many criticized the plea deal that levied several million dollars in fines but resulted in no criminal prosecutions as woefully inadequate for the severity of the devastation. Separately, the utility settled claims totaling more than $25 billion with fire victims, insurers, and government agencies for this and other fires.[56] Shortly after this settlement, PG&E was sued again by residents and businesses affected by the Kincade Fire of 2019. After recently emerging from bankruptcy, the utility was facing another potential $600 million in losses to finance $7.5 billion in additional wildfire damages.[57]

As the search for new financial mechanisms for funding disasters continued, markets experienced a growth in popularity of catastrophe bonds. These are bonds on which investors receive a return on investment if the catastrophe event triggers do not occur; if there is a defined catastrophe, then the funds in the bonds are used to support response efforts. The paradigm is similar to insurance. Investors like catastrophe bonds because they are somewhat independent from overall economic performance, whereas most other financial instruments are tied to broader economic trends. These bonds also tend to have shorter maturity, usually three to five years. These were some of the best-performing assets during the global financial crisis of 2008, but as investors increasingly bought them up in the years that followed, many sequential disasters triggered response payouts, lowering some of the investment enthusiasm for these bonds.[58]

Bonds were not enough. Planners began to recognize the need for a suite of institutionalized financial tools that could pay for preparedness and response, particularly in lower-resourced countries. The World Bank in 2016 established a "Pandemic Emergency Financing Facility" (PEF) designed to provide financing for poor countries experiencing pandemics and other serious outbreaks. The PEF was funded through country donations and World Bank–issued bonds. In emergencies it issued cash to support response or insurance to mitigate near-term threats. While the creativity of this financial instrument was praised for bringing in more than donations to help with pandemics, it was criticized for being slow to trigger. This was the case for an Ebola outbreak in the Democratic Republic of Congo in 2018, for which there was an initial failure for the outbreak to meet activation criteria, which in turn slowed disbursement. Funds triggered for COVID-19 may have been too late in the pandemic's acceleration to adequately contain and mitigate its impacts.[59] The World Bank has since shuttered the PEF. Debate and discussion continue on advancing a better financed and more comprehensive model for financing prevention, preparedness, and response.

The role of public-private partnerships in disaster preparedness and response also made its way into the public consciousness at this point. COVID-19 underscored the central role of pharmaceutical companies in dealing with public health crises; it also aired the hard truth that vaccines aren't actually "free," even when they are being provided free to the public to stem a pandemic. They have to be paid for. The vaccines and other pharmaceuticals that had been stockpiled for potential outbreaks like anthrax or smallpox had typically been paid for through joint investment between companies and the federal government. With no commercial market for these products, government investment in development and the promise of purchase when the products were ready created a market that helped some companies decide that it was worth it to get into biodefense pharmaceuticals. For COVID-19, that basic public-private partnership model held. The federal government invested nearly $30 billion in "Operation Warp Speed," the effort to engage the biotechnology and pharmaceutical sectors in developing vaccines for the pandemic and providing them to the federal government.[60] Not all companies took government R&D funds—Pfizer/BioNTech developed its vaccine without government investment, leveraging its U.S. purchase contract to minimize downstream risk.[61] Unlike Russia and China, which promoted government-developed vaccines, the United States chose to place its resources into the private sector. Many of these for-profit companies profited from their contributions to the pandemic, as had many companies before them that had provided vaccines, antivirals, and personal protective equipment to the Strategic National Stockpile for smallpox, anthrax, influenza, and other health threats. This is the very definition of a public-private partnership, one that pays for and leverages the technical and manufacturing expertise extant within the private sector while providing benefits to the public that has paid for the service.

As wealthy nations chewed up manufacturing capacity to purchase enough vaccine for their own populations, poorer countries were left behind. Calls began to mount for the release of patents designed to protect companies' intellectual property. Critics began to argue as soon as vaccines became available that the companies' intellectual property claim should be waived during the emergency to allow greater access to their manufacturing processes and thus support vaccine access in low- and middle-income countries. This view failed to consider that intellectual property at that time was not actually the bottleneck to global vaccine availability and to acknowledge the greater ecosystem in which the companies were operating.[62] This is a system that requires investors to be confident in a return on investment for the product at hand, and one that is predicated on faith that in the future they will not be punished for their efforts by being stripped of intellectual property—the primary element that actually allows companies to succeed. Vaccine hoarding by wealthy nations was a foundational reason for the lack of equity (and indeed a likely contributor to prolonging the pandemic by creating ample opportunity for problematic viral variants to emerge abroad). Liability issues for companies donating to countries that lacked legal frameworks for dealing with adverse events were also concerns, both for the companies and for potential patients. But the central point of failure really had its roots in a global planning failure to establish an effective benefits-sharing, funding, and overall operating model well in advance of the pandemic. Vaccine nationalism, manufacturing capacity limitations, and the need for companies to return profits to their investors were very well understood dynamics of pandemics and the medical countermeasure enterprise. Some planning for pandemic influenza benefits sharing was realized.[63] But international and national efforts to build structures that would address these dynamics or resolve such limitations were anemic at best until millions of people began to die.

This era saw the private sector retain its place of prominence in preparedness and response. The sector continued its path toward involvement in disasters with increasing use of financial markets and other efforts to bring new resources into disaster management and to better quantify risk. These efforts were generating some novel ideas but still lacked cohesive direction and a strong quantitative basis for investment decision support that values risk and resilience in the face of increasing disasters.

SIGNS OF CHANGE AMONG NONPROFITS

The philanthropic community continued its pace during this time without major change, settling into comfortable fundraising and response formulas. But a sense of disaster fatigue was setting in, and signs of change were on the horizon.

Sustainment of preparedness funding was still a struggle as most funding was still targeted to response and recovery, and with so many disasters, the windows of attention were seemingly shorter and shorter before the next disaster and appeal for assistance. Furthermore, the line between NGO as donor and NGO as implementer was blurring. NGOs were refining business models to solicit funds and pay for programs, including through federal grants and contracts.

The role of emergent community-based organizations in disaster response has been described throughout the history of disaster research. But given growing limitations on the larger, established nonprofits, the smaller groups' place in the contemporary landscape became heightened during this time. As the larger groups became stretched across increasing numbers of disasters, or limited due to more restrictive organizational policies, community-based organizations were increasingly acknowledged as a key part of response. Some funding models have attempted to account for the role of community-based organizations that may not have as easy access to government funds or mass donation solicitation campaigns.[64] The large NGOs overwhelmingly dominated the nongovernmental disaster philanthropy industry during this era.

COVID-19 was an enormous disaster matched by unprecedented disaster giving. During 2020 approximately $20 billion was awarded globally for pandemic relief through disaster philanthropy. Of this, corporations led the way, accounting for 44 percent of all dollars, followed by high-net-worth individuals at 27 percent. Donor-advised funds (by which investors give to a public charity for an immediate tax break and funds are disbursed over time) from three of the largest wealth-management companies (Charles Schwab, Vanguard, and Fidelity) gave an additional $14.6 billion. Community foundations accounted for the largest number of grants provided, more than half. When donors specified recipient groups, 35 percent of these funds were expressly directed toward Black, indigenous, and people of color (BIPOC) communities. The numbers are skewed by the large donations of one high-wealth individual, Mackenzie Scott, for both the larger proportion of donations from high-wealth individuals and from funds focused on BIPOC communities, and thus it is unclear if this indicates a trend or merely a temporary surge in funding.[65]

ACADEMIA TRIES TO MAKE SENSE OF A CHANGING WORLD

Academic alliances began forming that advanced new approaches in academic research and structures for funding it. An effort was growing to build hazard and disaster institutions in addition to the smaller programs that already existed across various university fields.

As international frameworks in disaster resilience matured and transitioned from the United Nations' Hyogo Framework of 2005 to the Sendai Framework of 2015, the call for coordinated effort from the scientific community continued to grow. In response, the Disaster Prevention Research Institute at Kyoto University convened its second Global Summit of Research Institutes for Disaster Risk Reduction with the theme "Development of a Research Road Map for the Next Decade." The summit sought to advance understanding of how academic disaster centers could support the newly established Sendai Framework. The effort identified the need for a forum for collaboration and knowledge sharing.

It also led directly to the establishment of the Global Alliance of Disaster Research Institutes (GADRI).[66] This was followed by the creation of the North American Alliance of Hazards and Disaster Research Institutes (NAAHDRI) out of a series of U.S. meetings. Its purpose was to bring together disaster research institutes into a collective entity for collaboration and advocacy for the disaster discipline.[67] Fields such as disaster medicine were holding symposiums on how to develop a more strategic research agenda with stabilized funding for disaster medicine and public health preparedness.[68] Universities were also looking at how to better reconcile foundational research with an increasing need for applied and translational research.[69]

Research studies continued apace. The researchers who studied the disaster literature in China found a rise in papers that may have been an effect of Wenchuan earthquake–specific research; but they also found in general a dramatic rise in number of disaster articles on Web of Science (a journals database) from 2008 to 2017 compared to the prior decade.[70] They concluded that the event "strengthened international cooperation to build a disaster science discipline" and increased a focus on disaster mitigation. Fernandez and Ahmed examined research trends since 2007, finding that the number of scientific publications per year that mentioned the phrase "build back better," an approach that gained traction after the Indian Ocean tsunami of 2004, rose steeply, from 3 in 2007 to 107 in 2018.[71] Mitigation and resilience were gaining ground, at least within the landscape of academic publishing.

Disaster research continued to seek its place as a distinct field within and beyond academia. Traditional academic institutions are built around principal investigators and research programs; incentive structures are based on the production of boundary-expanding knowledge within disciplines from these people and programs. Yet disaster science does not sit neatly within a given discipline. Its nature is cross-disciplinary and applied, providing it with no obvious home within these institutions or clear funding lines from the agencies that pay for them. This constriction perpetuates the canon on which research efforts tend to be built: discipline-specific, project-specific funding, usually carried out within a complementary school or program, but one that has no dedicated focus on disaster science and research.

This reality has sizable impacts on the academic workforce available to produce the evidence base for good disaster decision-making. Even in a time of increasing disasters and a growing number of disaster centers and academic programs, stable funding and career tracks for disaster scientists at a larger scale were still elusive. At the time of this writing, there are a number of academic centers and initiatives coming online focused on pandemic response and readiness, with many more in the works and likely to emerge in various iterations within academia.[72] This echoes the establishment of threat-specific academic centers in response to the lived disaster experiences of earlier eras. How this ultimately fits within a broader societal strategy to prepare for pandemics, other biological threats, and other kinds of disasters remains to be seen.

———————————

The Ebola crisis finally resolved in 2016. At least, this particular Ebola crisis did; the disease continues to emerge and cause smaller periodic outbreaks. Just a few years after the West Africa crisis ended, COVID-19 would emerge and result in a pandemic of much greater proportion. Pandemics were happening with greater frequency, no longer existing in the realm of rare events. And all the while, other disasters continued to rage with increasing frequency and intensity. The clustering of events left little room to breathe, to learn and apply lessons from the last disaster. Some lessons were learned; others had to be relearned. Many were never fully applied. With each disaster, the learnings seemed to surprise us. Meanwhile, disasters and the lack of mitigation in place for them continued to harm people, economies, and ecosystems, and science seemed to become more a source of conflict as much as a repository of solutions.

This era can perhaps best be understood across the sectors analyzed as one in search of a new business model for managing risk in the face of increasing catastrophes. Whether seeking new governance models, financial instruments, philanthropic approaches, or

adequately incentivized applied research, the diffuse problems created by the dysfunction and disincentivization were coming into
focus. Across four domains—politics, business, philanthropy, and
academia—the systemic dysfunction continued to make elusive the
achievement of rhetorical goals to get a handle on disasters.

PART II

HOW ORGANIZATIONS RESPOND
TO DISASTERS AND WHY THEY BEHAVE
THAT WAY

5

DISASTER POLITICS

THE DISASTERS described in part 1 portray a kind of relentless-
ness of hazards inflicting themselves on human populations.
The responses to them can be understood to some degree or
another through a complex matrix of governance, industry, philanthropy, and research. This chapter explores disasters and disaster
risk in the context of the U.S. domestic political sphere, while identifying central pressure points in international institutions. It aims to
identify the incentives and structures that lead to the decisions that
get made, whether through action or inaction. The political and policy landscapes are quite complex and warrant extensive treatment;
here we identify variables that contribute to decisions, many of which
have to date gone unexplored, but which reveal foundational contributions to the dysfunction and disincentivization plaguing disaster
preparedness.

PREPAREDNESS AND THE POLITICAL
DISINCENTIVE

Political polarization and dysfunction dominate many discussions of
governance these days. So much so that it is tempting (and not entirely

incorrect) to blame partisanship and tribalism for the woes of our policy outcomes. Partisan politics can easily explain how spending bills and other important legislation get jammed up, in the United States if not elsewhere.

The COVID-19 disaster and many of the breakdowns highlighted in the first half of this book were founded less in failures of imagination than in failures to act. Officials had the information they needed but were unwilling to take proportional action. The structures within which they operated were indeed as dysfunctional as the partisan tribalism of the moment has made them, but beneath this political turmoil is evidence that the structures of policy making itself and of political advancement had also disincentivized it.

Understanding why the nation's leaders—elected and nonelected alike—are disincentivized to meaningfully address risk is critical to emerging from the cycle of disaster, reaction, response, disaster.

We can start with voters—the people who provide jobs to the elected officials making the important decisions. Do voters value their candidates' support for preparedness, or for response, when choosing a president? Andrew Healy and Neil Malhotra evaluated the ways in which voters reward presidents' disaster decisions. They found that the electorate tends to reward disaster relief spending (i.e., response) with votes but on average shows little interest in preparedness spending. "Our central finding is that voters offer scant incentive to presidents to pursue cost-effective preparedness spending, but do encourage them to send in the cavalry after damage has been done and lives have been lost."[1] A government that responds to the incentives of disaster relief rather than disaster preparedness, they wrote, is a government that will underinvest in preparedness.

Why would this be? The study authors posited that a series of preferences may explain this self-defeating phenomenon. Preparedness spending is abstract and its benefits difficult to observe. How does the absence of a disaster prove that disaster prevention spending was worthwhile? Relief spending often comes in the form of tangible, direct payments to individuals, whereas preparedness spending is diffused across targets that are more broadly for the public good. Relief expenditures can also be directly attributed to the presidential administration spending them: How can politicians no longer in office take credit for preparedness spending that may have occurred in the decades preceding a disaster? Simply put, elected politicians are rewarded for short-term spending decisions that occur within their own election cycle. Taken together, the incentives that govern decision-making around getting elected and reelected run contrary to the kinds of decisions we need with respect to disasters.

THE TENSIONS OF DISASTER FEDERALISM

Further complicating decision making is the complex interplay that occurs across levels of government. The U.S. government exists at federal, state, and local scales. This well-accepted trifurcation has implications for how federal agencies are empowered to respond to disasters, and how the legislation and regulations that guide the disaster cycle are created.

The United States, and many other countries, bases its democratic governance on a system of federalism. The federal structure posits the existence of a federal government for larger governance issues but defers to smaller subdivisions for those more localized in nature. In the United States, these divisions are states and territories, with states delegating authority to different degrees to local counties or localities. The U.S. Constitution defines enumerated powers (those that reside with the federal government) and concurrent powers (those shared with the states). Anything not covered is under the purview of the states/territories.[2] This concept is perhaps most clearly articulated in the Constitution's Tenth Amendment, which reads, simply, "The powers not delegated to the United States by the Constitution, nor prohibited by it to the States, are reserved to the States respectively, or to the people."

The powers enumerated for the federal government range from tax collection to incurring debt on behalf of the nation, oversight of national defense, and regulation of commerce among groups of states (and with foreign nations). The authority to regulate interstate commerce is where much of the federal government's direct authority over disasters resides. Catastrophes can drastically affect the conduct of business between and among states. Outside of this interstate commerce clause and a few other narrowly defined criteria, states must invite the federal government to support the state response. This value of states' rights versus federal powers is a recurring tension dating back to the founding of the Republic. This dynamic persists throughout partisan politics, with conservative ideologies seeking to restrain unchecked federal powers, and liberal ideologies seeking to expand the reach and authority of federal programs. The concurrent powers shared between the federal government and states include the ability to levy taxes, build roads, and establish courts. In practice these play out with state courts and federal courts, interstate highways and local roads, and state and federal taxes.

Like so many things, disasters become politicized, and it happens at all levels of government. Peter Burns and Matthew Thomas described historical patterns of state-local political conflict that they argue directly influenced New Orleans's response to and recovery from Hurricane Katrina. Such patterns, they wrote, are often rooted in two areas: money and control over urban affairs. In New Orleans, long-standing tensions such as these revealed themselves in city-state arguments over the amount and availability of recovery money and control over rebuilding.[3] During COVID-19, many Americans have experienced firsthand how tensions between state and local government can affect their well-being: from mask mandates to school closure to vaccine requirements, governors and mayors have often found themselves unaligned.

At the federal-state level, the stakes and the politics ratchet even higher. The real federal power in disasters is in the money. Many federal programs don't actually compel state participation in federal disaster structures, but they do make funding contingent on it. States can go their own way, but in turn they would give up billions of dollars in federal assistance.[4]

September 11 was a watershed moment in reframing national thinking about the division of labor for disasters in the United States. According to the political scientist Peter Eisenger, the attacks "exposed a federal system that was ill-prepared to craft and implement a coherent program to protect the nation's cities." They revealed a tension between the national nature of national security and the highly localized effects of breaches in national security barriers. In an analysis of homeland security spending, Eisinger posits that the attacks came decades into a trend that began during the Nixon administration of unfunded federal mandates for cities and states in areas like education and wastewater management and suddenly demanded an altered mindset that acknowledged that homeland security was a different kind of problem.[5]

Curtis Brown, who is cofounder of the Institute for Diversity and Inclusion in Emergency Management and has served in leadership roles in emergency management and disaster policy in prominent regional, state, and federal positions, remarked in an interview as part of the research for this book, "In disaster response operations, the priority is on saving lives and reducing disaster impacts on individuals and critical infrastructure. For the most part, that is what has led the decision making." But he adds that for more abstract threats and less dramatic disasters, one is competing against a myriad of other priorities for officials' attention. "You're trying to constantly convince them through briefings, participation, and exercises to demonstrate what the political cost would be for not making these investments and not prioritizing it."

PREPAREDNESS, DISASTERS, AND MONEY

In the United States the funding of federal programs requires the president to draw up a request and for Congress to decide whether to grant that request. A friendly Congress may meet the request with minimal deliberation, while an adversarial Congress may cut or even increase it. Budgeting divisions within Congress and the executive branch require the development of numerous individual requests and bills, creating a busy dynamic and sometimes complex political maneuvering on the Hill during appropriations season so that a dozen appropriations bills can ultimately pass both chambers, are signed by the president, and see the government funded for another fiscal year.

When it comes to disasters, funding can flow from several sources: (1) annual appropriations to address prevention and increase preparedness and resilience; (2) emergency spending outside that cycle to address an emergent event; and (3) appropriations into standing accounts, like the Disaster Relief Fund, which provide a ready source of money for the executive branch to draw on when needed.

An early analysis of homeland security funding looked at spending through the lens of the federalist representation and processes for allocating resources. It found that political considerations often outweighed security risk assessments. In particular, key committee members responsible for drafting funding legislation would promote funding priorities for their district or state (i.e., where the voters elect them) over national interests. This trait is not unique to homeland security spending and exposes an important incentive governing legislative drafting: national interests can be less impactful on legislators' lawmaking decisions than those of defined geographic areas within the nation. So, when faced with national spending priorities, a bias toward constituents can take precedence.[6]

But national political incentives can be at odds with the national interest, too. The Healy and Malhotra study showed how electoral politics correlates with the availability of postdisaster resources, finding that election battleground states—those most competitive during a presidential election—get more than twice as many disaster declarations as uncompetitive states.[7] Disaster declarations translate into dollars. This apparent incentive for presidents to declare disasters with partiality is ultimately set by the voters. Voters reward elected officials for relief and recovery funding, despite the higher value of preparedness investments. There is no evidence that voters hold politicians accountable for preparedness, even though it demonstrably improves disaster outcomes and saves six taxpayer dollars in response for every one spent to prepare.[8]

The sandbox of disasters and money is full of contradictions. We don't pay enough in advance to prevent or prepare, so we end up paying out a lot later to respond and recover. We fund agriculture better than we fund public health. We allow rebuilding in risk-prone areas. Critics argue against the dearth of federal spending on resilience and disaster mitigation. They cite the abundance of spending on response and recovery that creates a disincentive for states and localities to invest in preparedness and mitigation.[9] "Clearly, the federal grants that we get on the state level and local level influence priorities and investments because everybody wants that federal money," notes emergency management expert Brown, "and as the federal government comes out with a pot of money, it influences what the priorities are."

This dynamic holds for infectious diseases. And given the widespread and prolonged impact of COVID-19, a hard look at these dynamics is critical to understand how we got to where we are. For years, government scientists understood that there are about twenty viral families—coronaviruses and influenza viruses among them— that are pandemic prone. They represent the most concerning threats as far as high-consequence infectious diseases go. They might emerge in a form we've seen before, like Zaire ebolavirus, or they might throw a curveball, like SARS-CoV-2 (more commonly known as COVID-19), but the pitcher is recognizable. What knowing that means from a preparedness perspective is that you could actually plan for outbreaks even if you don't know the specific virus you would be up against one day.

The *New York Times* reported that in 2017 an NIH research scientist submitted an idea to agency leadership to pursue prototype vaccines for viral families of known concern.[10] Outside experts had been recommending this for years.[11] The idea was that if you advanced research on technology for each family to a certain point or, better yet, created "platforms" that could be used across a range of potential pathogens or families, you would be much more ready to hit "go" when the time came. You could potentially have some of the clinical trial and regulatory hurdles—a major bottleneck—already addressed, much like we do each year with the new seasonal influenza vaccine. Dr. Anthony S. Fauci, then director of the U.S. National Institute of Allergy and Infectious Diseases, found it "really doable."[12]

But it wasn't doable enough to make it into the president's budget request. We don't know whether NIH never requested it or if the request was shot down during the vetting process, but we do know that the White House never asked the Hill for money for NIH to do this work until the nation was in full-blown pandemic crisis.

The incentive to fund preparedness is simply not a politically salient one. The story is similar at the Biomedical Advanced Research and Development Authority (BARDA), the agency where the advanced development of any such vaccine prototypes begun at NIH might continue. In what is known as a "professional judgment budget" projection (not an actual request, just a statement of likely future need), career BARDA experts predicted in 2016 that the agency would need to request dedicated funding for emerging infectious disease by FY 2018.[13] The amount was small—$200 million—but its presence was noteworthy. The addition of a dedicated "BARDA EID" (emerging infectious disease) funding line that the professionals felt should be added to the budget was a critical acknowledgment that the threat needed to be addressed more than it had been to date. But when the official FY2018 budget request came, the president didn't ask for that money. The judgment that it was needed remained in successive reports, but with a start date pushed back year by year. The professional judgment budget for EID was being ignored. The U.S. Department of Health and Human Services wasn't asking for this money, and Congress wasn't following up to ask why the experts thought an EID budget line was needed but not actually being requested. Nor did they appropriate the money even in the absence of a request, which they could have done.

We issued a request to HHS under the Freedom of Information Act in June 2021 to access internal budget deliberation and decision documents related to BARDA's annual requests. Our goal was to understand where in that process funding for EID may have been requested but then rejected. This could reveal where the specific barriers have been for the support of dedicated EID funding for advanced medical countermeasure development, informing us where the points of disincentivization occur. Two years later, HHS still had not provided any of the requested documentation. As such, we are unable to identify if these funds were indeed requested at some stage, and if so, at what point they were pulled from the official request that went to Congress—and therefore where the failure to request the funding occurred.

GOVERNING BY EMERGENCY SUPPLEMENTAL

For decades the United States has witnessed a rising reliance on funding disaster response via emergency appropriation. To better understand the funding and political dynamics at play, we reviewed data

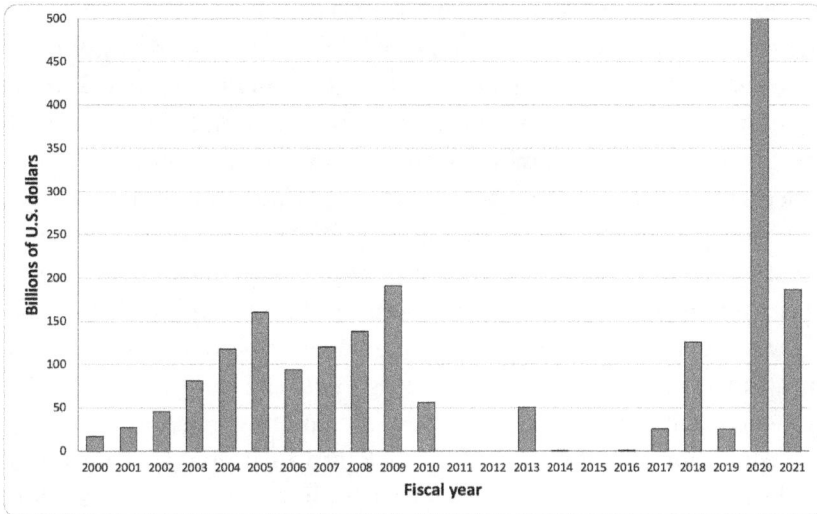

FIGURE 5.1 Supplemental appropriations by fiscal year, FY 2000–2021.

Graph by authors.

from the Congressional Budget Office on supplemental appropriations beginning with FY 2000.[14]

Figure 5.1 shows an upward trend. Congress gradually increased funding for emergencies and disasters over this time through a reliance largely on irregular supplemental appropriations bills passed in the immediate aftermath of a crisis. Coming into 2020, the tall bar represents unprecedented emergency spending for COVID-19.

What looks like a dip in spending in the early 2010s is actually a function of the passage of the Budget Control Act, commonly referred to as "sequestration," a budgeting stricture in effect from FY 2012 to FY 2021. This law created a more focused and proactive funding model during that time. It required stringent caps on discretionary appropriations, but it simultaneously allowed for something called a disaster relief adjustment, which meant that the standing disaster account (the Disaster Relief Fund from which FEMA draws) could be replenished during the annual appropriations process outside of the budget caps that limited discretionary spending. Doing this lessened the reliance on reactive supplemental appropriations, which is why the figure shows a drop in supplemental spending.

The way that the Budget Control Act corralled emergency spending was a good thing. It removed replenishment of the disaster relief account from the budget-restricted and hyperpolitical process of the regular annual appropriations, a process that often led to the standing disaster fund not getting as much money as disasters demanded in a given year and in turn placed more pressure on Congress to pass emergency supplemental bills. The Disaster Relief Fund is the primary mechanism by which the government supports response to emergencies and major disaster declarations under the Stafford Act.[15] By allowing this account to be funded adjacent to other annual appropriations, but outside their spending caps, the Budget Control Act removed one of the primary drivers for emergency appropriations, instead driving disaster spending back into an annual appropriation. It allowed disaster costs to be covered, and in a responsible fashion, and made room in the rest of the budget for other priorities. It had bipartisan support, and although the Budget Control Act is no longer in effect, this particular provision has been extended.

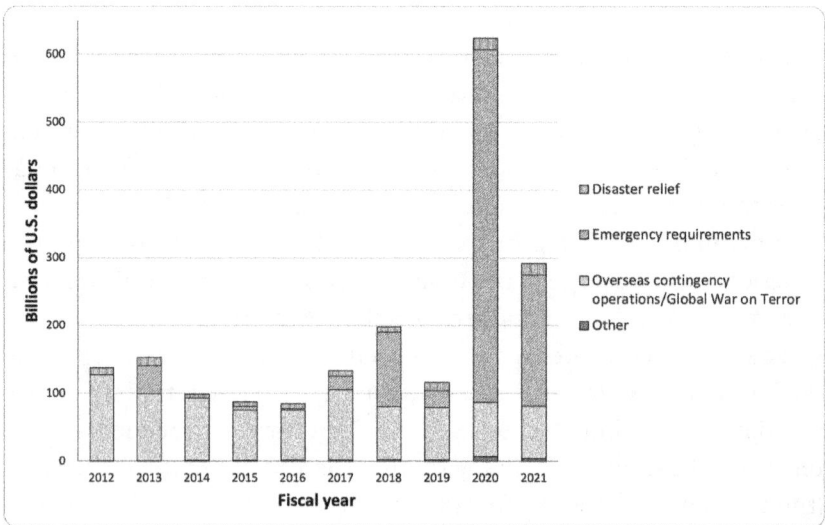

FIGURE 5.2 Adjustments to discretionary spending by fiscal year under the Budget Control Act, FY 2012–2021.

Graph by authors.

Figure 5.2 provides a close look at adjustments under the act across the fiscal years during which it was in effect, revealing spikes in "emergency requirements" that exceeded what the DRF could provide in those years.[16] Upticks are seen in FY 2013 with Hurricane Sandy and FY 2018 with the California wildfires and a difficult hurricane season (Harvey, Irma, and Maria). What this tells us is that in 2013 and 2018, and to a lesser extent 2017 and 2019, Congress returned to its old approach, passing reactive supplemental appropriations bills funding "emergency requirements" to respond to these unforeseen disasters. This need both resulted from and contributed to a systemic dysfunction in annual appropriations and planning, and, by extension, in underpreparedness for disasters.

An underappreciated issue with "emergency" spending is that emergency funding does not always go to emergency needs, or at least those promoted as the focus of the bill. These figures show that in many years, the majority of the "emergency" monies went to annual funding of overseas operations in the Global War on Terror. An emergency supplemental ostensibly for Katrina response in 2006 was a classic "Christmas tree bill" that included "emergency supplemental appropriations to the Department of State and related agencies for . . . educational and cultural exchange programs; . . . international broadcasting operations; and broadcasting capital improvements."[17] Some emergency spending, even when directly related to a recent disaster, is not allocated toward response but to longer-term mitigation and resilience building spent over years. The House put forward an emergency funding bill for Sandy that contained $17 billion to meet immediate needs and $33 billion for longer-term recovery and resilience.[18] Funding recovery through emergency spending may meet the short-term disaster need but denies a more strategic discussion of the needs and value of recovery in its own right, and the optimal ways of budgeting for future disaster recovery.

Emergency appropriations can be used for long-term needs if they receive an allowance to be spent over the long term. This may take the form of nonexpiring funds or an expiry of the funds a few years out. The agencies using such money thus have more time in which to spend it than they do funds appropriated for a given fiscal year. Some would argue that this flexibility is requisite to keep the agencies nimble as they respond to a disaster whose dynamics may still be unfolding and affecting communities for years. Others assert that the use of the mechanism and the granting of long lead times effectively sidestep the annual appropriations process and any funding caps that may apply to it.[19] It also makes fiscal conservatives uncomfortable because it challenges further oversight of the funds' expenditure.

Emergency supplementals are a fundamentally problematic way to pay for disasters. And yet, in the twenty-first century, emergency appropriations were becoming a go-to mechanism of U.S. presidents and congresses to finance response to natural disasters and health crises.

Looking at the availability of standing money for different kinds of disasters is revealing about the U.S. government's priorities. Even the agriculture department has a fund, the Commodity Credit Corporation. The CCC is a mandatory (not discretionary) fund for agricultural programs, providing for income support for farmers and promotion of U.S. agricultural exports; natural resource conservation and international food aid; and, indeed, disaster assistance. When a highly pathogenic strain of avian influenza struck poultry farms in the United States in 2014 and 2016, the USDA obligated $869 million for the response; nearly all this money came from the CCC.[20]

But H1N1, Ebola, Zika, COVID-19—they all came and went with no public health bank account from which to draw response funds. In 1983 Congress had recognized the value of such a fund, creating a Public Health Emergency Fund and allocating $30 million to it. Starting in 1993, appropriators avoided making any further allocations to the account. It has lain nearly empty for years, despite the lessons of COVID and the massive levels of emergency funding that were needed to respond to it. As of the middle of 2023, three and a half years into the COVID-19 crisis, Congress had not yet appropriated any money into the account.

HOW POLICY MAKERS DEAL WITH COMPETING RISKS

In 1972 Congress established the Office of Technology Assessment (OTA) to help it analyze and assess matters with a nexus to science and technology. Its charge was to translate an issue's complexity into relevant knowledge and illuminate trade-offs. It published on topics like nuclear proliferation and safeguards; reducing earthquake losses; vulnerability of electric systems to natural disasters and sabotage; the cost effectiveness of influenza vaccination; measuring the returns on research investment; and almost anything else across health, environment, power, law, technology, and other disciplines that intersect with policy making. According to a Harvard Belfer Center report, the OTA arguably helped Congress address its "low bandwidth for incorporating scientific and technical information into its policymaking process," that is, its low "absorptive capacity."[21]

Congress shuttered the office in 1995. Many reasons were cited, from cost, to redundancy with other federal reports, to accusations of political bias. Whatever the reason, Congress lost the OTA as a way to mitigate its absorptive capacity issues. Insufficient absorptive capacity is one reason that elected officials fail to adequately address every potential threat or risk. The constraints of budget caps are another. In other words, time and money. But every so often an event comes along that tips the scales and creates room for changing the formula—that in fact creates time and money.

The events of September 11, 2001, disrupted the status quo of security policy and led to a period of policy disruption that rippled into the decades that followed. A handful of other major disasters—especially Hurricane Katrina—caused a similar kind of disturbance in the policy fabric. Sudden events like this can become "focusing events"—in the disaster context, accidents, natural disasters, and deliberately caused catastrophes that can discernibly increase the attention paid to a policy problem. September 11 was a rare event that caught the public and policy makers by surprise, killed thousands of people, caused billions of dollars in damage, and revealed vulnerabilities across a wide spectrum of policy areas. Katrina, for its part, wasn't just a disaster—it was a catastrophe that overwhelmed the national emergency management system, which may explain the enormity of federal soul-searching that occurred thereafter.[22]

These kinds of disruptions work to influence change—or to at least create a perception that change is happening—through several means, notably by directly gaining the attention of elected officials. These major events spur policy makers to focus on policy making itself to prevent further system failures of the same kind. Congress shows it is taking charge by holding hearings: between September and December 2001, it held eighty-nine hearings on public risks from terrorism. The passage of many new laws followed. Disruptive events affect federal agencies in ways that may alter their involvement in the issue area subsequent to congressional demands, laws, or executive directives. In the case of 9/11, the federal government created an entirely new agency. At the executive level—the office of the president—one often sees a centralization of effort and sometimes the instatement of a "czar." But politics and public policy researchers Peter May, Joshua Sapotichne, and Samuel Workman found that capturing the attention of policy makers alone is "insufficient to motivate heightened levels of policymaking across the board."[23] Only those parts of the system with greater susceptibility to the intrusion of terrorism demonstrated an uptick in policy making activity after 9/11—border protection, transportation safety, information security—whereas areas like food safety, technological hazards, and natural disasters showed much less of a change. Even the massive reorganization that created DHS was in fact less paradigm shifting to federal agency involvement than one might have expected given the disaster that was 9/11. The reality was that there was the potential for much greater shifts in attention in areas perceived to be less susceptible to terrorism or to have a role in preventing or mitigating it. Even a 9/11 wasn't enough to foster the comprehensive and foundational reforms that could have improved federal and national readiness through substantial change.

WHAT CONSTITUTES A PROPORTIONAL RESPONSE

Congress may appear open to learning about emergent risks but often fails to act in a way that addresses what it has learned. From 1995 through 2019, Congress held 167 hearings on emerging infectious disease.[24] These hearings offered 167 opportunities for members of the House and Senate to hear 860 times from witnesses on the risk of emerging infectious disease, and what we as a nation were and were not doing to prevent, to prepare, and to be ready to respond and recover. The warnings these witnesses and sometimes the policy makers themselves conveyed predicted COVID-19 and the vulnerabilities of not preparing: the public health system is underresourced in a way that will quickly become apparent during a biological event; it is not clear who in the federal government will lead a pandemic response; the roles of federal and state governments are not clearly delineated; hospitals are unprepared for a significant surge in cases; the economic and social disruption caused by school closures will be substantial.

Why would Congress not act, or not in a way sufficient to meet the need? First, the work to understand why disasters happen, why their frequency is increasing, and how they can be prevented requires deep study and development of nuanced and strategic policy considerations. While hearings ostensibly communicate to the public that this study and solution development is occurring, the reality is that they often amount to discussion sessions. While they do provide a sense of oversight, it often lacks any real accountability for the executive branch to do what actually needs to get done. When they do produce legislative outputs, these often fail to address key issues. Second, low absorptive capacity, competing demands, competing risks, and limited budgets layer themselves into a tangled barrier that often defies meaningful action. Hearings are useful only insofar as they result in identification of a policy problem and a path toward solving it. Bills are often the preferred route of members of Congress to show they are solving problems. Members take enormous pride in the bills they introduce and especially in the number of bills—legislative "productivity" is a common metric used in political science evaluation. But bills are only useful to the extent that they actually get us to where we need to be. Prior to COVID-19, the American people were treated to three iterations of the foundational Pandemic and All-Hazards Preparedness Act and 161 chapters of the public health title of the United States legal code. There were essentially no authorities that the federal government lacked to allow it to take the needed steps toward better prevention and preparedness for pandemics. COVID-19 was still a disaster.

In the first twenty months of the COVID-19 era, members of Congress introduced 2,049 bills that had the word "Covid" in the bill title or summary.[25] Much of this legislation would not actually provide new legal authorities but would simply express what the bill sponsors wanted the executive branch to do, which in many cases it already had the authority to do, or would express to their constituents that they themselves were doing *something*. At its core, though, this collection of bills demonstrates a decided tendency for lawmakers to try to make laws—to act on the presumption that legislation is the solution to the problem, when in fact they have taken inadequate time to assess what the problem actually is.

It is possible that the mindset, programs, and advocacy machine put in place after 9/11 and anthrax may have skewed the United States toward disproportionate choices. In 2021 the *New York Times* published extensive coverage of biotechnology company Emergent Bio-solutions' deals with the federal government, citing large sums the U.S. government had paid to the company for more than a decade, mostly to support its development of anthrax vaccines for the Strategic National Stockpile.[26] The reporters concluded that government purchases for the stockpile have been driven by terrorist threats, and that Emergent's aggressive lobbying for the government to spend ever more on these threats crowded out spending that could have otherwise gone toward emerging infectious pathogens, like coronaviruses. The effects here may have been real, but it would be a mistake to blame undue lobbying influences alone for the failures of U.S. governance that led to the COVID-19 tragedy—the failure was present for decades across an ecosystem of imbalanced incentives and poor choices in the context of competing risks.

PERPETUATING INEQUALITIES

The table for disasters is often set well in advance of their occurrence. The same can be said for disaster inequities, which can be predicted along the lines of inequities hardwired within our society. In a sense, anything that preserves the status quo also preserves the inequities already built into our communities. Attempts to provide for "equal opportunities" can simply serve to preserve existing inequalities, and in some cases further widen them. Removing discriminatory practices and patterns in our organizational behaviors is important, and diligence against efforts to erode protections from discriminatory practices is critical. But such efforts on their own are insufficient. The legacies of discrimination are self-perpetuating, and removal of unfavorable practices does not stop the embedded discrimination already in motion.

An analysis by real estate giant Redfin found that legacies of redlining—a discriminatory practice of assigning grades to neighborhoods that were deemed risky for mortgage securities—influences disaster risk half a century after it was outlawed. In practice, redlining was used to isolate and segregate communities of color, particularly Black communities. The Fair Housing Act of 1968 made this practice illegal, but its legacy persists to this day. From a disaster perspective, formerly redlined communities are more likely to have homes in areas likely to be flooded as comparted to other, predominantly white neighborhoods. Low-income populations were in essence forced into living in areas at greater natural disaster risk, while those with higher incomes could get mortgages for property in safer areas. Today, majority minority communities are more likely to be affected by storms, and even global warming will discriminate, with formerly redlined communities averaging five degrees hotter due to dynamics of the way the neighborhoods were constructed.[27]

As the reality of climate change kicks in, communities no longer need to be redlined along racial lines to enable inequality: seemingly objective indicators of risk and income perpetuate these inequalities all on their own. In working to develop standard measures for climate-related risks to housing, agencies like the Federal Housing Finance Agency risk depressing property values in majority minority communities, furthering the wealth gap, and pushing communities of color into even more climate-vulnerable areas. Evidence from Hurricane Harvey reveals patterns in loan eligibility that disadvantaged communities of color. Access to information on risk and financial mechanisms for upward mobility, if kept equal, will widen these disparities.[28]

Sociologists Junia Howell and James Elliott also look at the increasing costs of disasters along with widening inequalities and find that not only is this occurring, but it is poised to get worse with increasing disasters. Their analysis identifies a dynamic by which inequality is driven by more than one cause, positing several compounding factors, such as differences in access to government assistance, disruption to housing and income, and inequitable opportunities to access resources that flow into disaster areas.[29] While more research is needed, the increase in income inequality, racial disparities, and disaster impacts all appear to be linked somehow.

Among these compounding drivers of inequality, differences in access to government is perhaps one of the most critical. This stems from the notion that unequal access to government officials leads to unequal access to resources that flow into postdisaster areas. Political science and public policy professor Daniel Aldrich noted this as a significant factor for recovery in his analysis of Japan's 3/11 triple disaster. This notion of *vertical capital*, or the connectedness of a community through the systems of governance, can predict who gets access to resources and who does not.[30] Often the most expeditious route to increasing the volume of assistance is to use existing outreach mechanisms, which tend to favor historically advantaged communities.

In discussing some of the dynamics of inequity, Curtis Brown notes that "there's this dynamic within government and bureaucracies. It's very slow to recognize the needs of marginalized and underserved communities and prioritize them. And that's because they're marginalized. They don't have the interest groups that the influential advocacy groups do to really push the resources and the policies and the direction to support them." He adds that a lack of data compounds the problem because the true impacts are undermeasured, and as a result, not taken into account operationally or politically.

And in disaster response itself, it is critical to acknowledge that elected officials are in fact rewarded for recovery dollars they bring to their constituencies—but not for preparedness funding, despite increasing evidence on the outsized savings it brings in terms of both lives and livelihoods.[31] When it comes to disaster policy, like many other policies, voters reward elected officials on some aspects of the job, but not always on the strategies that the data suggest they should care more about.

DISASTER POLITICS SCALED GLOBALLY

Disasters affecting one country directly can have cascading impacts across supply chains and economies. They can affect everything from human migration to natural resources and ecosystems to the global economy. The mix of stakeholders engaged in disasters is also often a plurality of domestic and international organizations. But while disasters may not respect borders, humans do. The system of governance we use to manage disasters, whether governmental or nongovernmental, must be organized by a set of principles and bureaucratic mechanisms to operationalize those principles.

How these systems function and what their underlying approaches are toward disaster risk reduction are influential across all levels of governance and across disaster stakeholders. High-profile institutions are creating common frameworks for disaster management. These institutions are not stand-alone entities but rather are built and managed by nation-states, ranging from the very rich to the very poor, all with agendas and national interests that seep their way into the functioning of international organizations, the frameworks created, and the operations that follow.

The intergovernmental community has gathered around disasters for some time. Recent decades have seen these efforts become more distinct from conflicts and other transnational concerns. The United Nations issued a handful of disaster-related resolutions in the 1960s, most related to a set of severe earthquakes and hurricanes that occurred during that time. Hints toward more formalization occurred in the 1970s, with Resolution 2816 creating the United Nations Disaster Relief Office. Then the United Nations declared 1990–1999 the "International Decade for Natural Disaster Reduction." The decade ended with an impetus to emphasize the need for disaster prevention as the central way to avoid the impacts of disasters. It culminated in the Hyogo Framework for Action 2005–2015, updated in 2015 by the Sendai Framework for Disaster Risk Reduction 2015–2030. Today's U.N. Office for Disaster Risk Reduction is tasked to implement the Sendai Framework.[32]

Sendai was endorsed by the United Nations General Assembly in 2015 and provides a strategic global framework for disaster risk

reduction through 2030. It recognizes the sovereignty of and responsibility of nation-states for disaster risk reduction, while also recognizing that it is under the purview of not solely nations but also local
governments, the private sector, and other stakeholders at all levels.
Its four areas of focus are to understand disaster risk, strengthen
disaster risk governance, invest in disaster risk reduction for resilience, and enhance disaster preparedness for effective response
and building back better in recovery. It provides seven targets:
reducing disaster mortality, reducing the number of people affected
globally by disasters, reducing direct economic loss in relation to
GDP, reducing the damage to critical infrastructure and disruption
to basic services, increasing the number of countries with risk
reduction strategies, enhancing international cooperation with
developing countries, and increasing access to hazard early warning
systems.[33]

Throughout the Sendai framework (and much international doctrine) is a ceding of responsibility and implementation to nation-
states. With a framework as sweeping as one for disaster risk reduction, achieving consensus among all nations would be a challenge. A
close look at the targets reveals them to be largely nonspecific and
without a binding mechanism.[34] Sendai offers priorities that most, if
not all, nations can agree to and are likely already doing, but it notably does not require handing over any sovereignty or accountability
to an international body or to have processes dictated to independent
nations.

While the United Nations was evolving on disasters, it was also
maturing on a particular subset of them—those biological in nature.
The WHO, a UN organization, had adopted International Sanitary
Regulations in 1951, ultimately replacing them with the International Health Regulations (IHR) in 1969. (Separate mechanisms were
developed for the intentional bioweapons threat, with the Biological
Weapons Convention entering into force in 1975.) As the century
turned, the framing of the emerging infectious disease problem
turned, too. In 2000 the UN Security Council adopted Resolution
1308, which expressed the council's grave concern over the extent of
the HIV/AIDS pandemic and emphasized that conditions of violence
and instability were dramatically exacerbating its spread.[35] This was

the first UNSC resolution that directly connected an infectious disease with security threats, and it was one of the first signs of a rhetorical and programmatic shift both within and outside of UN structures that began to morph emerging infectious disease beyond a health issue into a security issue, which in turn had implications for the level and kinds of funding that would begin to go toward addressing the infectious disease problem.

The IHR, designed to govern information sharing among the international community regarding health risks, were modified over the years that followed, with a significant overhaul occurring in 2005 after the SARS pandemic. The 2005 revision was a major acknowledgment that the expectations that had previously existed were insufficient to meet the threat of infectious disease in a highly globalized economy. The new regulations carried more stringent requirements for disease reporting and data sharing but did not solve the problem of how nations could actually pay to build preparedness and response capacity in a way that might stop a pandemic before it got started. Further, implementation has demonstrated a hesitance to sanction violations and weaknesses in coherence and coordination in high-profile international responses.[36]

The WHO is the primary intergovernmental organization tasked with international public health and is governed by a World Health Assembly (WHA). WHA sets policy for the WHO, and it was WHA membership that voted on the passage of and updates to the IHR. These regulations are one of the few tools to which states parties are required to adhere, although noncompliance is difficult to sanction, and there are no formal penalties associated with it.[37] Almost everything else the WHO issues is guidance. Nor is the WHO resourced to be the first responder to every outbreak, as was made clear by Ebola in West Africa, and by COVID-19.

It is only relatively recently that the international community has come around to addressing the need for a more comprehensive shared governance and financing construct for preparedness and response to health crises. These conversations continue at pace in light of the devastation COVID-19 wrought. The World Bank and WHO have worked to establish a "financial intermediary fund" that, with donations from nations and philanthropies, will operate as a standing account for pandemic prevention, preparedness, and response activity.[38] The fiscal challenges of COVID-19 with respect to global vaccination in particular are shining a light on how public-private partnerships could be constructed *in advance* to help ensure vaccine availability and equity; such advance market commitments and obligations for the sharing of benefits, if well constructed, could mitigate future financing issues related to vaccine equity and should be considered during the development of new or revised global governance agreements with respect to medical countermeasures.[39]

The World Bank Group is another international apparatus, one designed to better finance and otherwise foster development. It comprises the International Bank for Reconstruction and Development, International Development Association, International Finance Corporation, Multi-lateral Investment Guarantee Agency, and International Center for Settlement of Investment Disputes, entities that are among the largest and most influential organizations active in international development finance. In relation to disasters, the bank has key roles in disaster risk financing and in creating knowledge to be used by the group members and other actors in seeking more informed approaches to disaster risk financing.[40] But, like other international organizations, the influence of major donor countries is hard to escape, sometimes pushing bilateral interests over global ones, or attaching conditions to funding.[41]

Similar to many nations, international institutions embody a quasi-federalist model. Nations are part of a global community that presses for compliance with treaties or norms and through which large sums of money flow. Countries that are members of international institutions may sign agreements, make commitments, and give or take money, but ultimately nation-state autonomy is preserved.

The United Nations and its agencies are dependent on donor nations to fund their operations, provide troops to peacekeeping missions, and otherwise offer technical and logistical support above and beyond baseline operations. This further divides the world into donor nations and aid recipients. Often the development of goals for such institutions is focused on the interests of major donor nations. The example of the Millennium Development Goals shows how well-intentioned performance measures were tilted toward the perspectives of aid organizations and institutions from wealthier countries, arguably creating inaccurate perceptions of aid beneficiary countries.[42] Many argue that countries in Africa were routinely low ranking, creating perceptions that some countries were much worse off than they actually were.[43]

Even the staff members of the United Nations and similar international organizations are often well connected politically in their home countries and retain loyalties that can steer international organization values and behaviors. Major donor countries are disproportionately represented among UN staff. It is not clear if this is a causal relationship or merely a side effect of the influence of major donors. But the phenomenon is noteworthy, especially when representation and implicit bias can influence policy preferences and bureaucratic implementation.[44]

———————

Political accountability is driven by reaction to disasters. When presidents get shots in the arms of their people, voters react. When they activate emergency management agencies like FEMA or the National Guard to support a state in need, this shows strength. Most important, when the dollars flow in, voters respond. The incentive structure to deal with disasters only really kicks in when elected officials are reacting to it. There is so much more political incentive to react to these problems than to work proactively against them.

Resolving this self-defeating reality will require, at a minimum, a reimagining of congressional activity. The U.S. Congress will need to embrace potential solutions like integrating its budget oversight and allocation across committees of jurisdiction; providing a standing fund for public health disasters; and considering more mandatory spending approaches. On a global scale, we must also figure out how to pay for and implement preparedness and response globally when we know that nations will continue to act in their own self-interest. This end remains elusive. Much of the funding for global preparedness has come in the form of bilateral donations—one country provides another with resources. This patchwork of funding has at once provided critical support while remaining insufficient to meet the need. There have been some efforts toward a more inclusive multilateral approach, such as through the United Nations and the World Bank. Rethinking investment targets and developing structures through which nations commit but which transcend national interests of donors is necessary, and models are appearing that may help reach these goals.

Political structures are but one element in the disaster ecosystem, but they play an outsized role in how well prepared we are. Politicians wield outsized influence due to their spending authority—not only in what they do spend, but in the downstream effects of decisions not to spend. Other aspects of political governance, including how the leadership mantle is wielded, influence national readiness and response and ripple beyond borders into the global sphere. Any realistic solutions must mitigate the vagaries of individual leadership styles and the particular pressures of election systems and cycles, being focused instead on securing and enacting sustainable frameworks and approaches inherently oriented toward the public good.

6

DISASTER MARKETS AND
THE PRIVATE SECTOR

D *ISASTER CAPITALISM* is a term generally used to describe the exploitation of disasters for profit.[1] The role of the private sector in disasters is often relegated to this turn of phrase, and, indeed, there are many guilty parties who routinely seek opportunity in disasters with little regard for the plight of the disaster survivors. With rebuilding to be done, there is money to be made. And with economies wiped out, they can be rebuilt in the interests of profiteers seeking to further enrich themselves. But as we have seen in the preceding chapters, the role of corporations in disasters is much more complex. In many ways the private sector is an important force for good, bringing approaches and resources that would otherwise not be used. Likewise, its entities are operators of essential infrastructure and drivers of the economic engines of recovery.

The private sector—just like every other sector—is driven by underlying motivations that influence whether and how it involves itself in disaster management, and many of these are predictable. Some private sector actors may be motivated by optimizing investment opportunities; others, by mitigating risk, managing uncertainty, protecting market share, rejuvenating economies in which they operate, and even, simply, acting on good intentions. The players in the private sector are as diverse as in any other, and oversimplifying to one type would at best provide a limited viewpoint, and at worst stunt an opportunity to leverage the good while improving the rest. While this chapter does not purport to represent the full field of private sector actors, it does seek to identify trends in how various private sector entities engage with disasters. With an understanding of broader trends, we hope to better understand the value propositions necessary to better reconcile capitalism with resilience.

OUTSOURCING DISASTER MANAGEMENT

The idea that certain functions are "inherently governmental" and that others are not is central to understanding what kinds of activities the federal government is willing to outsource. What constitutes an "inherently governmental function"? The question does have a straightforward answer, at least in the legalese language of the Federal Acquisition Regulations (FAR) of the United States: " 'Inherently governmental function' means, as a matter of policy, a function that is so intimately related to the public interest as to mandate performance by Government employees."[2] The FAR goes on to state that these functions typically fall into one of two categories: the act of governing (i.e., the discretionary exercise of government authority), and monetary transactions and entitlements. It lists criteria that help define what this means, such as the interpretation of U.S. laws so as to take or not take actions, determine and advance U.S. political and other interests, or significantly affect the life, liberty, or property of private persons. Activities such as directing criminal investigations, leading military personnel, or conducting foreign relations are inherently governmental.

The list goes on, but essentially amounts to meaning that anything falling outside leadership or money is eligible for private support. Contract support for emergency planning and response is common and often occurs in ways invisible to the beneficiaries. The CDC outsourced planning for COVID-19 vaccine distribution and administration to Boston Consulting Group (BCG), one of many contracts HHS awarded to the group for COVID-19 support. The *Washington Post* reported disputing views over whether the CDC contract was well handled, but it illustrates the extent to which contractors are tasked with implementing major governmental efforts for the public good.[3] BCG was deployed to a fifth of U.S. states as part of federal and state vaccine distribution efforts, and other consulting companies, including McKinsey and Blue Shield, were similarly contracted.

Privatization of government services is as old as the government itself—older, in fact. Military contractors supported the Continental Army and Navy during the Revolutionary War. The Pinkerton National Detective Agency provided President Lincoln with personal security during the Civil War. But it wasn't until after World War II that privatization—what some call "government by proxy"—grew into the institutionalized, privatized bureaucracies we know today in areas like military, atomic energy, and space contracting.[4] The Reagan era famously spun off ever more of the nation's public operations to the private sector as part of its privatization strategy to reduce the size of government.

Since 1979 FEMA had been the central federal authority for disaster management in the United States. While the private and nonprofit sectors had always played a major part in disaster response, their role expanded during the Clinton era as FEMA underwent reorganization as part of the administration's efforts to privatize emergency management policy. This continued under George W. Bush, whose first budget director, Mitch Daniels, said, "The general idea—that the business of government is not to provide services but to make sure that they are provided—seems self-evident to me."[5] The administration was equally clear that there needed to be a larger role for states.

The Homeland Security Act of 2002 accelerated the privatization of previously federal emergency management functions. It moved twenty-two agencies, including FEMA, under the new Homeland Security Department. The sociologist Kevin Gotham notes how, over the next few years, constant reorganizations and shifting of programs and resources "eroded the agency's capacity to coordinate and deliver resources to disaster-impacted communities."[6]

It is difficult, on the one hand, to imagine the myriad responsibilities of the government being accomplished through federal employees alone. There are too few of them, the need is too great, and the expertise extant within the private sector cannot be easily shifted into a public model. Yet not everyone agrees that privatization is necessarily good, or at least not in the way it is frequently carried out. Gotham further notes that "by providing assistance to communities affected by disasters, the state aids its citizens, asserts its power, and reproduces its sovereignty. In shifting emergency management responsibilities from government to market, privatization addresses disaster victims not as citizens and members of an aggrieved community but as atomized customers, clients, and consumers. In doing so, privatization obscures liability and accountability for problematic post-disaster outcomes, and disarticulates public purposes from post-disaster recovery and rebuilding activities." A by-product of this approach is the creation of revolving doors of public and private leaders.

The "revolving door" is really a somewhat complex ecosystem in which federal needs and individual opportunity are entangled. Privatization creates new jobs outside of government that were once within it. These may be operational roles or professional ones. Individuals who worked within government have options in the private sector. As the post-9/11 era wore on, the federal government intensified efforts to integrate emergency management into homeland security functions, doing so in a way that outsourced or privatized much of the emergency management element. What began to grow was a complex web of public-private contracting to support these critical functions.[7] The advent of "homeland security" and the establishment of the department also meant the sudden emergence of a market for lobbying and other strategy jobs. According to one analysis of disclosure forms, 157 registered lobbyists listed "homeland," "security," or "terror" on their forms as areas of their portfolios at the beginning of 2002; by April 2003 the number had jumped to 569.[8]

Looking beyond the United States, the trend to privatize disaster response and recovery functions can vary from more centrally controlled government approaches to more outsourcing. But a common thread is that even when the government controls the authorities for disaster response, it doesn't necessarily translate into control by the people. Additionally, with most of the world's recovery capacities (like transportation, shipping and logistics, and medical supply chains) being in the private sector, the integration of public and private partnerships is inevitable.

CRITIQUES OF CAPITALISM

Notions of capitalism as the root of disaster vulnerability are finding a rise in popularity as critics seek to understand the costs of development and its impacts on the world's poor.[9] Indeed, this is a tempting lens through which to view these challenges. The challenges in disaster resilience, and sustainability more broadly, permeate nearly every aspect of human activity, and capitalism as a fundamental economic framework makes it an easy target.

This approach to understanding disasters finds fault in perverse incentives and behaviors of corporations, as well as governments, in perpetuating poverty to accumulate greater wealth among the world's elite. Evidence across these approaches ranges from descriptive data of inequalities, circumstantial evidence purporting cause and effect, and smoking-gun examples of decisions where the tradeoffs of wealth and poverty were clearly known. Incentives that reward growth and disincentivize sustainable development often lead to powerful calls for deconstruction of the current world order, and replacement with a more equitable model based on case studies of local demonstration projects. It is important to turn our attention toward the egregious inequities under a surface language that purports to fight for a common good for all.

As consciousness of the perils of development grow, companies are engaging to address these concerns. Sometimes these efforts are genuine, and other times they merely change the cover on the same book. This latter approach when dealing with environmental concerns is referred to as greenwashing. The term was coined in the 1980s in response to hotels promoting towel reuse as environmentally friendly when in fact it was designed as a cost saving measure. The general principle is that greenwashing occurs when organizations spend more effort and resources to make their products appear more environmentally friendly than in actually making their outputs more environmentally friendly.[10] This trend's pervasiveness makes it difficult for the average consumer to differentiate genuine efforts from greenwashing. In his book *Unnatural Disasters*, Gonzalo Lizarralde expands this to concepts of sustainability and resilience by showing how this trend is entering further into the consumer space, noting that getting community buy-in is often more about getting sign-off on prefabricated ideas made without their input.

This phenomenon is often discussed in critiques of neoliberalism. Neoliberalism is loosely defined as the privatization of functions designed for public benefit. And it is increasingly seen as the primary source of failings in development, humanitarian assistance, and disasters. A natural step in this critique is to call for the dismantling of underlying systems, including capitalism itself. While this may be tempting in its simplicity and totality, it calls for a total revolution that lacks pragmatism. And as a consequence, there is little room left to work within the structures that will continue to exist despite the outcry from academics and advocates and that are perpetuated by the choices of individuals, organizations, and governments. While the deconstruction of these structures warrants further deliberation, the more realistic path forward is to reevaluate the fundamental incentive configurations that operate within them.

The value of resilience (that is, an economic incentive to work toward it) has been articulated under some specific investment criteria, such as the value of certain building mitigation investments, but in other key areas the articulation is lacking, such as in bond investments and environmental, social, and governance (ESG) ratings that routinely undervalue risks of climate change and other disruptions.[11] Understanding how this valuation of resilience fits within broader value frameworks for the private sector just might illuminate new approaches that don't require the societal deconstruction that would undoubtedly lead to intense conflict and misery in the transition toward a theorized greater good that may or may not ultimately be realized through more radical approaches.

RECONCILING SOCIETAL AND CORPORATE INCENTIVES

Companies exist at an intersection of many forces. They have expectations from shareholders for creating value across different time horizons. They have customers who demand both affordability and, increasingly, sustainability and ethical behavior. They are being asked to meet the short-term needs of their businesses without compromising their viability or the ability of future generations to achieve their goals. These pressures have been formalized in the notion of a triple bottom line: environmental, societal, and financial.

The environmental bottom line focuses on an organization's environmental impact and sustainability. This can take the form of preventing environmental damage from processing (e.g., improved toxic waste management) or from the advent of more sustainable innovations (e.g., energy efficient technologies). The societal bottom line is the goal of corporate social responsibility (CSR). Often, when we think of CSR, we think of corporate giving. But it actually encompasses the broader social responsibility ecosystem within an organization that includes things internal to the organization like fair wages and valuing diversity, as well as external relationships with the communities within which a company operates or otherwise affects by its organizational behaviors. The financial bottom line is focused on achieving expectations for creating shareholder value and operating in a way that promotes profitability and growth. Where organizations seek to be is in a "sweet spot" that can achieve all these goals simultaneously. Doing so requires a complex and balanced approach.[12]

The evolution of more effective corporate social responsibility will mean no longer resigning social responsibility to the periphery but instead actively finding shared value across society and making it central to the business model. Currently, the notion of trade-offs and constraints is often used to understand social responsibility. A common example is that it is more expensive to be more environmentally conscious, increasing the cost of doing business. But this thinking ignores the costs that corporate social *irresponsibility* imposes on business, such as the ways that pollution increases societal costs, leading to lower economic activity and depressing potential market size, and even shifting costs from production to taxes as government and communities need to cover the societal costs imposed for short-term profitability. Paying farmers higher wages through fair trade practices can be seen as redistribution of profits away from a company, but under a shared value perspective it is strengthening local clusters of institutions that can also translate into supply chain efficiency and yields.[13] So can new approaches to calculating Net Present Value, one of the complex equations used to determine the value of a proposed project with modifiers to account for sustainability.[14] What this all suggests is that the math we use to value resilience looks at the wrong variables or at least is an incomplete picture and is thus consistently producing wrong answers and incentivizing harmful behaviors.

PUBLIC-PRIVATE PARTNERSHIPS: AN INEVITABLE INTERDEPENDENCY

There are times when the public-private model fails. When it does so, it can be spectacular. The opposing party cannot resist the opportunity to say, "I told you so" (see Solyndra scandal), and the media cannot resist the headlines. It is tempting to look at the amassing of private sector profits among homeland security contractors, or challenges with biotech delivering on its COVID-19 vaccine commitments, as evidence that a profit-driven model pollutes the public good.

But there are many more examples of where these partnerships go right. They are simply less well publicized. Much of our disaster response and recovery capacity exists in the private sector, and thus successful disaster response and recovery does not happen without support and collaboration across public-private partnerships. Private companies are ultimately driven by internal interests, and public-private partnerships are most effective where those are aligned with public interests. They tend to fall apart when those interests diverge, or when they are not adequately satisfied by accommodations from one party or the other (e.g., liability shields for private companies, or deep price discounts for public purposes).

An important truth is that some expertise simply exists more plentifully in the private sector. Applying commercial logistics processes offers lessons to improve humanitarian disaster response, as does integration of business intelligence system principles into disaster management situational awareness and decision support schemas.[15] New financial instruments, such as catastrophe bonds, and new insurance products are also adding resources and financial signals to the disaster ecosystem, with enormous potential in reshaping the disaster resilience landscape.[16] But like any new ideas in disaster management, there are trade-offs. Insurance schemas need to have markets in order to function, and there are serious equity issues with vulnerability that is not profitable if it is not carefully managed and regulated.[17] And under these schemas, the need for government and charitable assistance would not realistically disappear but perhaps could be more targeted toward those most in need.

The private sector brings insights and resources that would otherwise not be accessible to the field of disaster management. At the same time, it will always be driven to some extent by organizational and shareholder interests. Even corporate social responsibility activities ultimately have some relationship to corporate objectives. They are an extension of a company's values. They may foster a positive image. They also often support the communities where businesses operate, creating an indirect benefit in terms of reputation, as well as social and economic health that benefits all. The balance between altruism and self-interest varies by organization, but questions are inevitably asked when money is spent, on what it is spent, and how this relates to core organizational goals. A for-profit company will always be interested in profitable activities, and the key to ensuring that capitalism works for disaster prevention and response is to find public-private models that support both business and public interests.

DIVERSITY AS A COMPETITIVE ADVANTAGE

The private sector has had a mixed record in terms of diverse, equitable, and inclusive business practices. It would be a mistake to say that private sector approaches should be fully emulated, yet there are examples of diversity initiatives that show promise. Indeed, there is a growing body of evidence showing how essential diversity, equity, and inclusion efforts can be to being competitive and effective. When done well, the needs of the communities that form the context of companies' operations are more integrated into those operations, and in times of disasters, business response, continuity of operations, employee assistance, and corporate social responsibility impacts can be more effective.

Initiatives like the Business Opportunities for Leadership Diversity (BOLD) have sought, among other things, to help corporations value the competitive advantage that cultural diversity brings them. Research into the value of diversity found that in some circumstances it led to greater innovation, while in others it led to more turnover among top employees. Looking closer at the relationship between diversity and organizational performance, the Diversity Research Network found that the context of diversity within the organization, and specifically the group/team dynamics that facilitate diversity, is key in experiencing value from diversity. In their work, HR practices like training, coaching, and development were important mitigators for diversity having a negative effect on performance. Some causes of the negative impacts were linked to overly competitive cultures and aggressive growth-oriented strategies at the expense of engagement.[18]

Sociologist Cedric Herring further explored the linkage to business performance, utilizing data from U.S. businesses in the late 1990s. His analysis concluded that diversity is associated with increased sales, customers, market share, and relative profits. While inconclusive as to precisely why diversity leads to better business performance, potential reasons posited range from creative competition to the introduction of more diverse ideas and creativity into business strategies. The research acknowledges the potential disruption diversity can cause but notes that "within the proper context, diversity provides a competitive advantage through social complexity at the firm level."[19]

What this research shows us is that diversity needs to be coached and integrated into the value chain methodically and thoughtfully. It is also a hard truth that in an environment where access to opportunities has been drawn on racial lines, directly and indirectly, tensions exist. Navigating this will require greater investments in time and effort and will likely increase the cost of doing business, but the payoff will be nothing less than greater reach and value to those served by our agencies and organizations, and greater equity in the outcomes.

Ultimately, the private sector brings to the table a wide and unique array of strategies for engagement. These range from direct contracted assistance to the development and maintenance of critical infrastructure on which civil society relies, to robust operations management and evaluation approaches, to many quasi-philanthropic approaches.

Celebrations and critiques of the performance of the private sector in disasters are equally valid, and both are worthy of investigation to better understand their dynamics and underlying incentives. Unchecked incentives to increase shareholder value can lead to egregious behaviors, and the market should not be relied on to adjust to fix abhorrent behavior. But with better understanding of capitalistic incentives, there can be a net value added to the creation of disaster resilience that can simultaneously bring new approaches and resources into the field, while also reducing pressure on government and charitable entities so they can focus more fully on the most vulnerable.

Many emerging risks remain inadequately valued in financial decision making, leading to unintended downstream costs. An approach that advocates for improved integration of risk and resilience modifiers in decision making could move us toward a culture of investing in resilience. Embrace of the triple bottom line, balanced score cards, and other strategic and tactical approaches is requisite.

How this ultimately gets implemented may require a shift in how value is articulated within the private sector, and among those who patronize its services. Greater scrutiny of sustainability by consumers and investors is already leading to a rethinking of how to value preparedness. ESG ratings are an initial attempt to requantify investments toward a more balanced approach. There are shortcomings to this approach, and it remains a work in progress.[20] Some mix of regulation and tax incentives may also help incentivize/disincentivize different behaviors. Watchdog nonprofits can also help to illuminate best practices and expose shortcomings. Perhaps what will be most critical are better data, coming from applied research to establish a foundation of evidence on which more resilience-oriented corporate investments and operations can be based. But as we will see, academia has its own challenges in answering these types of questions.

7

DISASTER NONPROFITS

DISASTER GIVING, and the role played by nonprofits and NGOs in particular, is central to the disaster relief mission space. Under structures like those presented by FEMA or by global entities like the UN and WHO, philanthropy organizations provide a critical backstop that serves those who would otherwise be unable to access private insurance, financing, and even emergency government assistance programs.[1] Domestically and internationally, this paradigm creates a complex interplay of government services, local and nonlocal (including foreign) assistance from nonprofits, and hybrid nonprofits that have some official designations from nations, like the Red Cross and Red Crescent.[2] When functioning well, these charities can be an essential part of disaster preparedness, response, and recovery. But they are largely independent organizations operating within a complex environment, and what is needed does not always match what is coordinated. To better understand this dynamic, it is important to understand how and why nonprofits function the way they do, and how their underlying business model drives certain actions over others.

In developing this book, we have been confronted with a fundamental question, the answer to which remains murky: What do we mean by nonprofits? Are we talking about foundations that are strictly focused on raising and making grants? Or charitable organizations that are providing programs and services in areas of need? In seeking

TABLE 7.1 Philanthropic organization types and features

Type	Organization description	Tax status	Grant-maker	Service provider
Donation managers	Solicit and receive donations and/or utilize institutional funds such as endowments to provide funds for charitable purposes. Many foundations fall under this category.	Nonprofit	X	
Program and service providers	Provide direct services and implement programs. May provide research, program implementation, or both. Typically funded through solicited donations, grants, service contracts, and other fundraising mechanisms. Some organizations in this category may provide subgrants, but typically for partners in direct program/service delivery.	Nonprofit		X
Hybrid charities	Solicit, receive, and/or provide donations for the purposes of grant-making *and* provide direct programs/services.	Nonprofit	X	X
Corporate social responsibility entities	Use company profits and other resources to support charitable activities, through direct grant-making, in-kind services, employee giving, volunteering, or other approaches. CSR approaches may vary, with some purely grant-making and others purely program-delivery in nature.	Funds originate in a for-profit entity but may be managed by a created nonprofit entity	X	X

answers, we begin to see that these questions posit a false dichotomy. Many foundations that are known for philanthropy have become more engaged in operations, and numerous nonprofits that provide services on the ground are also grant-makers themselves. Sometimes grant-making takes the form of relatively small giving from national organizations to community-based organizations. Other times it means the provision of large grants for partnership consortia to fund big, strategic initiatives. The general categories of entities operating within the philanthropic sector are roughly summarized in table 7.1.

PHILANTHROPIES: GIVING, RECEIVING, AND SPENDING

Nonprofits and philanthropic organizations operate along a continuum from giving to direct service provision. What they have in common is that they are all are ultimately reliant on donors in some way. Whether the donations come from institutions or individuals, that giving is an important signal for how nonprofits seek support and choose what to prioritize. The Gates Foundation may prioritize global health issues for fundraising and giving because that is a chief concern of Bill and Melinda Gates, and the Red Cross may highlight its disaster response in soliciting donations and recruiting volunteers because that has been its remit for some time. These are different types of nonprofits, but they still respond to signals from their funding sources or decision makers. These signals may be where we need to start looking; we need to understand the spaces where philanthropy and nonprofits do good work but at times do not make the investments that will pay off more in the long run.

It is well established that preparedness generally has significant value over response and recovery spending. The United Nations estimates that $6 billion in appropriate risk management investments would have benefits valued at $360 billion.[3] A U.S. analysis of mitigation projects finds $6 of benefit for every dollar spent on mitigation from federal grants alone, with some retrofits and hazard-specific investments saving far more.[4] But while disaster risk reduction and prevention show more value, the community of donors continues (with some exceptions) to be overwhelmingly focused on the acute response phase. And with it, so is the activity of the nonprofit community in the disaster space.[5] Philanthropy spends a lot on response, and one of many reasons for that is that individuals who donate to philanthropies are motivated to give in reactionary fashion.

It would be easy to point a finger at nonprofits, accusing them of short-sightedness. But many lament the difficulty in fundraising for preparedness and need to operate within the parameters of the resources available for the purposes in which the funding is provided. To better understand the context for how nonprofits solicit funds and operate within a disaster setting, we need to understand the signals for the fundraising that fuels their capacity for engagement on disaster issues.

THE DYNAMICS OF POSTDISASTER GIVING: WHY GIVE?

At the core of nonprofit performance is philanthropic giving. Giving (whether by individuals or corporations) is often driven by emotion, and when it comes to disasters, emotions peak in their immediate aftermath. Gregory Witkowski, a senior lecturer for nonprofit management at Columbia University's School of Professional Studies who was interviewed in the development of this book, notes that "people give in an effort to do something in the face of the destruction caused by a disaster. Perhaps they know someone impacted directly or have a connection to the place but certainly also see how a disaster can upend lives and want to do what they can to help."

A variety of factors drive the emotional connection to a disaster. It may be influenced by the aid agencies themselves in their calls for donations, by proximity to the disaster (physical and through knowing impacted family or friends), or by the media coverage that many rely on to tell the story of impact and need. One analysis of giving after the Asian tsunami disaster of 2004 found that media attention had a dramatic impact on disaster giving. An additional print story or an additional minute of televised news coverage from a major news service could lead to increases in donations by as much a 17–21 percent on the day of publication or newscast.[6] The media is understood as an important facet of sense-making functions for the public, for its role in creating access to information, and for amplification of certain stories and aspects of stories. Even with the growth of social media, traditional media still employs a multitude of strategies that shape understanding via these newer media platforms.[7]

Emotional appeal as a primary driver to capture the resources necessary to meet needs in disasters steers efforts toward those that bring in more resources. It creates a vicious cycle rooted in the best of intentions. Emotional appeals attract resources to do good work. But the work that is highlighted is the most photogenic, the most appealing to the emotions of donors, gradually steering aid to one type of "help" but leaving significant blind spots in the types of assistance that are less emotionally salient or are otherwise hard to describe. As businesses that require donations to maintain staff and infrastructure, NGOs capitalize on emotional appeals to underwrite their work and build their reputations as organizations worthy of supporting. Thus an incentive for overpromotion of response and recovery efforts and a programmatic bias toward acute need foster a business model that is not optimal for the most effective investments in disaster resilience. Donor behaviors and fundraising strategies mutually reinforce this paradigm.

Who gets funding is driven in part by who is set up to receive it. The disaster aid industry is a robust complex with sophisticated mechanisms for capturing funding. These can range from agency contract vehicles for assistance that lay dormant but can be activated when needed to canned appeals to donors to support a given response. Undoubtedly, right now, there are websites and press releases ready to go for the next disaster to appeal for donations, with placeholders for details and photos of the event. These processes are built on in-depth knowledge of when and how people give, informed by data on giving from prior disasters, and budgeted into personnel, supplies, and broader playbooks for responding in standardized ways (or at least as standardized as is possible in a disaster setting). Deviating somewhat from the chronic criticism of the aid industry, we recognize these preparatory processes as important. This type of response—efficient, fast, and substantial—is critical in aftermath of a tragedy. But it is not complete. Templated response provides order for the responding organizations, partners, and beneficiaries, but imposing systems on chaotic environments inevitably leaves some people out and focuses on what is known and predictable.

The actions of these organizations can also have unintended consequences, including the undercutting of local markets with injections of free commodities. For decades, the provision of food aid to disaster-stricken areas and the response to other humanitarian crises has therefore aimed to incorporate concomitant development of various frameworks and models aiming to avoid these negative impacts to local economies.[8]

The unpredictable and less visible needs are where emergent organizations come into play. These are organizations not traditionally geared toward response and recovery, but which extend their operations to meet the needs of survivors, sometimes emerging as new organizations that didn't exist prior to the disaster.[9] They do not have sophisticated marketing and development teams and often aren't set up to capture the resources coming in to help disaster survivors. They are often based in the community prior to the disaster and there long after the cameras lights fade and the recovery goes on outside of the broader public's eye. The larger NGOs will often provide subgrants to local service providers, which helps if they happen to fall within the mission area or programming of the larger NGO.

Issues of trust also continue to be an important factor in the giving landscape. Whereas NGOs benefited from a decreasing trust in government and quasi-government institutions during the Asian tsunami, years later, after many high-profile scandals and frustration with response efforts, trust in NGOs has leveled off and even declined slightly. According to the *Edelman Trust Barometer 2021*, businesses are the most trusted institutions, and the only group among government, the media, businesses, and NGOS to be considered both ethical and competent. According to the barometer's data, NGOs have a positive ethics score but a negative competency score.[10]

Witkowski observes, "There's less trust. And that seems to be generational more than anything else. So we're on a bad incline in that sense because the younger generation seems to have less trust in institutions." He adds, "I do think it's notable that the Red Cross remains a powerful brand despite a lack of trust in so many other organizations." Why some groups buck the trend of deteriorating trust versus others is unclear. But in the business of nonprofits, trust is often essential for harvesting donations.

When deciding where to give, donors (individual, organizational, and others) look for a combination of trusted brands, direct impact, and convenience of donation. Smaller and emergent organizations may only be able to offer the direct relief aspect. Larger nonprofits may have to work hard to demonstrate the case that a donation to a behemoth organization will reach those directly in need (a look at fundraising materials reveals a plethora of high-resolution photos of the NGO team helping survivors, usually in organization-branded attire). Transparency and trust are also key but pose an additional barrier for smaller and emergent nonprofits that lack the sophisticated accounting and communications infrastructure to bring in external auditors and build brand reputation and awareness. Some notable exceptions are trusted community institutions that are well known within a smaller geographic area.

Thus the market for giving is biased toward larger nonprofits who do essential work but may lack the penetration and agility to help many survivors who are among the most vulnerable. This also drives a trend in shorter-term assistance, moving from one disaster to the next to meet the acute need and to demonstrate value to emotionally driven donors.

THE COMPLEXITIES OF CHARITABLE RESPONSE

Nonprofits don't work in a vacuum. Tax laws, customs restrictions, governmental politics, and other factors all influence the ability to access and operate in different disaster areas. And while many non-profits leverage the images of their compassion and heroism serving those most in need, this can become a liability when events outside of their control prevent their ability to do the job, and they receive full blame for what are actually shared failures.

Jason Friesen is the founder and executive director of Trek Medics International, a nonprofit focused on improving access to emergency medical systems across the globe. He has also served in response and leadership roles for other NGOs in various disaster settings. While being interviewed in the development of this book, he noted, "Donors, beneficiaries, governments, the private sector, they all want different things. That's a given. They all may be working towards the same ends, but how they think they're going to get there or what they think that the path to those ends are, or what those ends actually look like once you take it out of the kind of abstract language that gets tossed around in reconstruction, well, everybody's got a different definition of what that means."

The aid response to the Haiti earthquake in 2010 ushered in mas-sive commitments of aid—$13.5 billion in total—from all sectors, with about a quarter from private charities and the rest from nations. But there was little to show for it five years after the earthquake. Exposés by NPR and ProPublica, among others, attempted to break down some of these challenges and to shine a light on purported versus actual effort on the ground.[11] But reports like these, even though they may be factually correct, can be misleading.

Friesen noted that "while very thorough from their perspective, it was a one-sided story. It is the trend to point the fingers at the inter-national NGOs, which certainly deserve a lot of criticism. There's no doubt about it. But it goes back to the public's expectation that you're going to walk into an earthquake in an extremely impoverished country and be able to clean things up just because you've got a ton of money." He further noted from his work in Haiti and other countries that the issue of corruption is also often left out of the reporting and public eye:

> Not just corruption at the highest levels, but the endemic corruption. From top to bottom, that is frankly quite a normal thing. In many impoverished countries that have problems with corruption to begin with, they now have been deeply affected by a catastrophic disaster and are being overwhelmed with international NGOs that are flush with cash. In countries with endemic corruption there is often a mentality at all levels that you need to "get while the getting's good," but among the media it almost seems politically incorrect for them to report on that aspect of relief because it runs counter to the "innocent victim" narrative they're putting forth.

In one sense, many nonprofits end up setting themselves up for criticism. By fundraising as saviors for the most in need and doing the job that no one else can or will, they also take on an implicit liability when things don't go well. And so when there are failures, that strategy backfires. But that is never the whole story. Disaster response is a cacophony of good intentions, opportunism, and agendas from a myriad of organizations. Nonprofits are one part, doing important work, but with an implicitly biased model focused on the most visible and acute needs, driven by the very donors who may be demanding better.

THE GROWTH OF CORPORATE SOCIAL RESPONSIBILITY

In 2000 less than a third of the largest corporations donated to disaster relief, but fifteen years later more than 90 percent had, with average donations increasing by a factor of ten.[12] This growth of engagement of the private sector has been driven by a range of factors. Tax incentives have always been an incentive for for-profit companies to engage in giving, but evidence is mounting that there is value to an organization beyond the direct monetary benefits that tax incentives provide.

Corporations and smaller for-profit organizations work within the context of the communities in which they have a presence. Organizations are often motivated to invest in the communities they serve, for the sake of reputation management, being seen as a good citizen, and by the knowledge that investments in the community are investments in the employees and the context in which they work and live. Additionally, the behaviors of some organizations may also be strong motivators for others. A major pledge for a disaster from a well-reputed company is often followed by donations from others, taking cues from the company's behaviors and setting the bar for subsequent donations.[13]

Some organizations create mechanisms for employees to provide direct donations to worthy causes through charity drives, payroll deductions, and even secondments of employees to support nonprofits. Organizations are increasingly part of the disaster landscape, and there are many ways in which they overlap. These corporate philanthropy strategies vary in their operational approaches, with some organizations managing aspects within the organization, while others may spin off a nonprofit entity that is independent from the main for-profit corporation.

The private sector has many philanthropic resources to provide and is increasingly an important part of the disaster preparedness, response, and recovery cycle. With more sophisticated giving coming from the private sector alongside corporate social responsibility strategies comes the potential for more positive impacts, as well as competition. It will be important to leverage these private sector philanthropic resources where they are available, while recognizing the limits of their reach. An article by the *Harvard Business Review* noted an important reality: "Disasters in underdeveloped economies, where few deep-pocketed businesses are present, are unlikely to attract significant corporate donations. So governments, NGOs, nonprofits, and individuals should be prepared to shoulder much of the burden when disaster strikes those regions."[14]

CONCERNS OVER FRAUD

With disaster giving comes fraud when organizations or individuals seek to dishonestly capitalize on others' generosity. Giving is particularly vulnerable to fraud because of the urgent need that leads to expedited giving. In the aftermath of Hurricane Katrina, the FBI investigated fifteen websites presented as charities in Florida.[15] The research found that the size and structure of charity markets did not seem to have a correlation;[16] having larger and more established charities versus smaller ones made no difference in the risk of fraud.

The occurrence of fraud negatively affects almost all the incentives for charitable giving. When money does not go where it is supposed to go, it has an impact on an organization's brand reputation and erodes donor confidence in their money actually doing good. Witkowski notes that "there's a concern about any kind of potential fraud following a disaster. And so the larger organizations have a name reputation, and people are drawn to that." He also notes that as corporate giving has increased, corporations will often align CSR efforts with trusted nonprofit brands as part of their strategies to mitigate fraud.

With concerns over fraud come increasing requirements and best practices for evaluating nonprofits. The concerns have created a market of due diligence resources, similar to business intelligence for for-profit organizations. In some cases, it's a nonprofit business evaluating nonprofits. Groups such as GuideStar have a variety of tools for conducting due diligence for nonprofit organizations. These include tax documents, compensation reports, and profiles. Some information is freely available while some is under a subscription model for enhanced analysis.[17] These are generally powerful and useful resources for evaluating more established organizations involved in disaster response. But the lack of response history and administrative records may make some of the most important response organizations that are embedded in communities less visible to the donor community. Current mechanisms for evaluating nonprofits have blind spots that inadvertently leave response areas for which localization and flexibility are most important lacking sufficient support.

EMERGING MODELS OF NONPROFITS

As NGOs and nonprofits grow in the disaster space, questions begin to emerge. How big should they be? How much should they be relied on to do the work for which governments are responsible? Or for which the private sector should be paying? After all, if everyone is benefiting from the work of NGOs, shouldn't everyone be contributing? And what is the balance between what donors want and how to meet the needs of those in the field? How does one reconcile how someone wants to spend their money versus how communities want to spend it?

These questions and many more have similarly challenged the humanitarian aid industry, a not-so-distant cousin of disaster relief. But the question is largely academic. NGOs set the terms of their response and often even help build the criteria under which they are evaluated. Because when people are depending on charity to do what they themselves aren't able or willing to do, then there isn't much influence available to them beyond making requests and suggesting priorities.

This is not to say that the nonprofit community is detached from response, but that the incentives that govern the various actors in disasters can leave gaps in community needs, especially if the needs are prolonged, and after the emotional appeal and attention of the media and donors comes to an end.

Emerging models of nonprofits seek to upend the current operational gaps and create more of a continuum of value. Long-term recovery coalitions are popping up in areas affected by disasters. These are often led by nonprofit organizations that convene community human service organizations and liaise with emergency management structures to inform and guide recovery priorities. Collaborations with local chambers of commerce and the business community also create important bridges between these worlds of for-profits and not-for-profits and culminate in essential services and economic activity critical for overall community-based recovery. Looking at broader trends at global and national scales, nonprofit organizations are also emerging to help bridge these gaps.

The Coalition for Epidemic Preparedness Innovations (CEPI) was created to bridge the public, private, civil society, and philanthropic communities in the infectious disease preparedness mission space.

Fostering investment in pharmaceutical research and development under a nonprofit banner, the group helps manage discoveries and intellectual property with the private sector to bring vaccines to scale when needs and facilitating market signals emerge for broader deployment.[18] Only a few years into its tenure when COVID hit, CEPI has been an important facilitator of industry response efforts throughout the pandemic. It is the kind of organization that could have served in advance of the pandemic as a facilitator between the public and private sectors on issues like manufacturing capacity, intellectual property, and equitable vaccine availability had it been sufficiently resourced and viewed as a model in this light.

The creation of the 100 Resilient Cities initiative took on the bold experiment of fostering resilience investments by funding chief resilience officers in cities throughout the world. The program brought together experts and resources from the for-profit and nonprofit sectors to catalyze broader resilience building in a way that transcended the various sectors, with initial support from the philanthropic sector. Unfortunately, the program was discontinued under new leadership from the Rockefeller Foundation. Its results had been mixed, and some programs spun off into other philanthropic efforts while others sunsetted.[19]

While new models attempt to break through and expand the models of nonprofits and means of philanthropic engagement in the disaster space, the monitoring and sharing of information on these dynamics have also given rise to conferences, meetings, and other collaboration venues to convene peers within and across professional arenas. Resource hubs and thought leadership sharing venues such as the Center for Disaster Philanthropy have also been created to continue to build the communities of practice in disaster philanthropy and nonprofit engagement in disasters.

––––––––––––––––––

Nonprofits are often rightly praised for doing the job that no one else will. But they are also vilified when perceived as inflexible to the needs of the disaster survivors. There are public calls for more responsiveness but also quick criticism of any sense of fraud or waste. This creates a challenging environment in which these groups are criti-cized for being at once both too slow and too fast. Nonprofits are driven by their mission, but they are fueled by their funders. Strategic planning and development of new ideas for long-term funding that doesn't have a blueprint is hard to fundraise for; bringing in funding for an acute need that is all over the news is easier. So their operations bias toward the emotional response, which brings the resources to do the work more focused and celebrated on disaster response. At the same time, there is growing concern of donor fatigue in disasters, where, with the sheer abundance of disasters occurring, the drama fades into the baseline.

As we grow more emotionally numb to the increasing number of disasters, perhaps there is an opportunity to reexamine how this sec-tor engages in disasters and to explore emerging models of charita-ble support that are as holistically beneficial to disaster resilience as they are emotionally satisfying to the patrons of these organizations. Philanthropies must acknowledge that they can increase the good they do by making their fundraising and implementation strategies more inclusive of long-term needs.

Much as there are ratings for the transparency of nonprofits, such as GuideStar, from a fiscal perspective, more transparency on impacts and value realized from each dollar donated could transition toward more prevention-oriented investments. Of course, to do this, we would need better data on the value of preparedness, at higher resolutions. Educating donors, individuals, and institutions on where giving is most valuable could also help steer this industry toward a more bal-anced involvement in disasters. With increasing disasters and more and more crowding for attention in appeals for funding, the current model is increasingly under strain, providing opportunities for inno-vation and new models of giving and supporting disaster survivors in preparedness, response, and recovery.

8

DISASTER ACADEMICS

I **N THE** extensive history of scientific inquiry, disaster research is quite young. The scholar Samuel Prince's work on the explosion in Halifax Harbor described in the introduction was undertaken in 1917.[1] The Disaster Research Center, among the earliest dedicated disaster research centers based in the social sciences, was founded in 1963 in the United States at Ohio State University (later moved to the University of Delaware). While its founding was deeply rooted in the scientific method and under the stewardship of now highly regarded scholars Enrico Quarantelli, Russel Dynes, and others, the initial patrons were not from traditional scientific foundations. The original research proposals that seeded the center were not selected for funding by the National Science Foundation. Rather, it was the Office of Civil Defense and the Air Force Office of Scientific Research that funded the work. Driven by the cold war between the United States and the Soviet Union, early disaster research funding reflected what would become a familiar pattern of national security interests.[2]

As Quarantelli, Dynes, and others found early in their careers, disaster science doesn't fit neatly within academic and scientific funding categories. And while there is an increasing degree of disaster research activity, the lack of a unified theoretical foundation and funding entity for rapid research means that much of the work does not necessarily build on prior studies in the way that other fields are doing. Additionally, it is not always well suited to navigating the ethical issues with collecting data from disaster survivors, which, using qualitative methods, often requires survivor participation in surveys, interviews, focus groups, and the like.[3] This has led to calls for a disaster research "code of conduct" in recognition of the complexities of postdisaster research.[4]

The model of scientific research and the business of academia is not optimized for disaster research. Much high-quality work being is being funded and conducted but lacks the type of funding, support, and communities of practice that other fields have. We recognize that education and research are performed within all the sectors described in this book, but in this chapter we explore academia as the locus of research and educational activity. We look at what academia is optimized to do and identify the ways it overlays with how science, disasters, and academic organizations intersect.

ON SCIENTIFIC DISCOVERY

Science traditionally takes a reductionist approach to understanding. Through painstaking and tedious experimentation and observation driven by hypotheses to be tested, the scientific approach reveals the observable components of our world. Institutions have been built over the ages around the relentless pursuit of discovery, understanding, and educating the next generation of discoverers. From this, universities emerged with incentives for faculty advancement based on discovery, and refereed journals were created to publish findings for peer review and for others to replicate or disprove.

Stuart Firestein is a professor of biological sciences at Columbia University and also on the faculty advisory board for Columbia University's Institute for Ideas and Imagination. In speaking about traditional scientific inquiry in an interview for this book, he notes that "there was this notion that the place where we would make the most progress would be in a very reductionist approach to the questions we had . . . essentially, it amounts to a kind of a mechanistic view of where you learn what the parts do." He adds, "And that had been a dominating idea in science for quite a while. . . . I mean, Newton wrote down a bunch of laws, and from that, it turns out you not only can predict what keeps the planets moving in their orbits, but you know about how cannonballs fly and bridges stay up and all these other sorts of things."

Institutions have been built on this model of reductionism and have survived for centuries. What that translates into today are institutions that incentivize research based on outputs and publications. But not just any publications. Those with a high impact factor—a measure of how often others cite the publications in a journal—are preferred. For traditional reductionist discovery, this may be an appropriate measure. If you do work, and many others are using that work as a starting point for their own, you are in essence advancing the field. Working across scientific fields is more of a bonus.

Applied and translational research—like the important work of developing programs based on more fundamental research—is rarely incentivized through academic channels. Although foundations, the private sector, and government agency funders often prefer applied approaches that have contemporaneous impact on their areas of focus, scientific funders (of which there are dedicated subsets within government, nonprofits, and elsewhere) are focused on advancing the science and are, by design, relatively agnostic about its immediate practical impact.

Efforts have also been made to promote more interdisciplinary and transdisciplinary research, but institutional advancement incentives are slow to match this desire. There has been some progress, with entities like the National Science Foundation increasingly funding multidisciplinary awards for hazard and disaster research. While the advent of the scientific method has been critical for establishing valid discoveries, the approach is not without its limits. Firestein notes that much of what leads to understanding is how these principles work in different contexts, which is much more chaotic: "When is it the case that there is a single answer or single solution to a problem of any reasonable complexity?" He suggests, "I think an answer to this or a solution, a strategy for this, would be to embrace what I would call a pluralistic approach." He goes on to describe it as a genuine approach to bringing different ideas to the table and truly collaborating, one distinct from the often rhetorical promise toward "interdisciplinarity."

THE MESSINESS OF DISASTER RESEARCH

Disaster science is a messy field. It lacks clear boundaries and incorporates many approaches across multiple disciplines. Disaster research is often an application of other fields of research, frequently those of the social sciences, where much of the discretely identified "disaster" scholarly work is done. It does have some of its own theoretical frameworks, but these tend to be much less established than those of other fields. It is not clear if disaster research suffers from a lack of a unified approach, or if by its very nature it is a different kind of science, one that sits naturally at the intersection of many fields.

One study of social capital and vulnerability in disasters found six distinct areas around which this field of disaster research clustered: social capital and trust, tsunami and health, disability and community resilience, adaptation and governance, gender and livelihood, and LGBTQ+.[5] Meaning, all these areas of scientific inquiry were needed for just one aspect of disaster research. As of late 2021, the North American Alliance of Hazards and Disaster Research Institutes had ninety-nine member organizations representing research across a broad spectrum of social, physical, and medical sciences.[6] The Global Alliance of Disaster Research Institutes has members across all continents from forty-seven countries. It similarly has groups ranging across scientific fields, with areas of focus within the alliance on atmospheric and water-related disasters, earthquake and volcanic disasters, geohazards, and integrated disaster risk management.[7] There are also expansive networks of additional disaster centers that include centers of excellence in support of national security apparatus (e.g., those funded by ministries of defense and those focused on cybersecurity), health (e.g., medical countermeasure research), and supply chain (e.g., industry groups and global trade organizations). Each touches on disasters directly or indirectly, and in different ways.

For the more distributed branches of disaster science—those spread across a multitude of underlying disciplines—researchers often need to compete for funding, and for space in academic journals that are more focused on the primary scientific discipline, of which disasters are just one context for inquiry. For the intersectional work, there is a constant struggle to find sustained funding and resources, as well as to meet expectations within academia for advancement. While more journals have been developed in the disaster fields, high-impact values for these publication venues are elusive.[8] Because disaster science is often an overlay of multiple sciences studying complex questions (such as how social constructs interface with the built environment and external natural hazards), it requires collaboration and derivation of work from other fields. In essence, the discovery is inherently derivative of other discoveries, and the novelty of discovery is in its application. The types of impacts can be striking in terms of policy changes and direct improvements to lives and livelihoods, but these are outside the purview of the domain of scientific discovery and thus are not prized discoveries for academic career advancement, which is often judged by peers from a single field of study.

Academic institutions are working to balance this, to find a way to preserve the institutional foundations rooted in reductionist discovery, while forming bridges between research fields where definitions of discovery can be expanded and even incentivized. Nascent efforts are underway to form new institutes and institutions within academia toward this end. Researchers at the Berlin Social Science Center took a deep look at this tension of doing interdisciplinary research in "monodisciplinary deep structures." Their work applies to all interdisciplinary research, not just disaster science. They found that while the creation of interdisciplinary units did produce some positive results, most career-based incentives were still biased toward monodisciplinary incentives related to hiring processes, promotions, funding, and scientific publishing, and peer review processes were biased toward monodisciplinary research. As a result, *inter*disciplinary research is more often *multi*disciplinary, or many disciplines contributing in parallel with one another, rather than truly interdisciplinary.[9]

Firestein notes, "We treat an awful lot things like climate change or the pandemic, or any of the disasters that you want to talk about, as if there's a single event here, as if there's a single description or a single solution that will work. And we don't even know if the solution that will work will come exclusively from science. That's why I think it's important to include the humanities. Quite often, that solution may come from somewhere else entirely."

HOW ACADEMIC RESEARCH IS FUNDED

Much like other nonprofits, academic institutions rely on external funding to support their researchers. Income from endowments, tuition, and other fees pays for only so much and is usually reserved for the direct costs of delivering and administering educational programs. Most research faculty must write proposals for grants, contracts, and other kinds of awards that will fund the research they are trying to do.

In the United States, according to the National Science Foundation, the federal government spent $142 billion in FY 2019 on research and development.[10] NSF does not parse the proportion of this spending that goes to disaster-related research, so understanding the extent to which it funds this field relies on estimates. One external analysis of federal disaster science research support across all funders from 2011 to 2016 identified $69 billion over this six-year period.[11] This estimate would indicate that about 8 percent of the federal government's R&D budget goes to disaster-relevant science. More than half of this went to engineering, with other disciplines (medicine, public health, social science, emergency management) accounting for the difference. The study's authors noted that biosecurity (i.e., infectious threats) predominate on the health side, leaving less emphasis on noncommunicable health threats. Overall, they found that only twelve of the thirty-five U.S. "national disaster management capabilities" were allocated any funding, implying a lack of a coordinated strategy to address the research needs that would improve national preparedness and response across the disaster spectrum.

These figures likely represent only part of the federal funding for research, as billions are also spent for academic and research organizations to engage in mission support, such as the development and delivery of training programs, decision support tools, modeling, and related areas. This type of funding can be lucrative for universities but also highly restrictive in what it can and can't be used for, and it better reflects a consulting engagement rather than support for developing and growing the field of disaster science, once again coming into tension with the institutional incentives that govern professional advancement.

In addition to federal sources, many academic institutions also seek grants from foundations and corporate social responsibility funds. While these can be important sources of funding, they tend to be skewed more toward direct impact and service delivery. Some foundational scientific work has been done with philanthropic dollars, most notably for biomedical research, but most of the funding still goes to support human services organizations in response and recovery, with a smaller allocation for preparedness.[12]

One of the issues for any performer receiving federal disaster research funding is that it has been so inconsistent. As suggested by disaster medicine and public health researchers Tom Kirsch and Mark Keim, "There are few consistent disaster research funding sources. The limited funding available does not allow for the development of research expertise, a consistent researcher development path, or for the progression of the quality of the research."[13] The lack of a consistent and coordinated funding paradigm also makes it difficult to underwrite institutions dedicated to disaster science. This perpetuates the fragmentation of the field and creates competition for resources and attention in adjacent fields.

While we have been focusing on research into disasters themselves, when disaster strikes, efforts are also made to preserve research already underway. After major hurricanes like Katrina, scientific funders worked to support researchers affected by the storms.[14] The NYU research centers hit hard by Sandy may have been destroyed, but the government paid to rebuild them. The significant cost of rederiving wiped-out rodent lines came from FEMA and NIH grants.[15] FEMA paid $92 million to replace lost biospecimens. Of note, however, was that many of these centers remained in the path of future storms and flooding events. This is a cycle in which the government pays for research in flood zones, the research gets wiped out, and the government pays for it again, limiting any incentive for recipients to mitigate risk until grant requirements change or mitigation resources are made allowable in the grants. This is an important dynamic of the academic research enterprise, creating a nexus between the funder and the funded that is difficult to disentangle under the business model in play.

THE RESEARCH AGENDA DIVIDE

At the heart of disaster research should be a vector driving it toward what is most useful—for prevention, for mitigation, for resilience, for recovery. Some of these utilities may be generalizable to entire nations, or even the entire global population, while others may require nuanced attention to the particular needs of communities. How research agendas actually get established, however, is often not based in thoughtful analysis of need or utility.

The kinds of research that get supported are driven in part by the demands of universities and in part by funders' objectives. Research in the private sector is no exception, with pharmaceutical companies, for instance, vying for federal dollars for research regardless of whether it makes sense in the context of broader preparedness. Research agendas may also be directed simply by a principal investigator's curiosity to explore a given hypothesis—intellectual curiosity living at the heart of basic science but not always aligning with the kinds of applied science that disasters require. What rarely drives it are the needs of communities, particularly those that lack the resources to underwrite research. For instance, even though slow-onset disasters generally allow for more time to react and cause more damage, academic studies of humanitarian logistics for these disaster types are represented far less than those that study sudden-onset disasters.[16] The high complexity of disasters, combined with the difficulty of access to areas affected, may explain this, but that is ultimately unsatisfying when it is exactly there that the research focus is needed. The disconnect between research agendas and the communities that should be the beneficiaries further perpetuates the dynamic of solutions imposed on marginalized and poorer communities rather than codeveloped inquiries with those who would stand to benefit most from them.

The agenda is also influenced by the fabric of modern academia itself. Academic processes incentivize all kinds of activity on the part of the faculty pursuing tenure. Academic tenure refers to indefinite appointments granted to faculty upon meeting certain targets for teaching, research, and service. It is a kind of job security attractive to many who pursue academic careers. It serves many purposes, one of which is to allow faculty freedom of expression, research, and publication absent external pressures.[17] But achieving it requires adherence to stringent demands laid out by the university. The demands of tenure committees can be at odds with societal benefit. Departmental politics demand that tenure-track candidates publish in high-impact journals, yet there are few high-impact disaster journals. Solving disaster problems necessitates cross-disciplinary research, but the dearth of high-impact interdisciplinary journals means that meeting the publication demands of tenure committees is unattainable for those seeking to undertake and publish interdisciplinary science. One dynamic that may be changing in higher education is the rise of non-tenure-line faculty, who may have fewer strings attached to their research objectives as it relates to promotion and may therefore be more at liberty to pursue interdisciplinary research. One benefit of a tenure track, however, can be hard funding and more financial freedom to pursue research that is too early-stage or not attractive to traditional funders.

As mentioned earlier, peer-reviewed journal quality is often defined by a metric known as impact factor. This is a quantitative representation of how often research published in the journal is cited by others over a specified period of time (usually two to five years). This calculation tends to favor broader established journals encompassing a field (versus a niche within a field). Disaster research as a younger field with many specializations does not always fare well using these metrics. A landmark study that is used widely for policy making and program design may not have many citations, as the communities using the research are not publishing on their use in academic journals, even though the impact is significant. Alternatively, many other researchers may use an influential article proposing a new theoretical framework as a framing mechanism in their own papers, and the article may have many citations but little measurable impact outside of academia. This is not to say that peer review impact factors are not useful, but it is important to acknowledge that they are a myopic measure, with outsized importance in valuing academics. Because of this, they can steer work in directions that are often independent and disconnected from the policy and practice communities.

The academic service pillar is important, too, in that it relates to how research gets applied in the wider world. Service takes many forms, such as university committee membership, journal editorial positions, and professional societies for various disciplines. These tend to be more prized in academic circles. But service could also encompass uncompensated work to translate one's research into societal applications. As funders demand that researchers demonstrate the wider impacts of their research, understanding the ways in which the translation of new knowledge is or can be incentivized is important but may prove complicated by divergent appeal of incentives based on personal values, individual capacities, and misalignment of external engagement activity with grant cycles.[18]

The interplay of these dynamics leads to a significant introduction of bias as well. The actual production of research is biased toward wealthier countries. In countries with large research institutions, much of the disaster research is conducted by in-country researchers. With disasters such as the Sichuan earthquake in 2008 or Hurricane Katrina in 2005, 91 percent of authors of the papers published were from China and the United States, respectively. Alternatively, for Typhoon Yolanda in the Philippines in 2013, only 12 percent were from the Philippines, and only 3 percent of authors writing about the Haiti earthquake in 2010 were from Haiti.[19] Local perspectives and insights may be lost in these cases, and local institutions are not developed and strengthened when research itself is not reflective of its beneficiaries.

——————

The science of disaster studies is evolving, but it is still possible to look at the past few decades of research to understand trends in how this research is conducted. Evaluations of how communities respond to and recover from disasters require the application of an array of scientific disciplines and concepts within disciplines. Scholars have increasingly looked at levels of vulnerability in communities and levels of social capital to draw inferences about why communities are differentially responsive or resilient and predict how they may be so in the future based on factors like race, class, and the strength of social ties. Vulnerability and social capital coexist and likely interact within populations, but scholarship tends to separate them.[20]

Governments and philanthropies could do a much better job embracing funding vehicles that cut across disciplines and incentivize scientists to work together. Analyses of the impact of such cross-disciplinary awards on society and disaster resilience could go a long way toward demonstrating the potential value of this approach and, critically, convincing university leadership that their support of such an ecosystem and the scientists that make it up is worthy of twenty-first-century academia.

In opening the aperture and recognizing the importance of a pluralistic approach, we must assess the very foundation of the scientific institutions themselves. How we teach, how we research, and how we work to reduce the world into its component parts influence and are part of the underlying structures that guide what work is chosen and how researchers develop and sustain careers in their field. Some of the most important advances in disaster science may be measured in new and applied discoveries, but the ecosystem for those discoveries to be made will come from more boring, bureaucratic shifts in how we fund, administer, and otherwise incentivize research going forward.

PART III

IN SEARCH OF DISASTER RESILIENCE

9

HUMANS ARE BAD AT RISK, AND EVEN WORSE WITH UNCERTAINTY

SOME OF the dysfunctions we have uncovered occur within a given sector. Others cut across domains, creating a powerful ecosystem effect. To challenge these forces, a rewiring of incentives is necessary across the board. In these final chapters, we gather the threads of evidence over twenty years to identify core areas of dysfunction and disincentive and propose remodeling solutions that we believe are indeed achievable, if we decide they are important enough. But first, agreeing to make hard choices that could help better address disaster risk will require acknowledging that we are bad at risk to begin with.

RISK: PERCEPTION VERSUS REALITY

People have a hard time with risk. We don't judge it very well. One reason may be that humans possess two cognitive systems: one that intuits and another that reasons.[1] The brain's primitive amygdala (intuition) and evolutionarily advanced neocortex (reasoning) were designed for different purposes and often find themselves in tension. As a result, the reality of risk around us may diverge from what we are perceiving it to be.[2]

In thinking about the *Challenger* space shuttle disaster, author David Epstein wrote of a NASA culture that prized data.[3] When faced with a decision about whether to launch *Challenger* on January 28, 1986, decision makers felt that they couldn't sell the idea to their superiors that launching was risky unless they had data to back it up. But they didn't. They had guesses, but no hard evidence that O-rings that sealed the wall of the rocket boosters would definitely fail, or even a number to offer of what the estimated risk of failure might be.

NASA ran its space shuttles and their parts through test after test to ensure that they did not fail. It built in redundancy after redundancy just in case they did. This was proof that NASA did have concern for safety and for building an evidence base—data—to support safety-related decision-making. But when it came time to decide, NASA leaders did what humans do: they rationalized a choice of action in the face of extreme pressure and competing demands. They opted for a unidirectional reliance on their revered data: they might have opted for direction A—needing evidence to prove *safety*—but went instead for direction B—needing evidence to prove *risk*.

The decision arguably wasn't about data but about culture. It reflected a cultural reliance on a data-driven process that had worked for every other launch until that morning, but which was crippled in the face of uncertainty compounded by political pressure. A series of decisions preceded the final "go/no-go" decision. NASA management at Marshall Space Flight Center was making a decision under top NASA pressure to meet the launch schedule; if that slipped, it could have concrete implications for NASA's fiscal future. The contractor, Morton Thiokol, in turn needed to meet that demand to stay on schedule or at least not be a roadblock to it; NASA's future, and its own, may have depended on it.

A NASA culture that prized data caused leaders to make the (seemingly perverse) decision that absent data to prove the O-rings would fail, they would go ahead under the assumption that they would not. Yet absence of evidence is not evidence of absence. The O-rings did fail, and the shuttle and all its crew were lost.

To put it succinctly, humans are bad at risk. They make high-consequence decisions even when cognitively ill-equipped to do so.

Much of the debate about science today is characterized by a narrative that science has the facts and that we simply have to listen to them. But there are almost no real-world situations in which decisions are based purely on scientific data. Science does not have all the answers. Well, even so, we can produce a good risk assessment, right? But even the best risk assessments can't actually tell you what to *do* with that risk. If likelihood is low but consequences are high, do you go all out to prevent that disaster? What if you are dealing with a dozen such scenarios—do they all merit the same priority? Science informs risk assessment; it does not dictate its outcomes or how it should be used.

We often do a much better job reacting to disasters than managing their risk in advance. We are better at springing to action after the fact (nowhere is this more obvious than in the U.S. Congress). But that is an incredibly unsatisfying rationale for our lack of preparedness for disasters. Flaws in human nature may not be directly fixable, but bureaucratic structures can be designed to mitigate the negative effects of human impulses or flawed human reasoning. They can buffer problematic elements of institutional culture.

Experts have looked at the question of "organizational pathology" for disasters like *Challenger* and the Three Mile Island near–nuclear meltdown in 1979. The political scientist Maureen Casamayou explored three hypotheses for how excessive risk taking may have led to these events: structural and procedural blockages prevented information from reaching the right people; the right people received the warnings but didn't understand them; and the right people received and understood the warnings but deliberately ignored them due to external pressures.[4]

These disasters as case studies are distinct in one sense from the kind of disasters we write about in this book, in that our effort at hand is less about the way tactical information gets handled in close temporal proximity to an event and more about the handling of longer-term, strategic warnings. But there are lessons to be learned from such an analysis. The first hypothesis—*communications blockage*—holds that highly complex agencies like NASA and the Nuclear Regulatory Commission are bound to have communications breakdowns.

In the *Challenger* case, there may have been a winnowing of information on its way to top management such that it was thin or distorted by the time it made it to them. This cannot be said of many of the disasters described in this book, from hurricanes to floods to infectious diseases. While Congress, the White House, and the suite of executive branch agencies in place to execute their wishes comprise an incredibly complex and bureaucratic landscape, ample evidence in the public domain and in the very national experience with these kinds of disasters argues otherwise. That being said, when witnesses testify at congressional hearings, our experience tells us (and we expect that a content analysis of the record would demonstrate) that outside experts are more likely to be the ones bringing concerns about vulnerability and risk, whereas federal officials are more likely to advertise their successes, which could influence lawmakers' perception of a given risk.

Casamayou's second hypothesis—*misunderstanding or misperception*—posits that the communication must reach not only the person but also the person's mind. Summarizing social psychologist Leon Festinger, if received information causes a cognitive dissonance by disrupting preexisting opinions or knowledge, individuals may attempt to reduce that dissonance by either changing their behavior to conform to the new information or digging in and justifying reasons not to.[5] The wealth of concerning and relentless information delivered to decision makers about twenty-first-century disasters and our vulnerability to them could easily create such dissonance. Would they react by conforming to the new information—by accepting it and acting on it proportionally—or would they justify the status quo or a minimalist approach to change because the costs, be they political or fiscal, are simply too high? What we have often seen is that they are ready to act proportionally when the new information comes in the form of a disaster, but less so when it comes in the form of a strategic warning.

The final hypothesis—*external pressures that override the warnings*—conveys the reality that organizations are subject to forces from without. In the case of the Nuclear Regulatory Commission, there were organized interest groups advocating against nuclear power that may have pushed the NRC to consider safety, but other, more powerful forces were probably working in the opposite direction. NRC and NASA both had a great deal of external support for their missions—notably from Congress itself. Legislators "may have been insufficiently vigorous and penetrating in their oversight" of these agencies, resulting in a kind of neglect. Alleged mismanagement of funds at the shuttle program, combined with external forces, may have led to cutting corners. In the disasters described in this book, Congress itself is subject to external forces, notably from the administration and from interest groups, which encourage, if not force, congressional agendas in a particular direction, and from the public and particularly the electorate, who may be relatively disinterested in the nuts and bolts of preparedness and fail to reward it with public support or votes.

NASA fixed the O-ring problem. It never recurred. But seventeen years later a completely different technical problem founded in the same bureaucratic problem did occur when the agency tried to assess the hazard from a piece of foam that struck the shuttle during its launch. On February 1, 2003, the shuttle broke up on reentry, costing the lives of all astronauts aboard.

CHARACTERIZING OUR DYSFUNCTION

The disasters described in this book, and our collective responses to them, tell a story about priorities, about incentives and disincentives, and about the ways in which the people acting on behalf of the citizenry are not always incentivized to prioritize the most helpful things. Inevitably, this all relates to risk, which is exactly what disasters present before they happen. It is important to reflect on the repeated themes of our dysfunction, understanding that future efforts to prevent and mitigate disasters will be truly successful only if we acknowledge and address the flawed ways in which we deal with disaster risk.

A key through-line in the studied disasters is a kind of *insufficient receptivity to risk*. If we are poorly built to cognitively handle risk, this deficit finds its way into the way we govern our societies with respect to risk. National security affairs professor Erik Dahl writes that 9/11 wasn't really about a failure to connect the dots, or to imagine the worst that our adversaries could do, or to develop quality strategic-level intelligence assessments of bin Laden and al-Qaeda. The "problem was not too much intelligence and insufficiently imaginative intelligence analysts, but too little precise warning and insufficiently receptive policy makers."[6] Receptivity here is key. September 11 intelligence may have failed on a tactical level to alert authorities with respect to an imminent threat, but the real problem was that "in the years leading up to 9/11, national-level decision makers were insufficiently receptive to the warnings they received about the threat from bin Laden. This suggests that even if tactical intelligence on the threat had been available, it is unlikely that policy makers would have been prepared to listen and take the actions necessary to stop the attacks." Most of this book's disasters tell a similar story. They demonstrate a receptivity that is often post hoc. Policy makers had enormous amounts of strategic-level intelligence about the emerging infectious disease threat and the inherent risks it created, but their actions based on that intelligence were insufficient. Myriad recommendations from external and internal experts, including Congress's own Government Accountability Office, went either unheeded or only partially addressed, helping to lay the foundation for the disaster of COVID-19.

Similar warning signs were seen within the private sector leading up to the financial crisis of 2008. The widespread failures of NGOs in the response to the Haiti earthquake (among other disasters) and the insufficiency of the evidence base to integrate social and political dynamics into our preparedness investments are all outcomes of similar sectoral pathologies.

Members of Congress introduced thousands of bills after COVID-19 broke out under the presumption that legislation would be the solution to the problem, when in fact the problem was that they had taken inadequate time to assess what the problem actually was.[7] Nonprofits similarly produce voluminous reports on the number of people reached, the number of meals served, the number of blankets distributed. But the question to be answered of why so many were needed in the first place is harder to find. Even harder is the denominator—the number of people who needed assistance, many of whom may not actually be among the recipients of the aid. The focus is on the need served versus the need unserved. The private sector adds the lens of shareholder value to the mix, and researchers produce peer-reviewed scientific treatises behind journal paywalls and technical jargon that is necessary for advancement, but academic success is rarely measured in terms of real-world impact.

So we don't see the risk and don't act proportionally to real risk, and this creates a *thinking too small* mindset that poorly serves us for the disasters we face. Historian Daniel Immerwahr describes Washington, D.C., as a place "deadlocked between those determined simply to hang onto power and those seeking modest tweaks."[8] The political entanglement of competing agendas in an era of rampant political hostility exacerbates this reality. Washington is not a place for big thinking and initiatives, for tackling the most far-reaching problems of our time. Reticence from not one but both parties stymied meaningful climate change legislation until 2022, by which point many experts were warning that much of the damage to the environment was irreversible. President Biden's American Preparedness Plan—what his administration has termed a "moonshot" for pandemics—calls for $65 billion over seven to ten years, or $6.5 billion a year. To put this in perspective, President Kennedy's actual moonshot cost $98 billion over fourteen years; in today's dollars, about $90 billion per year.[9] It was a no-holds barred, must-win effort, properly incentivized by an enemy more visible than a virus. The Biden plan, which on an annual basis would cost about 1 percent of the Department of Defense's entire annual budget, wasn't taken up as a standalone bill in the middle of a pandemic that had claimed nearly 800,000 lives at the time—instead it became a pawn in the game to advance other agendas before Congress found itself in yet another election year.

Humans seek ways to manufacture certainty in a chaotic world and to create the illusion of simplicity as the world grows more complex. But the increasing complexity of our world is not reversible or containable, and rather than feverishly work to retain an old model of disaster engagement, it demands approaches adapted to where we are headed.

10

REIMAGINING THE MODEL

THE SCOPE of the disasters described in this book may feel overwhelming. Terrorist-made disasters, natural hazards, and disasters of our own unintentional design convene into a landscape of what feels something like routinized calamity. Layered with the dysfunctional way we choose to deal with these events, a kind of vicious spiral starts to emerge, leaving optimism behind it.

As practitioners of disaster science and policy, we come at this from a place of extreme frustration, but also one of cautious optimism. We can acknowledge that we build our own vulnerability to disasters. We can acknowledge that the dysfunctions that make us vulnerable occur within and because of a system characterized by a lack of incentives or a presence of disincentives. In this way, it finally becomes possible to reframe the problem much more honestly.

REMEDYING THE DYSFUNCTION

Moving from a status quo defined by an insufficient receptivity to risk to one that is not only receptive but willing to make disruptive structural change is required. Part of this means finding a willingness on the part of those in power to remedy the core dysfunctions driving underpreparedness and shifting the incentive structures that underlie them. As the public policy and international affairs professor Thomas Birkland wrote, "Changes in the appreciation of how problems come about, what causes them, and what can be done to change the conditions under which they grow worse are central to understanding social policy learning."[1]

REIMAGINING CONGRESSIONAL ACTIVITY

"Of all our recommendations, strengthening congressional oversight may be among the most difficult and important. So long as oversight is governed by current congressional rules and resolutions, we believe the American people will not get the security they want and need. The United States needs a strong, stable, and capable congressional committee structure to give America's national intelligence agencies oversight, support, and leadership."[2]

We would like to take credit for this recommendation—would like to be able to say it is a new idea of our own making that merits thoughtful consideration—but this is a recommendation of the 9/11 Commission, now nearly twenty years old, and the only one that has gone unimplemented. It is as relevant to all-hazards disasters today as it was to terrorism intelligence in 2004.

Modifications to the American congressional structure alone will not address all congressional problems. Campaign finance reform and the establishment of term limits would free up American legislators to do so much more than they currently have time for or are willing to take on. Reports from members themselves indicate that their time spent campaigning is well beyond what they would prefer, and that it does affect their ability to do their jobs.[3] Reforming campaign finance is an issue that looms large yet is unlikely to occur any time soon. The absence of term limits in the U.S. House of Representatives and Senate also impedes real change on hard issues. With no limits, members run again and again for reelection, wasting precious time in fundraising and campaigning that could be spent governing. The lack of limits relentlessly ties career politicians to the special interests that can assure their reelection. Some may think of special interests purely in terms of lobbyists, but in reality, constituents are special interests, too. Constituent demands may not line up with tedious but important work that is needed to prevent disasters or prepare their communities for them. Setting limits on the number of terms in which a legislator can serve could free them from some of the political and financial pressures of running and rerunning, but a pervasive sense of entitled incumbency prevents legislators from legislating themselves out of future terms.

In the meantime, disasters are worsening, and nearer-term solutions are needed. What else can we do to avoid the bureaucratic dysfunction that leads to failures like the loss of nearly one million American lives from an essentially predictable infectious disease? Homeland security expert Andrew Weis, who was interviewed in the development of this book, noted that "nine times out of ten people can agree on what the right policy outcome is, but getting there is really hard because of all the various stakeholders and interests." How can we better align interests toward common goals and meaningful actions?

The U.S. Congress and commentators must step back from their reflex reaction to view disasters such as COVID-19 solely as policy failures that can be quickly fixed with more hearings and more bills. Instead, they must look to solutions for the more foundational failures in the very way they govern. They have paid little attention to their own inattention to the distal drivers, like unsustainable land use practices and climate change, or the proximal vulnerabilities, like inadequate supplies of vaccines and treatments, and, critically, public health infrastructure. They are so used to governing by continuing resolution, by omnibus, and by emergency supplemental that they have forgotten what it means to strategically budget and appropriate. Congress is so poorly structured and incentivized to legislate in a way that actually mitigates risk and creates resilience that dramatic shifts are necessary to avoid another century of relentless reactivity. Individual brains may be insufficiently wired to deal well with risk, but it may be possible to suggest collective checks that address the inadequacies that individual deficits create at a shared level.

One way to deal with certain kinds of disasters from a budgetary perspective is via the development of integrated budgets. This is an approach that defies the siloes of individual department requests and instead creates a single budget across relevant departments. Precedent for this exists in the form of a 1984 law by which Congress required a new Arctic Research Commission, directing the director of the Office of Management and Budget (OMB) to consider all federal agency requests as one integrated request. But appetite for this approach in security and disasters has been nonexistent. In 2018 the former lawmakers and policy makers who make up the Bipartisan Commission on Biodefense proposed to Congress that it require OMB to submit an integrated budget request for biodefense.[4] Similar to the 9/11 Commission recommendation, they also asked Congress to structure itself in a way that it could receive this budget and reflect on it synergistically, across authorizing and appropriating committees. This proposal met with resounding silence on Capitol Hill. Now, in the wake of the kind of disaster the Biodefense Commission feared, Congress must reconsider.

Policy makers need to acknowledge that the shadow budget they are using to fund disaster response and relief is ad hoc, is nonstrategic, and fails to create lasting and strategic investment that can increase resilience and reduce the ultimate costs to taxpayers.[5] We need data to understand the mosaic of disaster spending, and the relationship between preparedness and response. But even in the absence of data, there is obvious low-hanging fruit that can improve preparedness right now. The advance infusion of dollars into a public health security emergency fund is requisite. No reinventing of the wheel is necessary—the tool is already available, and the regularity of public health events that could have benefited from it is a clear signal that its premise is sound.[6] Another approach to improve public health resilience that some have advised is for the government to designate certain health security spending as mission-critical and exempt these programs from the budget caps that restrict discretionary spending.[7]

Congress is so central to everything carried out by the executive branch that it must better appreciate its role in making prevention and preparation the preferred course, even when reaction is easier and ostensibly valued more by voters.

ASKING HARD QUESTIONS OF INTERNATIONAL
MODELS OF ASSISTANCE

Some of the issues faced by the United States in its own management of disaster funding are mirrored in international disaster assistance dynamics. Systems like the United Nations and its affiliates are not standalone organizations. They are composed of and funded by nation-states each with their own constituents and self-interests. The notion of stronger international institutions is often romanticized, only to result in disappointment when they are slow to act and under-perform in response situations. And administrative frameworks that are rooted in strong values often lead to operational structures that are designed not to offend, effecting coordination of donors through appeals and clusters rather than directing assistance based on defined community need.

One approach that could resolve some of these challenges is the development of requirements for adherence to more detailed or sophisticated activity metrics, and the establishment of consequences for lack of adherence. To have more binding approaches often requires nation-by-nation ratification of treaties, an imperfect approach but one that can be helpful in establishing minimum standards and acceptable global norms. The alternative is a kind of reasonable resignation to the limits of international organizations and understanding that there will always be limits on the impacts that can be achieved. The idea here is that there are important functions that can be accomplished through world bodies, but that expectations are greater than what can reasonably be expected when national interests do not align well with global need. The nearer-term answer is probably a combination of both of these approaches.

Where there is international consensus that aligns with strong disaster science and involves community perspectives, codification of these principles in the form of treaties and more robust mechanisms is the next logical step from current frameworks. Creating performance standards and accountability mechanisms to ensure timely responses of organizations in line with community needs is occurring and will require sanctions for working against the interests of the global community and the survivors of disasters. Further, investment targets for countries for disaster mitigation and prevention should be a requirement for membership in international organizations, much like paying dues or adhering to other membership obligations.

But this progress will be painfully slow. Much of the book of international law remains to be written, and there are no easy answers that solve all the problems. As long as the world is defined by the boundaries of nation-states as the principal political divisions, intrastate politics and interests will be a powerful guiding force, which is why the interests of nation-states require increased attention when conveying the value of resilience building.

REDEFINING DISASTER PHILANTHROPY

Disaster assistance will always be needed, and with it response support from nonprofits fueled by disaster philanthropy. The emotional appeal for assistance is not a bad thing. The fact that we feel empathy for those affected by disasters and are compelled to act is a defining feature of our humanity. It would be a mistake to deny the positive nature of this compassion. As a dominant driver of humanitarian business models, however, and the fundraising that goes with it, it can starve approaches that would create a more holistic way to address disasters.

Preparedness saves lives and money but is much more difficult to fundraise for. It is less photogenic and emotive to communicate bureaucratic and administrative processes, such as convening stakeholders for writing plans, than is a boots-on-the-ground response. So this default pathway to capture "low-hanging fruit" and follow our hearts and the hearts of others in the heroism prevails in the disaster aftermath. Yet, as we have seen, this can lead to strategies that overlook the capacities and nuances in the disaster-affected communities and pull attention from the root cause of the severity of the disaster: the lack of mitigation, insufficient preparedness, and oftentimes generations of inequities that created unnecessary vulnerabilities.

Governance structures for nonprofits and philanthropies should build on the communications and financial stewardship structures they already use to shift the conversation to one that is more holistic and inclusive of long-term community needs, and indeed to avoid needing their support in the future. Only in this way can we distinguish nonprofits' long-term fundraising goals from the style of short-term quarterly shareholder updates used by the private sector. The size and scope of response should be seen both as a success in terms of deployments and needs met and as a failure in allowing the vulnerabilities that put so many lives and livelihoods at risk to grow in the first place.

Independent oversight of nonprofits already exists in terms of their adherence to financial transparency and how much money reaches those in need. Perhaps development of a "contribution to value scorecard" would better capture where money is having the highest return on investment, versus the highest profile with limited return, based on overall impact on lives and livelihoods. Developing metrics that afford meaningful capacity to monitor and evaluate organizations would be no small task. But robust models with clear metrics and onsite inspections exist in other sectors, such as those used for healthcare accreditation. In these models, the cost is borne by the organization seeking accreditation, but the evaluation is done independently. Additionally, novel uses of emerging technologies such as blockchain provide new approaches to following the money.[8] With growing disasters and more dissonance in nonprofits clamoring for the attention of prospective donors, demonstration of impact and value created is needed much more than emotional appeals.

REFRAMING RISK AND FINANCIAL DECISION MAKING

New models are emerging to target the gap between market incentives and public good. The development of the triple-bottom-line framework has laid a theoretical foundation that is just beginning to be implemented. This is a foundation that explicitly acknowledges that there is a business case for societal good, for resilience valuations to be built into private sector decisions about resilience within specific types of transactions and business environments.

We need to acknowledge that we construct artificially comprehensive methods of valuing investments, with layers of assumptions hidden amid the sophistication of valuation models. Many emerging risks (climate change, disaster vulnerability) are not adequately valued in financial decision making, leading to investments in development strategies that end up being costlier in the long run. Better integration of risk and resilience modifiers in decision making is needed to ensure that investments drive us toward resilience rather than away from it. Independently verified case studies and examples of when it does work well could be used to lay a new foundation for effective social impact investing.

Achieving the sweet spot in the triple bottom line requires more than good marketing, as we have seen with criticisms of greenwashing. It requires linkages with strategy in tangible ways and hard data demonstrating the value across stakeholders who may be incentivized differently. It also requires avoiding the trap of aiming to incentivize one behavior while inadvertently incentivizing another potentially more harmful behavior. In traditional business literature, this folly may come in the form of rewarding individual results when teamwork is the desired goal or rewarding short-term profitability in lieu of long-term sustainability through mechanisms such as bonuses and employee evaluations.[9] Yet the means to mitigate these impulses already exist in the private sector. Tools like the balanced scorecard work to ensure that organizational leadership is aware of the balancing of different focus areas above the bottom line. They may include, for instance, scoring financial performance, project management, customer service, and employee development.[10] This can draw more attention to the value of resilience in different areas for decision support. But of course, it must still compete with shareholder and organizational interests.

A reimagined business model also requires addressing the tension between collaboration and competitiveness. Collaboration is necessary to prevent and mitigate disasters, but a competitive, market-driven environment can interfere with that. Sharing data across competitors is generally not in the interests of two companies that compete with each other, and antitrust rules even forbid it in some circumstances. Some emerging models of using nonprofits as arbiters of data sharing across industry stakeholders are creating interesting paradigms for side-stepping or accommodating concerns over business-competitive data that has significant use for public good. Pharmaceutical and healthcare supply chain companies collaborate with nonprofits like the Coalition for Epidemic Preparedness

Innovations (CEPI) and Healthcare Ready, respectively, as two examples of this model.

For this approach to be successful, we will need better ways to distinguish between good actors and those merely looking to appear that they are doing good. It will require others, including in academia and advocacy circles, to acknowledge that the private sector can be a force for good as much as it can be a detriment to disaster resilience. Understanding the difference, and educating consumers on how to recognize it, will help strengthen market signals in this regard, create more direct incentives for positive resilience and equity building efforts, and disincentivize efforts that would diminish the gains that have been made.

PROMOTING PLURALISM, PREVENTION, AND CAREER PATHS IN DISASTER SCIENCE RESEARCH

Deep and even siloed research is important. Reductionist research is responsible for almost everything we understand about the world today. But science in the twenty-first century should not be limited by that model. And yet it is. Few funding vehicles require or incentivize interdisciplinary approaches to asking questions, generating data, and solving problems. The creation of cross-disciplinary research programs and promotion incentives for researchers is essential and should be implemented in sustainable, institutionalized frameworks. Both governments and philanthropies should make conscious choices to issue funding vehicles and awards that reward pluralism, and these should not be outliers, but the new norm.

There are emerging models that can build more translational and cross-disciplinary approaches to conducting and utilizing research. The creation of special funding announcements for interdisciplinary work and the establishment of interdisciplinary centers has proven the value of such approaches. It has also highlighted the challenge of building a career path without more sustained and foundational investments, in terms of both research funding and creating career ladders and performance evaluation schema for faculty and researchers that do not discount interdisciplinary and applied work. Without these, disaster research will inevitably remain in the siloed domains of other fields.

The funding of interdisciplinary work should also strongly emphasize the value of prevention. Academic research has often been
response-focused and backward-looking to the last disaster. We have
yet to really harness the ingenuity of the research enterprise, whether
academic or private, to develop cross-cutting solutions that can stop
disasters before they start and are closely tied to real, on-the-ground
needs in communities. What is needed is a holistic and generational
growth of the underlying data that will be a prerequisite for better valuation of risk, understanding of the role of politics, and improving
the overall integration of the multitude of science that overlaps to create our disaster and resilience ecosystems.

INVESTING IN DIVERSITY AND EQUITY

Finally, across all sectors discussed in this book, representation matters. Communities are affected by decisions that are often made thousands of miles away. How they are researched, what recovery priorities are defined, where businesses choose to invest, and where
charities target their assistance and deploy their teams influence outcomes at the community level. All these factors are bound by institutional and organizational rules designed to protect the interests of the
organization. Marginalized communities, by definition, are not well
represented in these paradigms. Increasing representation and diversity is the first step of many steps to reduce inequities in disasters.
Building the foundation for a new model of disaster management,
across all sectors, will require representation that looks more like the
communities served. From there, metrics that we already have for pre-
dicting inequities in response should be used for accountability in
all of the recommendations discussed here. It is not enough to merely
describe these challenges; we must hold ourselves to account when
we see history repeating itself again and again, just as we predicted.

FINDING THE PATH FORWARD

We envision that the road to a healthier disaster posture must be
characterized by a shift from the visible to the invisible. Instead of

attacking the most exposed flank of disasters—the law that didn't get passed, the program that didn't get funded—advocates inside and outside of key institutions and sectors should be asking what lies beneath. Politicians, industrialists, philanthropists, academicians— the individuals who make up the institutions most responsible for dealing with disasters must acknowledge the ways in which their structures and decisions are not serving their best intentions.

The common denominator is individuals. The aggregation of individual actions ultimately dictates the models in which the various aspects of civil society function. If students strive to become researchers in deterministic approaches, universities will respond with more programs and will advocate for more funding. But if those being served by academia demand more—demand an evolution to better reflect the complexity of the modern world and emergent scientific approaches—academic centers will need to work to meet this need, as we are seeing slowly take place. Some hardwired approaches will not change: consumers will buy products from companies, voters will reward elected officials for their work in response and recovery, and individuals will donate for disaster responses. Yet if we all shift to scrutinize companies that are building wealth from the communities in which they operate but not investing in their resilience; if we vote out public officials for leaving us vulnerable to so many disasters; if we decide to donate to causes that prevent the harm of disasters in the first instance—these old models become obsolete as their respective sectors respond accordingly.

At the heart of any global action are millions of forgettable interactions and transactions in which we as individuals participate and which, over time, accumulate into one of two things: increased vulnerability or increased resilience. Losing ourselves to the enormity and complexity of the world disempowers us from the changes we demand. Educating individuals in all communities and all organizations on how disasters are formed, how we perpetuate their damage, and how we have it within our power to reduce their impacts is perhaps the single most important thing that can be done to effect change at scale.

This book was inspired by the notion that much of what we do is guided by social instinct and muscle memory ingrained in our various incentive structures. By seeking to better understand the forces that consciously and subconsciously drive how make decisions, we can better design programs and inform our choices to ensure that the trend of increasing disasters is not one that has to continue, and that it is indeed within our power and our interests to work toward a brighter and more resilient future for all.

NOTES

INTRODUCTION

1. CRED and UNDRR, *Human Cost of Disasters: An Overview of the Last 20 Years (2000–2019)* (Geneva: Centre for Research on the Epidemiology of Disasters and UN Office for Disaster Risk Reduction, 2020).

2. T. Joseph Scanlon, "Disaster's Little Known Pioneer: Canada's Samuel Henry Prince," *International Journal of Mass Emergencies and Disasters* 6, no. 3 (1988): 213–32.

3. Enrico Louis Quarantelli, *Disasters: Theory and Research* (London: Sage, 1978); Russell R. Dynes, *Organized Behavior in Disaster* (Lexington, Mass.: Heath Lexington Books, 1970); Enrico L. Quarantelli and Russell R. Dynes, "Response to Social Crisis and Disaster," *Annual Review of Sociology* 3, no. 1 (1977): 23–49.

4. Jennifer Wilson and Arthur Oyola-Yemaiel, "The Evolution of Emergency Management and the Advancement Towards a Profession in the United States and Florida," *Safety Science* 39, no. 1–2 (2001): 117–31.

5. Engineering National Academies of Sciences, and Medicine, *Strengthening the Disaster Resilience of the Academic Biomedical Research Community: Protecting the Nation's Investment*, ed. Georges C. Benjamin, Lisa Brown, and Ellen Carlin (Washington, D.C.: National Academies Press, 2017), https://www.nap.edu/catalog/24827/strengthening-the-disaster-resilience-of-the-academic-biomedical-research-community.

6. Richard N. Wright, *Building and Fire Research at NBS/NIST 1975–2000* (Gaithersburg, Md.: National Institute of Standards and Technology, December 2003), https://www.nist.gov/publications/building-and-fire-research-nbsnist-1975-2000.

7. Robert Woods, "Ancient and Early Modern Mortality: Experience and Understanding," *Economic History Review* 60, no. 2 (2007): 373–99, https://doi.org/10.1111/j.1468–0289.2006.00367.x.

8. "Elimination of Malaria in the United States (1947—1951)," updated July 23, 2018, https://www.cdc.gov/malaria/about/history/elimination_us.html.

9. Michael E. Ruane, "Yellow Fever Led Half of Philadelphians to Flee the City. Ten Percent of the Residents Still Died." *Washington Post*, April 4, 2020, https://www.washingtonpost.com/history/2020/04/04/yellow-fever-led-half-philadelphians-flee-city-ten-percent-residents-still-died/; Samantha Snyder, "A Philadelphia Story," *Mount Vernon*, Fall 2020, https://magazine.mountvernon.org/2020/Fall/a-philadelphia-story.html.

10. K. E. Jones et al., "Global Trends in Emerging Infectious Diseases," *Nature* 451, no. 7181 (February 21, 2008): 990–93, https://doi.org/10.1038/nature06536.

11. Jeffrey Schlegelmilch, *Rethinking Readiness: A Brief Guide to Twenty-First-Century Megadisasters* (New York: Columbia University Press, 2020).

12. Neil Smith, "There's No Such Thing as a Natural Disaster," *Insights from the Social Sciences: Understanding Katrina*, June 11, 2006, https://items.ssrc.org/understanding-katrina/theres-no-such-thing-as-a-natural-disaster/; K. Chmutina et al., "Why Natural Disasters Aren't All That Natural," *Open Democracy* 14 (2017), https://www.opendemocracy.net/en/why-natural-disasters-arent-all-that-natural/.

13. Terry Cannon, "Vulnerability Analysis and the Explanation of "Natural" Disasters," *Disasters, Development and Environment* 1 (January 1994): 13–30; Kevin A. Gould, M. Magdalena Garcia, and Jacob A. C. Remes, "Beyond 'Natural-Disasters-Are-Not-Natural': The Work of State and Nature After the 2010 Earthquake in Chile," *Journal of Political Ecology* 23, no. 1 (2016): 93–114; Jean-Christophe Gaillard, Catherine C. Liamzon, and Jessica D. Villanueva, " 'Natural' Disaster? A Retrospect Into the Causes of the Late-2004 Typhoon Disaster in Eastern Luzon, Philippines," *Environmental Hazards* 7, no. 4 (2007): 257–70.

1. THE BIRTH OF THE MODERN ERA OF U.S. DISASTER MANAGEMENT AND ITS GLOBAL IMPLICATIONS (2001)

1. Genevieve J. Knezo, *Homeland Security and Counterterrorism Research and Development: Funding, Organization, and Oversight (RS21270)* (Washington, D.C.: Congressional Research Service, 2003).

2. Andrew L. Cherry and Mary Elizabeth Cherrys, "A Middle Class Response to Disaster: FEMA's Policies and Problems," *Journal of Social Service Research* 23, no. 1 (1997): 71–87.

3. Thomas Kean and Lee Hamilton, *The 9/11 Commission Report: Final Report of the National Commission on Terrorist Attacks Upon the United States*, vol. 3 (Washington, D.C.: Government Printing Office, 2004), 280–81.

4. United States Department of State Bureau of Diplomatic Security, "1993 World Trade Center Bombing," February 21, 2019, https://www.state.gov/1993-world -trade-center-bombing/.

5. Oklahoma City National Memorial and Museum, "Recovery: The Financial Impact of the Oklahoma City Bombing," accessed February 23, 2022, https:// memorialmuseum.com/wp-content/uploads/2019/09/okcnm-recovery-the -financial-impact.pdf.

6. Stephen J. Cozza et al., "Human Remains Identification, Grief, and Posttrau- matic Stress in Bereaved Family Members 14 Years After the September 11, 2001, Terrorist Attacks," *Journal of Traumatic Stress* (2020): 1137–43; Carey B. Maslow et al., "Chronic and Acute Exposures to the World Trade Center Disaster and Lower Respiratory Symptoms: Area Residents and Workers," *American Journal of Public Health* 102, no. 6 (2012): 1186–94.

7. Kean and Hamilton, *The 9/11 Commission Report*, 3:278.

8. Kean and Hamilton, 3.

9. United States Department of Justice, *Amerithrax Investigative Summary* (Wash- ington, D.C., February 19, 2010).

10. G. Pappas et al., "Psychosocial Consequences of Infectious Diseases," *Clinical Microbiology and Infection* 15, no. 8 (August 1, 2009): 743–47, https://doi.org/10.1111 /j.1469-0691.2009.02947.x.

11. Andrew Glass, "Bush Creates Office of Homeland Security, Oct. 8, 2001," *Polit- ico* (Washington, D.C.), October 8, 2016, https://www.politico.com/story/2016/10 /bush-creates-office-of-homeland-security-oct-8-2001-229212.

12. "Executive Orders Issued by President George W. Bush," 2009, https://george wbush-whitehouse.archives.gov/news/orders/.

13. "Actions Overview H.R. 3162—107th Congress (2001–2002)," https://www.con gress.gov/bill/107th-congress/house-bill/3162/actions.

14. Uniting and Strengthening America by Providing Appropriate Tools Required to Intercept and Obstruct Terrorism (USA PATRIOT ACT) Act of 2001, Pub. L. 107-56, October 26, 2001

15. An Act to Establish the Department of Homeland Security and for Other Pur- poses, Pub. L. 107-296, November 25, 2002.

16. Goldwater-Nichols Department of Defense Reorganization Act of 1986, Pub. L. 99-443, October 1, 1986.

17. United States Department of Homeland Security, "Who Joined DHS," 2015, https://www.dhs.gov/who-joined-dhs.

18. Peter Eisinger, "Imperfect Federalism: The Intergovernmental Partnership for Homeland Security," *Public Administration Review* 66, no. 4 (2006): 537–45.

19. Eisinger.

20. United States Congress, Senate Committee on Governmental Affairs, *Homeland Security Grant Enhancement Act of 2003: Report of the Committee on Governmen- tal Affairs, United States Senate, to Accompany S. 1245 to Provide for Homeland Security Grant Coordination and Simplification, and for Other Purposes, Together*

with Additional Views (Washington, D.C.: Government Printing Office, 2004), https://www.govinfo.gov/content/pkg/CRPT-108srpt225/html/CRPT-108srpt225.htm.

21. Aspen Institute, *Task Force Report on Streamlining and Consolidating Congressional Oversight of the U.S. Department of Homeland Security*, Justice and Society Program (September 2013), https://www.aspeninstitute.org/wp-content/uploads/files/content/docs/pubs/Sunnylands%20report%2009-11-13.pdf.

22. Associated Press, "DHS Most Overseen Department," *Charleston-Gazette Mail*, May 20, 2011, https://www.wvgazettemail.com/inside-washington-dhs-most-overseen-department/article_b7118d32-ff91-5fb1-9aa5-f57d369fd58a.html.

23. Public Health Security and Bioterrorism Preparedness and Response Act of 2002, Pub. L. 107-188, June 12, 2002; C. Stephen Redhead and Mary Tiemann, *Public Health Security and Bioterrorism Preparedness and Response Act (PL 107–188): Provisions and Changes to Preexisting Law (RL31263)* (Washington, D.C.: Congressional Research Service, August 21, 2002).

24. Office of the Director of National Intelligence, "Background and Authorities—ISE," 2020, https://www.dni.gov/index.php/who-we-are/organizations/national-security-partnerships/ise/about-the-ise/ise-background-and-authorities.

25. Joann Peterson and Alan Treat, "The Post-9/11 Global Framework for Cargo Security," *Journal of International Commerce and Economics* 2 (2009): 1–30, https://heinonline.org/HOL/P?h=hein.journals/jice2&i=35.

26. Doron Zimmermann, "The European Union and Post-9/11 Counterterrorism: A Reappraisal," *Studies in Conflict & Terrorism* 29, no. 2 (2006): 123–45.

27. Jason Bram, James Orr, and Carol Rapaport, "Measuring the Effects of the September 11 Attack on New York City," *Economic Policy Review* 8, no. 2 (2002): 5–20.

28. Gail E. Makinen, *The Economic Effects of 9/11: A Retrospective Assessment (RL31617)* (Washington, D.C.: Congressional Research Service, September 27, 2002).

29. Adam Blake and M. Thea Sinclair, "Tourism Crisis Management: US Response to September 11," *Annals of Tourism Research* 30, no. 4 (2003): 813–32.

30. Philip Auerswald et al., "The Challenge of Protecting Critical Infrastructure," *Issues in Science and Technology* 22, no. 1 (2005): 77–83.

31. Mark P. Mills, "On My Mind: The Security-Industrial Complex," *Forbes*, November 29, 2004, https://www.forbes.com/forbes/2004/1129/044.html.

32. Judith Reppy, "A Biomedical Military-Industrial Complex?," *Technovation* 28, no. 12 (2008): 802–11.

33. United States General Accounting Office, *September 11: More Effective Collaboration Could Enhance Charitable Organizations' Contributions in Disasters: Report to the Ranking Minority Member, Committee on Finance, U.S. Senate* (Washington, D.C.: GAO, 2002).

34. Ray Suarez, "Red Cross Woes," vol. 19, transcript, *A News Hour with Jim Lehrer* (2001); Hilary Fussell Sisco, Erik L. Collins, and Lynn M. Zoch, "Through the Looking Glass: A Decade of Red Cross Crisis Response and Situational Crisis Communication Theory," *Public Relations Review* 36, no. 1 (2010): 21–27.

35. Nicole Bolleyer and Anika Gauja, "Combating Terrorism by Constraining Charities? Charity and Counter-terrorism Legislation Before and After 9/11," *Public Administration* 95, no. 3 (2017): 654–69.

36. Elizabeth A. Bloodgood and Joannie Tremblay-Boire, "International NGOs and National Regulation in an Age of Terrorism," *VOLUNTAS: International Journal of Voluntary and Nonprofit Organizations* 22, no. 1 (2011): 142–73.

37. Avishag Gordon, "Terrorism as an Academic Subject after 9/11: Searching the Internet Reveals a Stockholm Syndrome Trend," *Studies in Conflict & Terrorism* 28, no. 1 (2005): 142–73, https://doi.org/10.1080/10576100590524339.

38. E. S. Reich, "Science After 9/11: How Research Was Changed by the September 11 Terrorist Attacks," *Scientific American*, September 1, 2011, https://www.scientificamerican.com/article/how-research-was-changed-by-september-11-terrorist-attacks; Knezo, *Homeland Security and Counterterrorism Research and Development*.

39. Reppy, "A Biomedical Military-Industrial Complex?"; U.S. Department of Health, Human Services, and National Institutes of Health, "NIAID Strategic Plan for Biodefense Research" (Bethesda, Md., 2002).

40. Marc Sageman, "The Stagnation in Terrorism Research," *Terrorism and Political Violence* 26, no. 4 (2014): 565–80.

41. Bart Schuurman, "Research on Terrorism, 2007–2016: A Review of Data, Methods, and Authorship," *Terrorism and Political Violence* 32, no. 5 (January 3, 2018): 1011–26, https://doi.org/10.1080/09546553.2018.1439023.

42. Henry A. Giroux, "The Militarization of US Higher Education After 9/11," *Theory, Culture & Society* 25, no. 5 (2008): 56–92; University at Albany, "Higher Education in a Post-9/11 World: Q&A with UAlbany Assistant Professor of Educational Administration and Policy Studies Jason Lane," news release, 2011, https://www.albany.edu/news/16124.php.

43. Erik J. Dahl, "The 9/11 Attacks: A New Explanation," in *Intelligence and Surprise Attack: Failure and Success from Pearl Harbor to 9/11 and Beyond*, 128–59 (Washington, D.C.: Georgetown University Press, 2013).

2. A PANDEMIC WARNING, EARTHQUAKES, TSUNAMIS, HURRICANE KATRINA, AND A BIRD FLU (2002–2007)

1. Erik W. Goepner, "Measuring the Effectiveness of America's War on Terror," *US Army War College Quarterly: Parameters* 46, no. 1 (2016): 107–20; Michael S. Baker, "Casualties of the Global War on Terror and Their Future Impact on Health Care and Society: A Looming Public Health Crisis," *Military Medicine* 179, no. 4 (2014): 348–55.

2. Lesley Rosling and Mark Rosling, "Pneumonia Causes Panic in Guangdong Province," *British Medical Journal (Clinical Research Edition)* 326, no. 7386 (2003): 416–16, https://doi.org/10.1136/bmj.326.7386.416.

3. David Shu-Cheong Hui, Poon-Chuen Wong, and Chen Wang, "SARS: Clinical Features and Siagnosis," *Respirology* 8 Suppl, no. Suppl 1 (2003): S20–S24, https://doi.org/10.1046/j.1440-1843.2003.00520.x.

4. World Health Organization, "Cumulative Number of Reported Probable Cases of SARS," Emergencies Preparedness Response, accessed February 3, 2021, https://www.who.int/csr/sars/country/2003_07_11/en/.

5. Institute of Medicine, *Learning from SARS: Preparing for the Next Disease Outbreak: Workshop Summary*, ed. Knobler Stacey et al. (Washington, D.C.: National Academies Press, 2004), https://www.nap.edu/catalog/10915/learning-from-sars-preparing-for-the-next-disease-outbreak-workshop.

6. World Health Organization, *Revision of the International Health Regulations: Report by the Secretariat* (Geneva: WHO, May 16, 2003).

7. John Pickrell, "Facts and Figures: Asian Tsunami Disaster," *New Scientist*, January 20, 2005, https://www.newscientist.com/article/dn9931-facts-and-figures-asian-tsunami-disaster.

8. Carla Kweifio-Okai, "Where Did the Indian Ocean Tsunami Aid Money Go?," *Guardian*, December 25 2014, https://www.theguardian.com/global-development/2014/dec/25/where-did-indian-ocean-tsunami-aid-money-go.

9. Kweifio-Okai.

10. Prema-Chandra Athukorala and Budy P. Resosudarmo, "The Indian Ocean Tsunami: Economic Impact, Disaster Management, and Lessons," *Asian Economic Papers* 4, no. 1 (2005): 1–39.

11. Joan C. Henderson, "Corporate Social Responsibility and Tourism: Hotel Companies in Phuket, Thailand, After the Indian Ocean Tsunami," *International Journal of Hospitality Management* 26, no. 1 (2007): 228–39.

12. Anawat Suppasri et al., "A Decade After the 2004 Indian Ocean Tsunami: The Progress in Disaster Preparedness and Future Challenges in Indonesia, Sri Lanka, Thailand and the Maldives," *Pure and Applied Geophysics* 172, no. 12 (2015): 3313–41, https://doi.org/10.1007/s00024-015-1134-6.

13. B. S. Goodwin, Jr., and J. C. Donaho, "Tropical Storm and Hurricane Recovery and Preparedness Strategies," *ILAR Journal* 51, no. 2 (2010): 104–19, https://doi.org/10.1093/ilar.51.2.104.

14. Georges C. Benjamin, Lisa Brown, and Ellen Carlin, eds., *Strengthening the Disaster Resilience of the Academic Biomedical Research Community: Protecting the Nation's Investment* (Washington, D.C.: National Academies Press, 2017), https://doi.org/10.17226/24827.

15. National Oceanic and Atmospheric Administration, "4 Hurricanes in 6 Weeks? It Happened to One State in 2004," 2019, https://www.noaa.gov/stories/4-hurricanes-in-6-weeks-it-happened-to-one-state-in-2004; Naim Kapucu, E. Berman, and X. Wang, "Emergency Information Management and Public Disaster Preparedness: Lessons from the 2004 Florida Hurricane Season," *International Journal of Mass Emergencies and Disasters* 26, no. 3 (2008): 169–97; United States

Congress, *A Failure of Initiative: Final Report of the Select Bipartisan Committee to Investigate the Preparation for and Response to Hurricane Katrina*, vol. 109 (Washington, D.C.: Government Printing Office, 2006).

16. Richard D. Knabb, Jamie R. Rhome, and Daniel P. Brown, "Tropical Cyclone Report: Hurricane Katrina, National Hurricane Center," *NOAA* (2011), https://www.nhc.noaa.gov/data/tcr/AL122005_Katrina.pdf; Carl Bialik, "We Still Don't Know How Many People Died Because of Katrina," *FiveThirtyEight* 26 (August 26, 2015), https://fivethirtyeight.com/features/we-still-dont-know-how-many-people -died-because-of-katrina/.

17. United States Congress, *A Failure of Initiative*, 109.

18. United States Congress, 109.

19. Steven Horwitz, "The Private Sector's Contribution to Natural Disaster Response," in *Bottom-Up Responses to Crisis*, ed. Stefanie Haeffele and Virgil Henry Storr (Cham, Swits.: Springer, 2020): 57–70.

20. "A Short History of FEMA," *Frontline*, 2005, https://www.pbs.org/wgbh/pages /frontline/storm/etc/femahist.html; FEMA, "History of FEMA," 2021, https:// www.fema.gov/about/history.

21. Benjamin, Brown, and Carlin, *Strengthening the Disaster Resilience*.

22. David M. Abramson, Yoo Soon Park, et al., "Children as Bellwethers of Recovery: Dysfunctional Systems and the Effects of Parents, Households, and Neighborhoods on Serious Emotional Disturbance in Children After Hurricane Katrina," *Disaster Medicine and Public Health Preparedness* 4, no. 21 (2010): S17–S27; David M. Abramson, Lori Ann Peek, et al., "Children's Health After the Oil Spill: A Four-state Study Findings from the Gulf Coast Population Impact (GCPI) Project," National Center for Disaster Preparedness, Columbia University, 2013, https://doi.org/10.7916/D8WQ0C4P; David M. Abramson, Tasha Stehling-Ariza, et al., "Prevalence and Predictors of Mental Health Distress Post-Katrina: Findings from the Gulf Coast Child and Family Health Study," *Disaster Medicine and Public Health Preparedness* 2, no. 2 (2008): 77–86; David M. Abramson, Richard M. Garfield, and Irwin E. Redlener, "The Recovery Divide: Poverty and the Widening Gap among Mississippi Children and Families Affected by Hurricane Katrina," National Center for Disaster Preparedness (2007), https://doi.org/10 .7916/D8NZ8GT5.

23. Keith Elder et al., "African Americans' Decisions Not to Evacuate New Orleans Before Hurricane Katrina: A Qualitative study," *American Journal of Public Health* 97, Supplement 1 (2007): S124–S129.

24. Glenn S. Johnson, "Environmental Justice and Katrina: A Senseless Environmental Disaster," *Western Journal of Black Studies* 32, no. 1 (2008): 42–52.

25. John Barnshaw and Joseph Trainor, "Race, Class, and Capital Amidst the Hurricane Katrina Diaspora," in *The Sociology of Katrina: Perspectives on a Modern Catastrophe*, ed. David L. Brunsma, David Overfelt, and J. Steven Picou, 103–18 (Lanham, Md.: Rowman & Littlefield, 2007).

26. Bradley W. Mayer, Jimmy Moss, and Kathleen Dale, "Disaster and Preparedness: Lessons from Hurricane Rita," *Journal of Contingencies and Crisis Management* 16, no. 1 (2008): 14–23.

27. Eric C. J. Claas et al., "Human Influenza A H5N1 Virus Related to a Highly Pathogenic Avian Influenza Virus," *Lancet* 351, no. 9101 (1998): 472–77, https://doi.org/10.1016/S0140-6736(97)11212-0.

28. J. C. de Jong et al., "A Pandemic Warning?," *Nature* 389, no. 6651 (1997): 554, https://doi.org/10.1038/39218.

29. Claas et al., "Human Influenza A H5N1 Virus."

30. H. Chen et al., "Establishment of Multiple Sublineages of H5N1 Influenza Virus in Asia: Implications for Pandemic Control," *Proceedings of the National Academy of Sciences of the United States of America* 103, no. 8 (2006): 2845–50, https://doi.org/10.1073/pnas.0511120103.

31. World Health Organization, *WHO Inter-country Consultation: Influenza A/H5N1 in Humans in Asia* (Geneva: WHO, 2005).

32. World Health Organization, "Cumulative Number of Confirmed Human Cases for Avian Influenza A(H5N1) Reported to WHO, 2003–2023, 24 April 2023," updated April 24, 2023, https://www.who.int/publications/m/item/cumulative-number-of-confirmed-human-cases-for-avian-influenza-a(h5n1)-reported-to-who-2003-2023-24-april-2023.

33. M. Gauthier-Clerc, C. Lebarbenchon, and F. Thomas, "Recent Expansion of Highly Pathogenic Avian Influenza H5N1: A Critical Review," *IBIS* 149, no. 2 (2007): 202–14, https://doi.org/10.1111/j.1474-919X.2007.00699.x.

34. Robert G. Webster et al., "Characterization of H5N1 Influenza Viruses That Continue to Circulate in Geese in Southeastern China," *Journal of Virology* 76, no. 1 (2002): 118–26, https://doi.org/10.1128/jvi.76.1.118-126.2002.

35. Ellen P. Carlin and Ryan Remmel, "Assessing U.S. Congressional Exposure to the Issue of Emerging Infectious Disease Risk Prior to 2020," *Health Security* 20, no. 3 (May–June 2022): 212–21, https://doi.org/10.1089/hs.2021.0205; Georgetown University Center for Global Health Science and Security, "Health Security Net," accessed January 21, 2021, http://healthsecuritynet.org.

36. World Health Assembly, *Strengthening Pandemic-Influenza Preparedness and Response*, Resolution WHA58.5 (Geneva: WHA, May 23, 2005); World Health Assembly, *Revision of the International Health Regulations*, Resolution WHA58.3 (Geneva: WHA, May 23, 20050.

37. World Health Organization, *Pandemic Influenza Preparedness Framework for the Sharing of Influenza Viruses and Access to Vaccines and Other Benefits*, 2nd ed. (Geneva: WHO, 2021).

38. National Research Council on Ocean Studies Board, *Tsunami Warning and Preparedness: An Assessment of the U.S. Tsunami Program and the Nation's Preparedness Efforts* (Washington, D.C.: National Academies Press, 2011).

39. Department of Homeland Security Appropriations Act, Pub. L. 109-295 (2007), October 4, 2006.

40. Keith Bea, *Federal Emergency Management Policy Changes After Hurricane Katrina: A Summary of Statutory Provisions* (Washington, D.C.: Congressional Research Service, 2007), https://fas.org/sgp/crs/homesec/RL33729.pdf.
41. Pandemic and All-Hazards Preparedness Act, Pub. L. 109-417, December 19, 2006.
42. Pandemic and All-Hazards Preparedness Act, S. Rept. 109-319, August 3, 2006.
43. Peter J. May, Joshua Sapotichne, and Samuel Workman, "Widespread Policy Disruption and Interest Mobilization," *Policy Studies Journal* 37, no. 4 (2009): 171–94, https://doi.org/https://doi.org/10.1111/j.1541-0072.2009.00335.x.
44. Implementing Recommendations of the 9/11 Commission Act of 2007, Pub. L. 110-53, August 3, 2007.
45. Shawn Reese, *Fiscal Year 2005 Homeland Security Grant Program: State Allocations and Issues for Congressional Oversight (RL32696)* (Washington, D.C.: Congressional Research Service, February 16, 2005); Clarence Lam, Crystal Franco, and Ari Schuler, "Billions for Biodefense: Federal Agency Biodefense Funding, FY2006–FY2007," *Biosecurity and Bioterrorism: Biodefense Strategy, Practice, and Science* 4, no. 2 (2006): 113–27.
46. Humanitarian Response, "What Is the Cluster Approach?," United Nations, Office for the Coordination of Humanitarian Affairs, accessed March 14, 2021, https://www.humanitarianresponse.info/en/coordination/clusters/what-cluster-approach.
47. Abby Stoddard et al., "Cluster Approach Evaluation: Final Draft, 2007," Humanitarian Policy Group, OCHA Evaluation and Studies Section, https://www.humanitarianresponse.info/sites/www.humanitarianresponse.info/files/2019/08/ClusterEvaluationFinal.pdf.
48. Horwitz, "The Private Sector's Contribution to Natural Disaster Response."
49. Kevin Fox Gotham, "Disaster, Inc.: Privatization and Post-Katrina Rebuilding in New Orleans," *Perspectives on Politics* 10, no. 3 (2012): 633–46, https://doi.org/10.1017/S153759271200165X.
50. Gotham.
51. Athukorala and Resosudarmo, "The Indian Ocean Tsunami."
52. Angela M. Eikenberry, Verónica Arroyave, and Tracy Cooper, "Administrative Failure and the International NGO Response to Hurricane Katrina," *Public Administration Review* 67 (2007): 160–70.
53. Stephanie Gajewski et al., "Complexity and Instability: The Response of Nongovernmental Organizations to the Recovery of Hurricane Katrina Survivors in a Host Community," *Nonprofit and Voluntary Sector Quarterly* 40, no. 2 (2011): 389–403.
54. Daina Cheyenne Harvey, Yuki Kato, and Catarina Passidomo, "Rebuilding Others' Communities: A Critical Analysis of Race and Nativism in Non-profits in the Aftermath of Hurricane Katrina," *Local Environment* 21, no. 8 (2016): 1029–46.

55. Pamela Jenkins et al., "Local Nonprofit Organizations in a Post-Katrina Landscape: Help in a Context of Recovery," *American Behavioral Scientist* 59, no. 10 (2015): 1263–77.

56. Elizabeth S. Merlot and Helen De Cieri, "The Challenges of the 2004 Indian Ocean Tsunami for Strategic International Human Resource Management in Multinational Nonprofit Enterprises," *International Journal of Human Resource Management* 23, no. 7 (2012): 1303–19.

57. Cailin Wang et al., "Emerging Trends and New Developments in Disaster Research After the 2008 Wenchuan Earthquake," *International Journal of Environmental Research and Public Health* 16, no. 1 (2019): 1–19, https://www.mdpi.com/1660-4601/16/1/29.

58. Shi Shen et al., "Visualized Analysis of Developing Trends and Hot Topics in Natural Disaster Research," *PLOS ONE* 13, no. 1 (2018): 1–15, https://doi.org/10.1371/journal.pone.0191250.

59. Adriana Leiras et al., "Literature Review of Humanitarian Logistics Research: Trends and Challenges," *Journal of Humanitarian Logistics and Supply Chain Management* 4, no. 1 (2014): 95–130, https://doi.org/10.1108/JHLSCM-04-2012-0008.

60. An Act to Establish the Department of Homeland Security and for Other Purposes, Pub. L. 107-296, November 25, 2002.

61. Department of Homeland Security Science and Technology Directorate, "Welcome to the Centers of Excellence," 2022, https://www.dhs.gov/science-and-technology/centers-excellence.

62. National Science Foundation, "NSF's Response to the Hurricanes," 2005, https://www.nsf.gov/news/news_summ.jsp?cntn_id=104474.

63. Amanda P. Cowen and Scott S. Cowen, "Rediscovering Communities: Lessons from the Hurricane Katrina Crisis," *Journal of Management Inquiry* 19, no. 2 (2010): 127–25.

64. Daniel P. Aldrich, "Ties That Bond, Ties That Build: Social Capital and Governments in Post Disaster Recovery," *Studies in Emergent Order* 4, no. December (2011): 58–68.

3. PANDEMIC, EARTHQUAKE, FUKUSHIMA, SUPERSTORM SANDY

1. Timothy C. Earle, "Trust, Confidence, and the 2008 Global Financial Crisis," *Risk Analysis: An International Journal* 29, no. 6 (2009): 785–92.

2. Eric Helleiner, "Understanding the 2007–2008 Global Financial Crisis: Lessons for Scholars of International Political Economy," *Annual Review of Political Science* 14 (2011): 67–87.

3. "Outbreak of Swine-Origin Influenza A (H1N1) Virus Infection—Mexico, March–April 2009," *Morbidity and Mortality Weekly Report* 58, no. 17 (May 8, 2009): 467–70.

4. "Emergence of a Novel Swine-Origin Influenza A (H1N1) Virus in Humans," *New England Journal of Medicine* 360, no. 25 (2009): 2605–15, https://doi.org/10.1056/NEJMoa0903810.

5. "Emergence of a Novel Swine-Origin Influenza A (H1N1) Virus in Humans."

6. "Outbreak of Swine-Origin Influenza A (H1N1) Virus Infection."

7. "Update: Novel Influenza A (H1N1) Virus Infections—Worldwide, May 6, 2009," *Morbidity and Mortality Weekly Report* 58, no. 17 (May 8, 2009): 453–58.

8. S. S. Shrestha et al., "Estimating the Burden of 2009 Pandemic Influenza A (H1N1) in the United States (April 2009–April 2010)," *Clinical Infectious Disease* 52 Suppl 1 (January 1, 2011): S75–S82, https://doi.org/10.1093/cid/ciq012.

9. U.S. Centers for Disease Control and Prevention, "2009 H1N1 Pandemic Timeline," updated May 8, 2019, https://www.cdc.gov/flu/pandemic-resources/2009-pandemic-timeline.html.

10. M. D. Van Kerkhove et al., "Estimating Age-Specific Cumulative Incidence for the 2009 Influenza Pandemic: A Meta-Analysis of A(H1N1)pdm09 Serological Studies from 19 Countries," *Influenza and Other Respiratory Viruses* 7, no. 5 (September 2013): 1–8, https://doi.org/10.1111/irv.12074.

11. M. P. Girard et al., "The 2009 A (H1N1) Influenza Virus Pandemic: A Review," *Vaccine* 28, no. 31 (July 12, 2010): 4895–4902, https://doi.org/10.1016/j.vaccine.2010.05.031.

12. "2009 H1N1 Pandemic Timeline."

13. Sarah A. Lister and C. Stephen Redhead, *The 2009 Influenza Pandemic: An Overview (R40554)* (Washington, D.C.: Congressional Research Service, November 16, 2009).

14. Rebecca Katz, Aurelia Attal-Juncqua, and Julie E. Fischer, "Funding Public Health Emergency Preparedness in the United States," *American Journal of Public Health* 107, no. S2 (2017): S148–S152.

15. Girard et al., "The 2009 A (H1N1) Influenza Virus Pandemic."

16. I. Mena et al., "Origins of the 2009 H1N1 Influenza Pandemic in Swine in Mexico," *eLife* 5 (June 28, 2016): 1–21, https://doi.org/10.7554/eLife.16777.

17. Institute of Medicine Forum on Microbial Threats, "The National Academies Collection: Reports Funded by National Institutes of Health," in *The Domestic and International Impacts of the 2009-H1N1 Influenza A Pandemic: Global Challenges, Global Solutions: Workshop Summary* (Washington, D.C.: National Academies Press, 2010).

18. AP, "Magnitude 7.0 Earthquake Shakes Japan; No Immediate Reports of Damage," *Los Angeles Times*, March 21, 2021, https://www.latimes.com/world-nation/story/2021-03-20/strong-earthquake-felt-in-japanese-capital-nhk-broadcaster-says-magnitude-7-2.

19. Charles R. Marmar et al., "Stress Responses of Emergency Services Personnel to the Loma Prieta Earthquake Interstate 880 Freeway Collapse and Control Traumatic Incidents," *Journal of Traumatic Stress* 9, no. 1 (1996): 63–85; Denis

Mitchell, René Tinawi, and Richard G. Redwood, "Damage to Buildings Due to the 1989 Loma Prieta Earthquake—a Canadian Code Perspective," *Canadian Journal of Civil Engineering* 17, no. 5 (1990): 813–34.

20. Jonathan Patrick, "Evaluation Insights Haiti Earthquake Response Emerging Evaluation Lessons," *Evaluation Insights*, no. 1 (2011), https://www.oecd.org/dac/evaluation/48432995.pdf

21. Thomas Kirsch, Lauren Sauer, and Debarati Guha Sapir, "Analysis of the International and US Response to the Haiti Earthquake: Recommendations for Change," *Disaster Medicine and Public Health Preparedness* 6, no. 3 (2012): 200–208.

22. Martin Gerdin, Andreas Wladis, and Johan Von Schreeb, "Foreign Field Hospitals After the 2010 Haiti Earthquake: How Good Were We?," *Emergency Medicine Journal* 30, no. 1 (2013): e8.

23. Vijaya Ramachandran and Julie Walz, "Haiti: Where Has All the Money Gone?," *Journal of Haitian Studies* 21, no. 1 (2015): 26–65.

24. Kenneth Pletcher and John P. Rafferty, "Japan Earthquake and Tsunami of 2011," *Britannica*, https://www.britannica.com/event/Japan-earthquake-and-tsunami-of-2011.

25. Pletcher and Rafferty; Thorne Lay and Hiroo Kanamori, "Insights from the Great 2011 Japan Earthquake," *Physics Today* 64, no. 12 (2011): 33–39.

26. Editors, "Fukushima Accident," *Britannica*, https://www.britannica.com/event/Fukushima-accident.

27. Tsutomu Shimura et al., "Public Health Activities for Mitigation of Radiation Exposures and Risk Communication Challenges After the Fukushima Nuclear Accident," *Journal of Radiation Research* 56, no. 3 (2015): 422–29.

28. Nathanael Massey, "Fukushima Disaster Blame Belongs with Top Leaders at Utilities, Government and Regulators," *Climatewire*, July 6, 2012, https://www.scientificamerican.com/article/fukushima-blame-utilities-goverment-leaders-regulators/.

29. Jinbong Choi and Seohyeon Lee, "Managing a Crisis: A Framing Analysis of Press Releases Dealing with the Fukushima Nuclear Power Station Crisis," *Public Relations Review* 43, no. 5 (2017): 1016–24.

30. Daniel P. Aldrich, *Black Wave: How Networks and Governance Shaped Japan's 3/11 Disasters* (Chicago: University of Chicago Press, 2019).

31. Jeffrey B. Halverson and Thomas Rabenhorst, "Hurricane Sandy: The Science and Impacts of a Superstorm," *Weatherwise* 66, no. 2 (2013): 14–23.

32. Eric S. Blake et al., *Tropical Cyclone Report: Hurricane Sandy (AL182012)*, National Hurricane Center (February 12, 2013), https://www.nhc.noaa.gov/data/tcr/AL182012_Sandy.pdf.

33. Blake et al.

34. Mark Zandi, "The Economic Impact of Sandy," *Moody's Analytics*, November 1, 2012.

35. NYC Emergency Management, *NYC's Risk Landscape: A Guide to Hazard Mitigation. Chapter 4.1: Coastal Storms* (November 2014), https://www1.nyc.gov/assets

/em/downloads/pdf/hazard_mitigation/nycs_risk_landscape_a_guide_to
_hazard_mitigation_final.pdf.

36. J. K. Pullium, "Disaster Response and Recovery," presentation to the Committee on Strengthening the Disaster Resilience of Academic Research Communities of the National Academies of Science), National Academies' Public Access
Records Office, Washington, D.C., March 2, 2016.

37. A. Hartocollis, "A Flooded Mess That Was a Medical Gem," *New York Times*,
November 10, 2012.

38. L. Ahlborn, *New York University Response to Committee Questions (Committee on
Strengthening the Disaster Resilience of Academic Research Communities of the
National Academies of Science)* (Washington, D.C.: National Academies' Public
Access Records Office, 2017).

39. David M. Abramson and Irwin Redlener, "Hurricane Sandy: Lessons Learned,
Again," *Disaster Medicine and Public Health Preparedness* 6, no. 4 (2012): 328–29.

40. David M. Abramson, Donna Van Alst, et al., "The Hurricane Sandy Place Report:
Evacuation Decisions, Housing Issues and Sense of Community," *2015 Briefing
Report Series of the Sandy Child and Family Health (S-CAFH) Study* no. 1 (2015)
https://doi.org/10.7916/D82806TN.

41. Lainie Rutkow, Holly A. Taylor, and Lance Gable, "Emergency Preparedness and
Response for Disabled Individuals: Implications of Recent Litigation," *Journal
of Law, Medicine & Ethics* 43, no. s1 (2015): 91–94.

42. Bruce R. Lindsay, *FEMA's Disaster Relief Fund: Overview and Selected Issues*
(R43537) (Washington, D.C.: Congressional Research Service, May 7, 2014).

43. William L. Painter and Jared T. Brown, *FY2013 Supplemental Funding for Disaster Relief* (R42869) (Washington, D.C.: Congressional Research Service, February 20, 2013), https://crsreports.congress.gov/product/pdf/R/R42892/13.

44. Congressional Budget Office, *Sequestration Update Report for Fiscal Year 2012*,
August 12, 2011, https://www.cbo.gov/sites/default/files/112th-congress-2011-2012
/reports/08-12-2011_sequestration.pdf.

45. Megan S. Lynch, *Lifting the Earmark Moratorium: Frequently Asked Questions
(R45429)* (Washington, D.C.: Congressional Research Service, December 3,
2020), https://crsreports.congress.gov/product/pdf/R/R45429.

46. Abhijit Bhattacharjee and Roberta Lossio, *Evaluation of OCHA Response to the
Haiti Earthquake: Final Report* (January 2011), https://www.unocha.org/sites
/unocha/files/dms/Documents/Evaluation%20of%20OCHA%20Response%20
to%20the%20Haiti%20Earthquake.pdf.

47. Aldrich, *Black Wave*.

48. Caroline Jorant, "The Implications of Fukushima: The European Perspective,"
Bulletin of the Atomic Scientists 67, no. 4 (2011).

49. Victor Nian and S. K. Chou, "The State of Nuclear Power Two Years After
Fukushima—the ASEAN Perspective," *Applied Energy* 136 (2014): 838–48.

50. "Counting the Cost of Calamities," *Economist*, January 14, 2012, https://www
.economist.com/briefing/2012/01/14/counting-the-cost-of-calamities.

51. "Counting the Cost of Calamities."
52. M. Kunz et al., "Investigation of Superstorm Sandy 2012 in a Multi-disciplinary Approach," *Natural Hazards and Earth System Sciences* 13, no. 10 (2013): 2579–98, https://doi.org/10.5194/nhess-13-2579-2013.
53. FEMA, *2018–2022 Strategic Plan* (Washington, D.C.: FEMA, 2018).
54. Congressional Research Service, *The 2009 H1N1 Influenza Pandemic: An Overview (R40554)* (Washington, D.C.: Congressional Research Service, November 16, 2009), https://crsreports.congress.gov/product/pdf/R/R40554.
55. "Report: Industry Earned Over $3 Billion on H1N1 Vaccine," *Pharmaceutical Processing World*, May 11, 2010, https://www.pharmaceuticalprocessingworld.com/report-industry-earned-over-3-billion-on-h1n1-vaccine/.
56. Massey, "Fukushima Disaster Blame Belongs with Top Leaders"; Union of Concerned Scientists, *The Minerals Management Service: Bad Science in the Name of Private Interests* (Cambridge, Mass: Union of Concerned Scientists, August 5, 2010), https://www.ucsusa.org/resources/attacks-on-science/minerals-management-service-bad-science-name-private-interests.
57. Arthur Gautier and Anne-Claire Pache, "Research on Corporate Philanthropy: A Review and Assessment," *Journal of Business Ethics* 126, no. 3 (2015): 202–14.
58. Elizabeth McAlister, "Soundscapes of Disaster and Humanitarianism: Survival Singing, Relief Telethons, and the Haiti Earthquake," *Small Axe: A Caribbean Journal of Criticism* 16, no. 3, 39 (2012): 22–38.
59. Kirsch, Sauer, and Sapir, "Analysis of the International and US Response."
60. Justin Elliott and Laura Sullivan, "How the Red Cross Raised Half a Billion Dollars for Haiti and Built Six Homes," *Pro Publica*, June 3, 2015, https://www.propublica.org/article/how-the-red-cross-raised-half-a-billion-dollars-for-haiti-and-built-6-homes.
61. Jacob Kushner, "Haiti and the Failed Promise of US Aid," *Guardian*, October 11, 2019, https://www.theguardian.com/world/2019/oct/11/haiti-and-the-failed-promise-of-us-aid.
62. Michael Berkowitz and Arnoldo Matus Kramer, "Helping Cities Drive Transformation: The 100 Resilient Cities Initiative. Interviews with Michael Berkowitz, President of 100 Resilient Cities, and Dr. Arnoldo Matus Kramer, Mexico City's Chief Resilience Officer," *Field Actions Science Reports*, Special issue 18 (2018); Joanne Fitzgibbons and Carrie L. Mitchell, "Just Urban Futures? Exploring Equity in '100 Resilient Cities,'" *World Development* 122 (2019): 648–59.
63. Jorge Morales-Burnett and Rebecca Marx, *The Rise of the Chief Resilience Officer* (Washington, D.C.: Urban Institute, 2022).
64. U.S. Department of Health and Human Services, "Scientific Research," updated January 5, 2016, https://www.phe.gov/Preparedness/planning/science/Pages/research.aspx.
65. Centers for Disease Control and Prevention, "Public Health Preparedness and Response Research to Aid Recovery from Hurricane Sandy Publication Repository," updated September 29, 2020, https://www.cdc.gov/cpr/science/sandy

-publications.htm; U.S. Department of Health and Human Services, "Hurricane Sandy Research Grants," updated December 21, 2017, https://www.phe.gov/Preparedness/planning/SandyResearch/Pages/default.aspx.

66. "Hurricane Sandy Research Grants."
67. National Academies of Sciences, Engineering, and Medicine, *Exploring the Translation of the Results of Hurricane Sandy Research Grants Into Policy and Operations: Proceedings of a Workshop in Brief* (Washington, D.C.: National Academies Press, 2017).
68. Honglei Yi and Jay Yang, "Research Trends of Post Disaster Reconstruction: The Past and the Future," *Habitat International* 42 (2014): 21–29, https://doi.org/10.1016/j.habitatint.2013.10.005.
69. Leiras et al., "Literature Review of Humanitarian Logistics Research."

4. EBOLA, HURRICANES, WILDFIRES, AND A PANDEMIC FOR THE AGES (2013–2021)

1. B. Le Guenno et al., "Isolation and Partial Characterisation of a New Strain of Ebola Virus," *Lancet* 345, no. 8960 (1995): 1271–74, https://doi.org/10.1016/S0140-6736(95)90925-7.
2. Centers for Disease Control and Prevention, "History of Ebola Virus Disease (EVD) Outbreaks," accessed May 24, 2021, https://www.cdc.gov/vhf/ebola/history/chronology.html.
3. Sylvain Baize et al., "Emergence of Zaire Ebola Virus Disease in Guinea," *New England Journal of Medicine* 371, no. 15 (2014): 1148–25, https://doi.org/10.1056/NEJMoa1404505.
4. B. P. Bell et al., "Overview, Control Strategies, and Lessons Learned in the CDC Response to the 2014–2016 Ebola Epidemic," *MMWR Suppl* 65, no. 3 (July 8, 2016): 4–11.
5. Bell et al.
6. White House, "FACT SHEET: Emergency Funding Request to Enhance the U.S. Government's Response to Ebola at Home and Abroad," news release, November 5, 2014, https://obamawhitehouse.archives.gov/the-press-office/2014/11/05/fact-sheet-emergency-funding-request-enhance-us-government-s-response-eb.
7. Jeff Schlegelmilch, "The Biggest Test Trump Faces with Hurricane Harvey," *Fortune*, August 28, 2017, https://fortune.com/2017/08/28/hurricane-harvey-houston-trump-response/.
8. National Oceanic and Atmospheric Administration, "Hurricane Harvey & Its Impacts on Southeast Texas," accessed June 9, 2021, https://www.weather.gov/hgx/hurricaneharvey.
9. John P. Cangialosi, Andrew S. Latto, and Robbie Berg, *National Hurricane Center Tropical Cyclone Report: Hurricane Irma (AL112017)* (Washington, D.C.: National Oceanic and Atmospheric Administration, June 30, 2018).

10. Richard J. Pasch, Andrew B. Penny, and Robbie Berg, *National Hurricane Center Tropical Cyclone Report: Hurricane Maria (AL152017)* (Washington, D.C.: National Oceanic and Atmospheric Administration, February 14, 2019).

11. "Major Hurricane Maria—September 20, 2017," National Oceanic and Atmospheric Administration, accessed June 23, 2021, https://www.weather.gov/sju /maria2017.

12. Pasch, Penny, and Berg, *National Hurricane Center Tropical Cyclone Report: Hurricane Maria (AL152017)*.

13. Leyla Santiago, "Puerto Rico's New Hurricane Maria Death Toll Is 46 Times Higher than the Government's Previous Count," *CNN.com*, August 28, 2018, https://www.cnn.com/2018/08/28/health/puerto-rico-gw-report-excess-deaths /index.html; Milken Institute School of Public Health, *Project Report: Ascertainment of the Excess Mortality from Hurricane Maria in Puerto Rico* (Washington, D.C.: George Washington University, 2018).

14. Doina Chiacu, "Trump Disputes Puerto Rico Storm Death Toll, Draws Outcry," Reuters, September 13, 2018, https://www.reuters.com/article/us-usa-puertorico -trump/trump-disputes-puerto-rico-storm-death-toll-draws-outcry-idUSKCN1 LT23H.

15. Charley E. Willison et al., "Quantifying Inequities in US Federal Response to Hurricane Disaster in Texas and Florida Compared with Puerto Rico," *BMJ Global Health* 4, no. 1 (2019): 1–6.

16. Samantha Rivera Joseph et al., "Colonial Neglect and the Right to Health in Puerto Rico After Hurricane Maria," *American Journal of Public Health* 110, no. 10 (2020): 1512–18.

17. "Hurricane Florence: September 14, 2018," updated March 29, 2019, https://www .weather.gov/ilm/HurricaneFlorence.

18. Stacy R. Stewart and Robbie Berg, *National Hurricane Center Tropical Cyclone Report: Hurricane Florence (AL062018)* (Washington, D.C.: National Oceanic and Atmospheric Administration, May 30, 2019).

19. Willison et al., "Quantifying Inequities."

20. John L. Beven II, Robbie Berg, and Andrew Hagen, *National Hurricane Center Tropical Cyclone Report: Hurricane Michael (AL142018)* (Washington, D.C.: National Oceanic and Atmospheric Administration, May 17, 2019).

21. National Centers for Environmental Information, "U.S. Billion-Dollar Weather and Climate Disasters: Overview," accessed January 11, 2022, https://www.ncdc .noaa.gov/billions/.

22. Armando González-Cabán, "The Economic Dimension of Wildland Fires," in *Vegetation Fires and Global Change–Challenges for Concerted International Action. A White Paper Directed to the United Nations and International Organizations*, ed. Johann Georg Goldammer, 229–37 (Remagen-Oberwinter, Ger.: Kessel, 2013).

23. National Centers for Environmental Information, "U.S. Billion-Dollar Weather and Climate Disasters: Overview."

24. Adam B. Smith, "2020 U.S. Billion-Dollar Weather and Climate Disasters in Historical Context," January 8, 2021, *Climate.gov*, https://www.climate.gov/disasters2020.

25. David Bowman et al., *Wildfires: Australia Needs National Monitoring Agency* (Berlin: Nature Publishing Group, 2020).

26. Nicolas Borchers Arriagada et al., "Unprecedented Smoke-Related Health Burden Associated with the 2019–20 Bushfires in Eastern Australia," *Medical Journal of Australia* 213, no. 6 (2020): 282–83, https://doi.org/10.5694/mja2.50545.

27. "Australia's 2019–2020 Bushfires: The Wildlife Toll," *World Wide Fund for Nature* (2020).

28. Cal Fire, *Top 20 Most Destructive California Wildfires*, April 28, 2021, https://www.fire.ca.gov/media/t1rdhizr/top20_destruction.pdf.

29. Smith, "2020 U.S. Billion-Dollar Weather."

30. Morgan McFall-Johnson, "Over 1,500 California Fires in the Past 6 Years—Including the Deadliest Ever—Were Caused by One Company: PG&E. Here's What It Could Have Done but Didn't," *Business Insider*, November 3, 2019, https://www.businessinsider.com/pge-caused-california-wildfires-safety-measures-2019-10.

31. Jeff Schlegelmilch and Irwin Redlener, "California Blackouts Are a Planned Disaster," *Hill*, October 11, 2019, https://thehill.com/opinion/energy-environment/465362-california-blackouts-are-a-planned-disaster.

32. Jeff Schlegelmilch, "3 Reasons Trump Is Wrong About California's Deadly Fires, and One Reason He May Be Right," *Hill*, November 13, 2018, https://thehill.com/opinion/energy-environment/416523-3-reasons-trump-is-wrong-about-californias-deadly-fires-and-one; Allan Smith, "Trump Threatens to Pull Federal Aid for California Wildfires," *NBC News*, 2019, https://www.nbcnews.com/politics/donald-trump/trump-threatens-pull-federal-aid-california-wildfires-n1075866; Saranac Hale Spencer, "Contrary to Viral Claim, Trump OK'd Aid for California Fires," Debunking Viral Claims, *FactCheck.org*, updated October 16, 2020, https://www.factcheck.org/2020/09/contrary-to-viral-claim-trump-okd-aid-for-california-fires/.

33. S. Mallapaty, "Where Did COVID Come From? Five Mysteries That Remain," *Nature* 591, no. 7849 (March 2021): 188–89, https://doi.org/10.1038/d41586-021-00502-4.

34. E. P. Carlin et al., *Opportunities for Enhanced Defense, Military, and Security Sector Engagement in Global Health Security*, EcoHealth Alliance (2021), https://www.ecohealthalliance.org/wp-content/uploads/2021/02/Opportunities-for-Enhanced-Defense-Military-and-Security-Sector-Engagement-in-Global-Health-Security.pdf.

35. Trust for America's Health, *The Impact of Chronic Underfunding on America's Public Health System: Trends, Risks, and Recommendations, 2020* (2020), https://www.tfah.org/report-details/publichealthfunding2020/.

36. David Marcozzi, "During Times of Crisis Our Health-Care Delivery Is Still Lagging," *Hill*, May 24, 2018, https://thehill.com/opinion/healthcare/389276-during-times-of-crisis-our-health-care-delivery-is-still-lagging.

37. Blue Ribbon Study Panel on Biodefense, *A National Blueprint for Biodefense: Leadership and Major Reform Needed to Optimize Efforts* (October 2015), https://biodefensecommission.org/reports/a-national-blueprint-for-biodefense/; Blue Ribbon Study Panel on Biodefense, "Transforming Medical Countermeasure Technology and Partnerships" (letter) (May 4, 2018), https://biodefensecommission.org/wp-content/uploads/2019/07/2018.05.04BRSPBMCMLetterEC.pdf.

38. Topher Spiro and Zeke Emanuel, *A Comprehensive COVID-19 Vaccine Plan*, CAP, July 28, 2020; Sharon LaFraniere, Chris Hamby, and Rebecca Ruiz, "Vaccine Maker Earned Record Profits but Delivered Disappointment in Return," *New York Times*, June 16, 2021, https://www.nytimes.com/2021/06/16/us/emergent-biosolutions-covid-vaccine.html.

39. Anita Patel et al., "Personal Protective Equipment Supply Chain: Lessons Learned from Recent Public Health Emergency Responses," *Health Security* 15, no. 3 (2017): 244–52, https://doi.org/10.1089/hs.2016.0129.

40. Cristina Carias et al., "Potential Demand for Respirators and Surgical Masks During a Hypothetical Influenza Pandemic in the United States," *Clinical Infectious Diseases* 60 Suppl 1, no. Suppl 1 (2015): S43–S51, https://doi.org/10.1093/cid/civ141.

41. Coronavirus Preparedness and Response Supplemental Appropriations Act, 2020, Pub. L. 116-123, March 6, 2020, https://www.congress.gov/bill/116th-congress/house-bill/6074; Congressional Budget Office, *CBO Estimate for H.R. 6074, the Coronavirus Preparedness and Response Supplemental Appropriations Act, 2020, as posted on March 4, 2020* (Washington, D.C.: CBO, March 4, 2020).

42. Coronavirus Aid, Relief, and Economic Security Act, Pub. L. 116-36, March 27, 2020, https://www.congress.gov/bill/116th-congress/house-bill/748; Congressional Budget Office, *Preliminary Estimate of the Effects of H.R. 748, the CARES Act, Public Law 116-136, Revised, with Corrections to the Revenue Effect of the Employee Retention Credit and to the Modification of a Limitation on Losses for Taxpayers Other than Corporations* (Washington, D.C.: CBO, April 27, 2020).

43. Cécile Philippe and Nicolas Marques, *The Zero Covid Strategy Protects People and Economies More Effectively* (Paris: Institut Économique Molinari, 2021); Ingrid T. Katz et al., "From Vaccine Nationalism to Vaccine Equity—Finding a Path Forward," *New England Journal of Medicine* 384, no. 14 (2021): 1281–83.

44. André Sapir, "Why Has COVID-19 Hit Different European Union Economies So Differently?," *Policy Contribution*, no. 18 (September 2020), https://www.bruegel.org/wp-content/uploads/2020/09/PC-18-2020-22092020-final.pdf.

45. Mark Eccleston-Turner and Harry Upton, "International Collaboration to Ensure Equitable Access to Vaccines for COVID-19: The ACT-Accelerator and the COVAX Facility," *Milbank Quarterly* 99, no. 2 (2021): 426–49.

46. Thomas J. Christensen, *A Modern Tragedy? COVID-19 and US-China Relations* (Washington, D.C.: Brookings Institution, May 2020), https://www.brookings.edu/research/a-modern-tragedy-covid-19-and-us-china-relations/; Min Ye, "The COVID-19 Effect: US-China Narratives and Realities," *Washington Quarterly* 44, no. 1 (2021): 89–105.

47. Vida Abedi et al., "Racial, Economic, and Health Inequality and COVID-19 Infection in the United States," *Journal of Racial and Ethnic Health Disparities* 8, no. 3 (2021): 732–42; Jack Cordes and Marcia C. Castro, "Spatial Analysis of COVID-19 Clusters and Contextual Factors in New York City," *Spatial and Spatio-temporal Epidemiology* 34 (2020): 1–11, https://doi.org/10.1016/j.sste.2020.100355; Tiana N. Rogers et al., "Racial Disparities in COVID-19 Mortality Among Essential Workers in the United States," *World Medical & Health Policy* 12, no. 3 (2020): 311–17.

48. Liz Hamel et al., "KFF COVID-19 Vaccine Monitor: April 2021," Kaiser Family Foundation, May 6, 2021, https://www.kff.org/coronavirus-covid-19/poll-finding/kff-covid-19-vaccine-monitor-april-2021/.

49. Jon Cohen, "U.S. Officials Welcome New Zika funding, but Say Delays Hurt," *Science*, October 3, 2016, https://www.sciencemag.org/news/2016/10/us-officials-welcome-new-zika-funding-say-delays-hurt.

50. Diane P. Horn and Baird Webel, *Introduction to the National Flood Insurance Program (NFIP)* (Washington, D.C.: Congressional Research Service, 2021).

51. *Stafford Act Assistance for Public Health Incidents (IN11229)* (Washington, D.C.: Congressional Research Service, March 22, 2021).

52. World Bank, *2014–2015 West Africa Ebola Crisis: Impact Update* (2016), https://www.worldbank.org/en/topic/macroeconomics/publication/2014-2015-west-africa-ebola-crisis-impact-update.

53. Horn and Webel, *Introduction to the National Flood Insurance Program*; Andrew G. Simpson, "FEMA Renews $1.3 Billion Reinsurance for Flood Program with 27 Carriers," *Insurance Journal*, January 6, 2020, https://www.insurancejournal.com/news/national/2020/01/06/553631.htm.

54. Katherine Chiglinsky and Elaine Chen, "Wildfire Risk Leaves Californians Without Homeowners Insurance," *Bloomberg*, December 4, 2020, https://www.bloomberg.com/news/features/2020-12-04/wildfire-risk-leaves-californians-without-homeowners-insurance; Chad Hemenway, "California Issues Moratorium on Insurers Non-Renewing or Cancelling Following Wildfires," *Insurance Journal*, November 5, 2020, https://www.insurancejournal.com/news/west/2020/11/05/589813.htm.

55. Lloyd Dixon, Flavia Tsang, and Gary Fitts, *California Wildfires: Can Insurance Markets Handle the Risk?* (Santa Monica, Calif.: RAND Corporation, 2020), https://www.rand.org/pubs/research_briefs/RBA635-1.html.

56. "California Utility PG&E Pleads Guilty to 84 Wildfire Deaths," *BBC*, June 16, 2020, https://www.bbc.com/news/world-us-canada-53072946.

57. Kavya Balaraman, "PG&E Foresees $600M or Greater Loss for Kincade Fire, Files to Securitize $7.5B in Fire Costs" May 4, 2020 (Washington, D.C.), https://www.utilitydive.com/news/pge-foresees-600m-or-greater-loss-for-kincade-fire-files-to-securitize/577238/.

58. Nicolas Rabener, "Avoiding Disaster with Catastrophe Bonds?," Enterprising Investor, CFA Institute, January 21, 2021, https://blogs.cfainstitute.org/investor/2021/06/21/avoiding-disaster-with-catastrophe-bonds/.

59. Bangin Brim and Clare Wenham, "Pandemic Emergency Financing Facility: Struggling to Deliver on Its Innovative Promise," *BMJ* 367 (2019): 367; Karin Strohecker, "Coronavirus Spread Triggers World Bank Pandemic Bond Payout," *Reuters*, April 20, 2020, https://www.reuters.com/article/health-coronavirus-pandemic-bonds/coronavirus-spread-triggers-world-bank-pandemic-bond-payout-idUSL8N2C861O.

60. Government Accountability Office, *Covid 19: HHS and DOD Transitioned Vaccine Responsibilities to HHS, but Need to Address Outstanding Issues* (Washington, D.C.: GAO, January 2022), https://www.gao.gov/assets/gao-22-104453.pdf.

61. Sydney Lupkin, "Pfizer's Coronavirus Vaccine Supply Contract Excludes Many Taxpayer Protections," *NPR.org*, November 24, 2020, https://www.npr.org/sections/health-shots/2020/11/24/938591815/pfizers-coronavirus-vaccine-supply-contract-excludes-many-taxpayer-protections.

62. Luciana Borio and Scott Gottlieb, "Patent Busting Won't Help Vaccinate the World Faster," *Wall Street Journal*, May 9, 2021, https://www.wsj.com/articles/patent-busting-wont-help-vaccinate-the-world-faster-11620591133.

63. World Health Organization, *Pandemic Influenza Preparedness Framework for the Sharing of Influenza Viruses and Access to Vaccines and Other Benefits*, 2nd ed. (Geneva: WHO, 2021).

64. Jeffrey Schlegelmilch et al., "A Philanthropic Approach to Supporting Emergent Disaster Response and Recovery," *Disaster Medicine and Public Health Preparedness* 14, no. 1 (2020): 158–60, https://doi.org/10.1017/dmp.2019.97.

65. Candid and the Center for Disaster Philanthropy, *Philanthropy and COVID-19: Measuring One Year of Giving* (Washington, D.C., 2021).

66. Global Alliance of Disaster Research Institutes, "About GADRI," 2021, https://gadri.net/about/about-gadri/.

67. North American Alliance of Hazards and Disaster Research Institutes, "A Brief History," 2021, https://www.naahdri.org/about/history/.

68. National Center for Disaster Medicine and Public Health, "Disasters and Health: State of Science Symposium 2019," 2019.

69. Berlin Social Science Center, "Interdisciplinarity and Research Creativity: New Ways of Generating Impact," 2019, https://www.wzb.eu/en/research/presidents-research-group/research-group/projects/generating-impact.

70. Cailin Wang et al., "Emerging Trends and New Developments in Disaster Research After the 2008 Wenchuan Earthquake," *International Journal of*

Environmental Research and Public Health 16, no. 1 (2019): 29, https://www.mdpi
.com/1660-4601/16/1/29.

71. Glenn Fernandez and Iftekhar Ahmed, " 'Build Back Better' Approach to Disaster Recovery: Research Trends Since 2006," *Progress in Disaster Science* 1 (2019):
1–8, https://doi.org/10.1016/j.pdisas.2019.100003.

72. Rutgers University, "Center for COVID-19 Response and Pandemic Preparedness," 2022, https://support.rutgers.edu/signature-initiatives/center-for-covid
-19-response-and-pandemic-preparedness/; University of Michigan, "New
$13.8M Center at U-M Will Study Infectious Disease, Pandemic Preparedness,"
news release, October 19, 2021, https://news.umich.edu/new-13-8m-center-at-u-m
-will-study-infectious-disease-pandemic-preparedness/; University of Liverpool,
"Liverpool Announces World Leading 'End-to-End' Pandemic Institute," news
release, September 13, 2021, https://news.liverpool.ac.uk/2021/09/13/liverpool
-announces-world-leading-end-to-end-pandemic-institute/; Columbia University, "Columbia University Mailman School of Public Health to Lead New York
City's Pandemic Response Institute," news release, September 29, 2021, https://
icap.columbia.edu/news-events/columbia-university-mailman-school-of
-public-health-to-lead-new-york-citys-pandemic-response-institute/.

5. DISASTER POLITICS

1. Andrew Healy and Neil Malhotra, "Myopic Voters and Natural Disaster Policy,"
American Political Science Review 103, no. 3 (2009): 387–406, https://doi:10.1017
/S0003055409990104.

2. "Federalism," in *Legal Information Institute Legal Dictionary and Legal Encyclopedia* (Ithaca, N.Y.: Legal Information Institute, Cornell Law School, 2022),
https://www.law.cornell.edu/wex/federalism.

3. Peter F. Burns and Matthew O. Thomas, "A New New Orleans? Understanding
the Role of History and the State-Local Relationship in the Recovery Process,"
Journal of Urban Affairs 30, no. 3 (2008): 259–71, https://doi.org/10.1111/j.1467-9906
.2008.00395.x.

4. Joe Wainscott, "Navigating National Incident Management System Training
Requirements," *Citeseer* (2008), https://citeseerx.ist.psu.edu/viewdoc/download
?doi=10.1.1.176.5379.

5. Peter Eisinger, "Imperfect Federalism: The Intergovernmental Partnership for
Homeland Security," *Public Administration Review* 66, no. 4 (2006): 537–45.

6. Eisinger.

7. Andrew Reeves, "Political Disaster: Unilateral Powers, Electoral Incentives, and
Presidential Disaster Declarations," *Journal of Politics* 73, no. 4 (2011): 1142–51,
https://doi.org/10.1017/s0022381611000843.

8. Healy and Malhotra, "Myopic Voters and Natural Disaster Policy."

9. Sadie Frank, Eric Gesick, and David Victor, "Are Federal Disaster Policies Making the Harmful Impacts of Climate Change Even Worse?," *Planet Policy*, Brookings Institution, March 26, 2021, https://www.brookings.edu/blog/planetpolicy/2021/03/26/are-federal-disaster-policies-making-the-harmful-impacts-of-climate-change-even-worse/; Brock Long, "Why Will FEMA Spend as Much in Past 2 Years as the Previous 37? Here's How Disaster Aid Works," *Hill*, June 3, 2019, https://thehill.com/opinion/energy-environment/446635-why-will-fema-spend-as-much-in-past-2-years-as-the-previous-37; Pew, "What We Don't Know About State Spending on Natural Disasters Could Cost Us," Fiscal Federalism, *Pew Charitable Trusts*, June 19, 2018, https://www.pewtrusts.org/en/research-and-analysis/reports/2018/06/19/what-we-dont-know-about-state-spending-on-natural-disasters-could-cost-us.

10. Gina Kolata, "Fauci Wants to Make Vaccines for the Next Pandemic Before It Hits," *New York Times*, July 25 (updated July 26), 2021, https://www.nytimes.com/2021/07/25/health/fauci-prototype-vaccines.html.

11. Blue Ribbon Study Panel on Biodefense, *A National Blueprint for Biodefense: Leadership and Major Reform Needed to Optimize Efforts* (October 2015), https://biodefensecommission.org/reports/a-national-blueprint-for-biodefense/. See recommendation 27.

12. Kolata, "Fauci Wants to Make Vaccines."

13. U.S. Department of Health and Human Services, Public Health Emergency Medical Countermeasures Enterprise, "Multiyear Budget Fiscal Years 2015–2019."

14. To quantify the volume of supplemental appropriation bills in recent decades, we obtained data from the Congressional Budget Office for all supplemental appropriations enacted during fiscal years 2000–2021. Using these data, we summed the enacted budget authority for supplemental appropriations by year. Data source: https://web.archive.org/web/20220121082357/https://www.cbo.gov/system/files?file=2021-12/Supplemental-Appropriations-2021-12-09.pdf

15. Bruce R. Lindsay, *FEMA's Disaster Relief Fund: Overview and Selected Issues* (R43537) (Washington, D.C.: Congressional Research Service, May 7, 2014).

16. The Budget Control Act of 2011 (BCA; P.L. 112–25) instated annual limits on discretionary spending for FY 2012–2021. Using "budget adjustments" relating to major disasters, emergencies, war, and limited other purposes, however, the BCA permitted Congress to enact discretionary spending in excess of its regular annual limits. We obtained data from the Office of Management and Budget on the total enacted adjustments under each BCA adjustment category for FY 2012–2021. Figure 5.2 describes only discretionary spending; it does not reflect mandatory spending, including the $1.9 trillion American Rescue Plan passed in fiscal year 2021 in response to the COVID-19 pandemic. Data source: https://web.archive.org/web/20210120164259/https://www.whitehouse.gov/wp-content/uploads/2021/01/sequestration_final_January_2021_speaker.pdf.

17. Emergency Supplemental Appropriations Act for Defense, the Global War on Terror, and Hurricane Recovery, 2006, Pub. L. 109-234, June 15, 2006.

18. William L. Painter and Jared T. Brown, *FY2013 Supplemental Funding for Disaster Relief* (R42869) (Washington, D.C.: Congressional Research Service, February 19, 2013).

19. Justin Bogie, "Congress Must Stop the Abuse of Disaster and Emergency Spending," *Backgrounder*, February 4, 2019, https://www.heritage.org/sites/default/files/2019-02/BG3380.pdf.

20. Government Accountability Office, *Avian Influenza: USDA Has Taken Actions to Reduce Risks but Needs a Plan to Evaluate Its Efforts. GAO-17-360* (Washington, D.C.: GAO, April 2017), https://www.gao.gov/assets/gao-17-360.pdf.

21. Grant Tudor and Justin Warner, *The Congressional Futures Office: A Modern Model for Science and Technology Expertise in Congress* (Cambridge, Mass., Harvard Kennedy School Belfer Center for Science and International Affairs, May 2019).

22. Peter J. May, Joshua Sapotichne, and Samuel Workman, "Widespread Policy Disruption: Terrorism, Public Risks, and Homeland Security," *Policy Studies Journal* 37, no. 2 (2009): 171–94, https://doi.org/10.1111/j.1541-0072.2009.00309.x.

23. May, Sapotichne, and Workman, "Widespread Policy Disruption."

24. Ellen P. Carlin and Ryan Remmel, "Assessing U.S. Congressional Exposure to the Issue of Emerging Infectious Disease Risk Prior to 2020." *Health Security* 20, no. 3 (May–June 2022): 212–21, https://doi.org/10.1089/hs.2021.0205

25. Search of www.congress.gov by the authors on November 21, 2021, for all bills introduced in the 116th and 117th Congresses with the word "Covid" (not case sensitive) in the title or in the summary provided by the Congressional Research Service. The date of the first bill was February 27, 2020.

26. Chris Hamby and Sheryl Gay Stolberg, "How One Firm Put an 'Extraordinary Burden' on the U.S.'s Troubled Stockpile," *New York Times* March 6, 2021, https://www.nytimes.com/2021/03/06/us/emergent-biosolutions-anthrax-coronavirus.html; Sharon LaFraniere, Chris Hamby, and Rebecca Ruiz, "Vaccine Maker Earned Record Profits but Delivered Disappointment in Return," *New York Times*, June 16, 2021, https://www.nytimes.com/2021/06/16/us/emergent-biosolutions-covid-vaccine.html.

27. Lily Katz, "A Racist Past, a Flooded Future: Formerly Redlined Areas Have $107 Billion Worth of Homes Facing High Flood Risk—25% More than Non-Redlined Areas," *Redfin.com*, March 14, 2021, https://www.redfin.com/news/redlining-flood-risk/.

28. Stephen B. Billings, Emily Gallagher, and Lowell Ricketts, "Let the Rich Be Flooded: The Distribution of Financial Aid and Distress After Hurricane Harvey," *Journal of Financial Economics* 146, no. 2 (November 2022): 797–819, https://doi.org/10.1016/j.jfineco.2021.11.006; Naveena Sadasivam, "How Homeowners of Color Are Threatened by Climate Change—and Climate Policy," *Grist*, June 23, 2021, https://grist.org/housing/fhfa-fannie-mae-freddie-mac-mortgages-climate-risk/.

29. Junia Howell and James R. Elliott, "As Disaster Costs Rise, So Does Inequality," *Socius* 4 (January 1, 2018), https://doi.org/10.1177/2378023118816795.

30. Daniel P. Aldrich, *Black Wave: How Networks and Governance Shaped Japan's 3/11 Disasters* (Chicago: University of Chicago Press, 2019).

31. Healy and Malhotra, "Myopic Voters and Natural Disaster Policy."

32. United Nations Office for Disaster Risk Reduction, "History," accessed August 10, 2021, https://www.undrr.org/about-undrr/history.

33. United Nations Office for Disaster Risk Reduction, "What Is the Sendai Framework for Disaster Risk Reduction?," accessed January 2, 2022, https://www.undrr.org/implementing-sendai-framework/what-sendai-framework.

34. Lucy Pearson and Mark Pelling, "The UN Sendai Framework for Disaster Risk Reduction 2015–2030: Negotiation Process and Prospects for Science and Practice," *Journal of Extreme Events* 2, no. 1 (2015): 1571001, https://doi.org/10.1142/S2345737615710013.

35. United Nations Security Council, "UN Security Council Resolution 1308 (2000) on the Responsibility of the Security Council in the Maintenance of International Peace and Security: HIV/AIDS and International Peace-keeping Operations," 2000.

36. Gian Luca Burci and Stefania Negri, "Governing the Global Fight Against Pandemics: The WHO, the International Health Regulations, and the Fragmentation of International Law," *New York University Journal of International Law and Politics* 53 (2020): 501–22.

37. Kumanan Wilson, Sam Halabi, and Lawrence O. Gostin, "The International Health Regulations (2005), the Threat of Populism and the COVID-19 Pandemic," *Globalization and Health* 16, no. 1 (July 28, 2020): 70, https://doi.org/10.1186/s12992-020-00600-4.

38. World Health Organization, "World Bank to Work Together with WHO to Set Up Secretariat at the World Bank, with WHO as Lead Technical Partner," news release, June 30, 2022, https://www.who.int/news/item/30-06-2022-world-bank-board-approves-new-fund-for-pandemic-prevention—preparedness-and-response-(ppr).

39. Michael Kremer, Jonathan D. Levin, and Christopher M. Snyder, *Designing Advance Market Commitments for New Vaccines* (Chicago: Becker Friedman Institute for Economics, December 2020), https://bfi.uchicago.edu/wp-content/uploads/2020/12/BFI_WP_2020175.pdf.

40. World Bank Group, "Who We Are," accessed January 20, 2022, https://www.worldbank.org/en/who-we-are.

41. Robert K. Fleck and Christopher Kilby, "World Bank Independence: A Model and Statistical Analysis of US Influence," *Review of Development Economics* 10, no. 2 (2006): 224–40; Bernhard Reinsberg, Katharina Michaelowa, and Stephen Knack, "Which Donors, Which Funds? Bilateral Donors' Choice of Multilateral Funds at the World Bank," *International Organization* 71, no. 4 (2017): 767–802.

42. Rolph Van der Hoeven, *MDGs Post 2015: Beacons in Turbulent Times or False Lights?* (New York: UN System Task Team, 2012).

43. William Easterly, "How the Millennium Development Goals Are Unfair to Africa," *World Development* 37, no. 1 (2009): 26–35.

44. Svanhildur Thorvaldsdottir, "How to Win Friends and Influence the UN: Donor Influence on the United Nations' Bureaucracy," paper presented at the 9th Annual Conference on the Political Economy of International Organizations (PEIO), 2016.

6. DISASTER MARKETS AND THE PRIVATE SECTOR

1. Naomi Klein, *The Shock Doctrine: The Rise of Disaster Capitalism* (New York: Macmillan, 2007); Antony Loewenstein, *Disaster Capitalism: Making a Killing Out of Catastrophe* (London: Verso Books, 2015).

2. Author redacted, "Definitions of "Inherently Governmental Function," in *Federal Procurement Law and Guidance* (Washington, D.C.: Congressional Research Service, 2014).

3. Isaac Stanley-Becker, "How the U.S. Vaccination Drive Came to Rely on an Army of Consultants," *Washington Post*, August 22, 2021, https://www.washingtonpost .com/health/2021/08/22/private-consultants-vaccination-drive-outsourced/.

4. Donald F. Kettl, "Performance and Accountability: The Challenge of Government by Proxy for Public Administration," *American Review of Public Administration* 18, no. 1 (1988): 9–28.

5. Jon Elliston, "A Disaster Waiting to Happen," *Illinois Times*, September 30, 2004, https://www.illinoistimes.com/springfield/a-disaster-waiting-to-happen /Content?oid=11439319.

6. Kevin Fox Gotham, "Disaster, Inc.: Privatization and Post-Katrina Rebuilding in New Orleans," *Perspectives on Politics* 10, no. 3 (2012): 633–46, https://doi.org /10.1017/S153759271200165X.

7. Gotham.

8. Charles Perrow, "The Disaster After 9/11: The Department of Homeland Security and the Intelligence Reorganization," *Homeland Security Affairs* 2, no. 3 (April 2006), art. 3, https://www.hsaj.org/articles/174.

9. Naomi Klein, "Disaster Capitalism," *Harper's Magazine* 315 (2007); Gonzalo Lizarralde, "Unnatural Disasters," in *Unnatural Disasters* (New York: Columbia University Press, 2021); Jim Y. Millen Kim, Joyce V. Irwin, and John Alec Gershman, *Dying for Growth: Global Inequality and the Health of the Poor* (Monroe, Maine: Common Courage Press, 2000).

10. Karen Becker-Olsen and Sean Potucek, "Greenwashing," in *Encyclopedia of Corporate Social Responsibility*, ed. Samuel O. Idowu et al. (Berlin: Springer, 2013).

11. K. Porter et al., eds., *Natural Hazard Mitigation Saves: 2019 Report* (Washington, D.C.: National Institute of Building Sciences, Multi-Hazard Mitigation Council, 2019); Jackie Ratner and Jeff Schlegelmilch, "We Can't Afford to Ignore Climate Risk," *Government Finance Review* (June 2020): 63–69.

12. D. K. Nguyen and S. F. Slater, "Hitting the Sustainability Sweet Spot: Having It All," *Journal of Business Strategy* 31, no. 3 (2010): 5–11, https://doi.org/10.1108 /02756661011036655; Andrew W. Savitz with Karl Weber, *The Triple Bottom Line: How Today's Best-Run Companies Are Achieving Economic, Social and Environmental Success—and How You Can Too* (San Francisco: Jossey-Bass, 2013).

13. Michael E. Porter and Mark R. Kramer, "Creating Shared Value: How to Reinvent Capitalism—and Unleash a Wave of Innovation and Growth," *Harvard Business Review*, 2011, https://hbr.org/2011/01/the-big-idea-creating-shared -value.

14. Andrea Liesen, Frank Figge, and Tobias Hahn, "Net Present Sustainable Value: A New Approach to Sustainable Investment Appraisal," *Strategic Change* 22, no. 3-4 (2013): 175–89, https://doi.org/https://doi.org/10.1002/jsc.1931; "Net Present Value Plus," *Global Footprint Network*, accessed October 6, 2021, http:// footprintnetwork.org/npvplus; "Net Present Sustainable Value," Smeal College of Business, Pennsylvania State University, accessed October 6, 2021, https:// majorsustainability.smeal.psu.edu/finance/concepts/net-present-sustainable -value/.

15. R. David Swanson and Ronn J. Smith, "A Path to a Public-Private Partnership: Commercial Logistics Concepts Applied to Disaster Response," *Journal of Business Logistics* 34, no. 4 (2013): 335–46; Jeffrey Schlegelmilch and Joseph Albanese, "Applying Business Intelligence Innovations to Emergency Management," *Journal of Business Continuity & Emergency Planning* 8, no. 1 (2014).

16. Darius Lakdawalla and George Zanjani, "Catastrophe Bonds, Reinsurance, and the Optimal Collateralization of Risk Transfer," *Journal of Risk and Insurance* 79, no. 2 (2012): 449–76.

17. Pierre Picard, "Natural Disaster Insurance and the Equity-efficiency Trade-off," *Journal of Risk and Insurance* 75, no. 1 (2008): 17–38, https://doi.org/10.1111/j.1539 -6975.2007.00246.x.

18. Thomas Kochan et al., "The Effects of Diversity on Business Performance: Report of the Diversity Research Network," *Human Resource Management* 42, no. 1 (2003): 3–21.

19. Cedric Herring, "Does Diversity Pay? Race, Gender, and the Business Case for Diversity," *American Sociological Review* 74, no. 2 (2009): 208–24, https://doi.org /10.1177/000312240907400203.

20. Ratner and Schlegelmilch, "We Can't Afford to Ignore Climate Risk."

7. DISASTER NONPROFITS

1. Bruce R. Lindsay and Shawn Reese, *FEMA and SBA Disaster Assistance for Individuals and Households: Application Process, Determinations, and Appeals* (45238) (Washington, D.C.: Congressional Research Service, June 22, 2018).

2. Emily Ying Yang Chan and Wilson Li, "Role of Government and NGOs," in *Orthopedics in Disasters: Orthopedic Injuries in Natural Disasters and Mass Casualty Events*, ed. Nikolaj Wolfson, Alexander Lerner, and Leonid Roshal, 47–59 (Berlin: Springer, 2016).

3. Marlena Hartz, "The Future of Disaster Philanthropy," paper presented at the Conference Board, London/New York, July 2017.

4. Multi-Hazard Mitigation Council, *Short Natural Hazard Mitigation Saves: 2019 Report* (Washington, D.C.: National Institute of Building Sciences, 2019).

5. Hartz, "The Future of Disaster Philanthropy."

6. Philip H. Brown and Jessica H. Minty, "Media Coverage and Charitable Giving After the 2004 Tsunami," *Southern Economic Journal* 75, no. 1 (2008).

7. Julian Marx, Milad Mirbabaie, and Christian Ehnis, "Sense-Giving Strategies of Media Organisations in Social Media Disaster Communication: Findings from Hurricane Harvey," paper presented at the Australasian Conference on Information Systems, Sydney, 2018, https://arxiv.org/pdf/2004.08567.pdf.

8. Cynthia Donovan et al., "Emergency Needs Assessments and the Impact of Food Aid on Local Markets," MSU International Development Working Paper no. 87, 2006, https://www.canr.msu.edu/resources/emergency-needs-assess ments-and-the-impact-of-food-aid-on-local-markets

9. Jeffrey Schlegelmilch et al., "A Philanthropic Approach to Supporting Emergent Disaster Response and Recovery." *Disaster Medicine and Public Health Preparedness* 14, no. 1 (2020): 158–60, https://doi.org/10.1017/dmp.2019.97.

10. Edelman, *Edelman Trust Barometer 2021*, https://www.edelman.com/sites/g/files /aatuss191/files/2021-03/2021%20Edelman%20Trust%20Barometer.pdf.

11. Richard Knox, "5 Years After Haiti's Earthquake, Where Did the $13.5 Billion Go?," *NPR*, January 12, 2015, https://www.npr.org/sections/goatsandsoda/2015/01/12/3761 38864/5-years-after-haiti-s-earthquake-why-aren-t-things-better; Justin Elliott and Laura Sullivan, "How the Red Cross Raised Half a Billion Dollars for Haiti and Built Six Homes," *Pro Publica*, June 3, 2015, https://www.propublica.org/article /how-the-red-cross-raised-half-a-billion-dollars-for-haiti-and-built-6-homes.

12. "Giving After Disasters," *Harvard Business Review* (January–February 2019): 17–20, https://hbr.org/2019/01/giving-after-disasters.

13. L. Ballesteros, T. Wry, and M. Useem, "Halos or Horns? Reputation and the Contingent Financial Returns to Non-Market Behavior," Wharton School, 2018.

14. "Giving After Disasters."

15. Hartz, "The Future of Disaster Philanthropy."

16. Rajeev K. Goel, "Uncharitable Acts in Charity: Socioeconomic Drivers of Charity-Related Fraud," *Social Science Quarterly* 101, no. 4 (2020): 1397–1412, https:// doi.org/10.1111/ssqu.12794.

17. Candid, "Guidestar," accessed December 24, 2021, https://www.guidestar.org/.

18. "CEPI," accessed December 24, 2021, https://cepi.net/.

19. Joanne Fitzgibbons and Carrie L. Mitchell, "Just Urban Futures? Exploring Equity in '100 Resilient Cities,'" *World Development* 122 (2019): 648–59,

https://doi.org/10.1016/j.worlddev.2019.06.021; Sylvia Croese, Cayley Green, and Gareth Morgan, "Localizing the Sustainable Development Goals Through the Lens of Urban Resilience: Lessons and Learnings from 100 Resilient Cities and Cape Town," *Sustainability* 12, no. 2 (2020): 550, https://doi.org/10.3390/su12020550.

8. DISASTER ACADEMICS

1. Russell R. Dynes and Enrico Louis Quarantelli, "The Place of the 1917 Explosion in Halifax Harbor in the History of Disaster Research: The Work of Samuel H. Prince" (1993).
2. E. L. Quarantelli, "The Early History of the Disaster Research Center," *History in the Making*, University of Delaware, Disaster Research Center, accessed March 6, 2022, https://www.drc.udel.edu/drc-vision-history/.
3. Greg Oulahen, Brennan Vogel, and Chris Gouett-Hanna, "Quick Response Disaster Research: Opportunities and Challenges for a New Funding Program," *International Journal of Disaster Risk Science* (2020): 568–77, https://doi.org/10.1007/s13753-020-00299-2.
4. J. C. Gaillard and Lori Peek, "Disaster-zone Research Needs a Code of Conduct," *Nature*, November 20, 2019, https://www.nature.com/articles/d41586-019-03534-z.
5. Timothy Fraser, Daniel P. Aldrich, and Andrew Small, "Connecting Social Capital and Vulnerability: Citation Network Analysis of Disaster Studies," *Natural Hazards Review* 22, no. 3 (2021), https://doi.org/doi:10.1061/(ASCE)NH.1527-6996.0000469.
6. North American Alliance of Hazards and Disaster Research Institutes, "Institutes, Centers and Laboratories," accessed December 30, 2021, https://www.naahdri.org/membership/institutes-centers-and-laboratories/.
7. Global Alliance of Disaster Research Institutes, "Global Alliance of Disaster Research Institutes," 2021, https://gadri.net/.
8. National Center for Disaster Medicine and Public Health, "Disasters and Health: State of Science Symposium 2019," Washington, D.C., 2019; Berlin Social Science Center, "Interdisciplinarity and Research Creativity: New Ways of Generating Impact," 2019, https://www.wzb.eu/en/research/presidents-research-group/research-group/projects/generating-impact.
9. Hendrik Woiwode and Anna Froese, "Two Hearts Beating in a Research Centers' Chest: How Scholars in Interdisciplinary Research Settings Cope with Monodisciplinary Deep Structures," *Studies in Higher Education* 46, no. 11 (2021): 2230–44, https://doi.org/10.1080/03075079.2020.1716321.
10. National Science Foundation, "Federal R&D Obligations Increased 10% in 2019; Largest Year-to-Year Change Since 2009," accessed December 2, 2021, https://ncses.nsf.gov/pubs/nsf21328. Table 5 outlines funding obligations by performer.

11. Thomas D. Kirsch and Mark Keim, "US Governmental Spending for Disaster-Related Research, 2011–2016: Characterizing the State of Science Funding Across 5 Professional Disciplines," *Disaster Medicine and Public Health Preparedness* 13, no. 5–6 (2019): 912–19, https://doi.org/10.1017/dmp.2019.14.

12. Candid and Center for Disaster Philanthropy, *Philanthropy and COVID-19* (Washington, D.C., 2020).

13. Kirsch and Keim, "US Governmental Spending."

14. National Science Foundation, "NSF's Response to the Hurricanes," 2005, https://www.nsf.gov/news/news_summ.jsp?cntn_id=104474.

15. L. Ahlborn, *New York University Response to Committee Questions (Committee on Strengthening the Disaster Resilience of Academic Research Communities of the National Academies of Science)* (Washington, D.C.: National Academies' Public Access Records Office, 2017).

16. Adriana Leiras et al., "Literature Review of Humanitarian Logistics Research: Trends and Challenges," *Journal of Humanitarian Logistics and Supply Chain Management* 4, no. 1 (2014): 95–130, https://doi.org/10.1108/JHLSCM-04-2012 -0008.

17. American Association of University Professors, "Tenure," accessed January 20, 2022, https://www.aaup.org/issues/tenure.

18. Nasreen S. Jessani et al., "Academic Incentives for Enhancing Faculty Engagement with Decision-makers—Considerations and Recommendations from One School of Public Health," *Humanities and Social Sciences Communications* 7, no. 1 (November 11, 2020): 1–13, https://doi.org/10.1057/s41599-020 -00629-1.

19. Gaillard and Peek, "Disaster-Zone Research Needs a Code of Conduct."

20. Fraser, Aldrich, and Small, "Connecting Social Capital and Vulnerability."

9. HUMANS ARE BAD AT RISK, AND EVEN WORSE WITH UNCERTAINTY

1. Daniel Kahneman, "Maps of Bounded Rationality: Psychology for Behavioral Economics," *American Economic Review* 93, no. 5 (2003): 1449–75, https://doi.org /10.1257/000282803322655392.

2. Bruce Schneier, "Why the Human Brain Is a Poor Judge of Risk," *WIRED*, March 22, 2007, https://www.wired.com/2007/03/security-matters0322/.

3. David Epstein, *Range: Why Generalists Triumph in a Specialized World* (New York: Riverhead Books, 2019).

4. Maureen Hogan Casamayou, *Democracy in Crisis: Three Mile Island, the Shuttle Challenger, and Risk Assessment* (Boulder, Colo.: Westview Press, 1993).

5. For a discussion on cognitive dissonance, Casamayou cites Leon Festinger, *A Theory of Cognitive Dissonance*, 4th ed. (Stanford, Calif.: Stanford University Press, 1968).

6. Erik J. Dahl, "The 9/11 Attacks: A New Explanation," in *Intelligence and Surprise Attack: Failure and Success from Pearl Harbor to 9/11 and Beyond* (Washington, D.C.: Georgetown University Press, 2013), 128–59.

7. Search of www.congress.gov by the authors on November 21, 2021, for all bills introduced in the 116th and 117th Congresses with the word "Covid" (not case sensitive) in the title or in the summary provided by the Congressional Research Service. The date of the first bill was February 27, 2020.

8. Daniel Immerwahr, "The Strange, Sad Death of America's Political Imagination," *New York Times*, July 2, 2021, https://www.nytimes.com/2021/07/02/opinion/us-politics-edward-bellamy.html.

9. Deborah D. Stine, *The Manhattan Project, the Apollo Program, and Federal Energy Technology R&D Programs: A Comparative Analysis (RL34645)* (Washington, D.C.: Congressional Research Service, June 30, 2009).

10. REIMAGINING THE MODEL

1. Thomas A. Birkland, *Lessons of Disaster: Policy Change After Catastrophic Events* (Washington, D.C.: Georgetown University Press, 2006).

2. Thomas Kean and Lee Hamilton, *The 9/11 Commission Report: Final Report of the National Commission on Terrorist Attacks Upon the United States*, vol. 3 (Washington, D.C.: Government Printing Office, 2004).

3. Tim Roemer, "Why Do Congressmen Spend Only Half Their Time Serving Us?," *Newsweek*, July 29, 2015, https://www.newsweek.com/why-do-congressmen-spend-only-half-their-time-serving-us-357995; Ciara Torres-Spelliscy, "Time Suck: How the Fundraising Treadmill Diminishes Effective Governance," *Seton Hall Legislative Journal* 42, no. 2 (2018): 271–310, https://scholarship.shu.edu/cgi/viewcontent.cgi?article=1136&context=shlj.

4. Bipartisan Commission on Biodefense, *Budget Reform for Biodefense: Integrated Budget Needed to Increase Return on Investment* (Washington, D.C., February 2018), https://biodefensecommission.org/reports/budget-reform-for-biodefense/.

5. Jeff Schlegelmilch, *Written Testimony of Jeff Schlegelmilch, Subcommittee on Legislative and Budget Process of the House Rules Committee* (Washington, D.C., U.S. House of Representatives, January 16, 2022).

6. Ellen P. Carlin and Jennifer B. Alton, "Now Is the Time to Resource the Public Health Emergency Fund," *The Hill*, February 28, 2020, https://thehill.com/blogs/congress-blog/healthcare/485163-now-is-the-time-to-resource-the-public-health-emergency-fund.

7. Bipartisan Policy Center, *Positioning America's Public Health System for the Next Pandemic* (Washington, D.C.: Bipartisan Policy Center, June 2021), https://bipartisanpolicy.org/download/?file=/wp-content/uploads/2021/06/Public

-Health-Report_RV2.pdf; Robert P. Kadlec, *Written Testimony of Dr. Robert P. Kadlec, House Rules Subcommittee on Legislative and Budget Procedures of the House Rules Committee* (Washington, D.C.: United States Congress, January 19, 2021), https://www.congress.gov/117/meeting/house/114328/witnesses/HHRG-117 -RU02-Wstate-KadlecR-20220119.pdf.

8. Chelsey Delany, "Bonds of Trust: Blockchain and disaster relief," *Blockchain Events*, *IBM*, 2020, https://www.ibm.com/blogs/blockchain/2020/01/bonds-of -trust-blockchain-and-disaster-relief/.

9. Steven Kerr, "An Academy Classic: On the Folly of Rewarding A, While Hoping for B," *Academy of Management Executive* 9, no. 1 (1995): 7–14.

10. Robert S. Kaplan and David P. Norton, "The Balanced Scorecard: Measures That Drive Performance," *Harvard Business Review* (1992): 172.

BIBLIOGRAPHY

Abedi, Vida, Oluwaseyi Olulana, Venkatesh Avula, Durgesh Chaudhary, Ayesha Khan, Shima Shahjouei, Jiang Li, and Ramin Zand. "Racial, Economic, and Health Inequality and Covid-19 Infection in the United States." *Journal of Racial and Ethnic Health Disparities* 8, no. 3 (2021): 732–42.

Abramson, David M., Richard M. Garfield, and Irwin E. Redlener. "The Recovery Divide: Poverty and the Widening Gap Among Mississippi Children and Families Affected by Hurricane Katrina." National Center for Disaster Preparedness (2007). https://doi.org/10.7916/D8NZ8GT5.

Abramson, David M., Yoon Soo Park, Tasha Stehling-Ariza, and Irwin E. Redlener. "Children as Bellwethers of Recovery: Dysfunctional Systems and the Effects of Parents, Households, and Neighborhoods on Serious Emotional Disturbance in Children After Hurricane Katrina." *Disaster Medicine and Public Health Preparedness* 4, no. 21 (2010): S17–S27.

Abramson, David M., Lori Ann Peek, Irwin E. Redlener, Jaishree Beedasy, Thomas Aguilar, Jonathan Sury, Akilah N. Banister, and Rebecca May. "Children's Health After the Oil Spill: A Four-State Study Findings from the Gulf Coast Population Impact (GCPI) Project." National Center for Disaster Preparedness, Columbia University, 2013. https://doi.org/10.7916/D8WQ0C4P

Abramson, David M., and Irwin Redlener. "Hurricane Sandy: Lessons Learned, Again." *Disaster Medicine and Public Health Preparedness* 6, no. 4 (2012): 328–29.

Abramson, David M., Tasha Stehling-Ariza, Richard M. Garfield, and Irwin E. Redlener. "Prevalence and Predictors of Mental Health Distress Post-Katrina: Findings from the Gulf Coast Child and Family Health Study." *Disaster Medicine and Public Health Preparedness* 2, no. 2 (2008): 77–86.

Abramson, David M., Donna Van Alst, Alexis Merdjanoff, Rachael Piltch-Loeb, Jaishree Beedasy, Patricia Findley, Lori Ann Peek, et al. "The Hurricane Sandy Place Report: Evacuation Decisions, Housing Issues and Sense of Community." *2015 Briefing Report Series of the Sandy Child and Family Health (S-CAFH) Study*, no. 1 (2015). https://doi.org/10.7916/D82806TN

An Act to Establish the Department of Homeland Security and for Other Purposes, Pub. L. 107-296, November 25, 2002.

Ahlborn, L. *New York University Response to Committee Questions (Committee on Strengthening the Disaster Resilience of Academic Research Communities of the National Academies of Science)*. Washington, D.C.: National Academies' Public Access Records Office, 2017.

Aldrich, Daniel P. *Black Wave: How Networks and Governance Shaped Japan's 3/11 Disasters*. Chicago: University of Chicago Press, 2019.

——. "Ties That Bond, Ties That Build: Social Capital and Governments in Post Disaster Recovery." *Studies in Emergent Order* 4 (December 2011): 58–68.

American Association of University Professors. "Tenure." Accessed January 20, 2022. https://www.aaup.org/issues/tenure.

Aspen Institute Justice and Society Program. *Task Force Report on Streamlining and Consolidating Congressional Oversight of the U.S. Department of Homeland Security*. Washington, D.C.: Aspen Institute, 2013. https://www.aspeninstitute.org/wp-content/uploads/files/content/docs/pubs/Sunnylands%20report%2009-11-13.pdf.

Associated Press. "DHS Most Overseen Department." *Charleston-Gazette Mail*, May 20, 2011. https://www.wvgazettemail.com/inside-washington-dhs-most-overseen-department/article_b7118d32-ff91-5fb1-9aa5-f57d369fd58a.html.

——. "Magnitude 7.0 Earthquake Shakes Japan; No Immediate Reports of Damage." *Los Angeles Times*, March 21 2021. https://www.latimes.com/world-nation/story/2021-03-20/strong-earthquake-felt-in-japanese-capital-nhk-broadcaster-says-magnitude-7-2.

Athukorala, Prema-Chandra, and Budy P. Resosudarmo. "The Indian Ocean Tsunami: Economic Impact, Disaster Management, and Lessons." *Asian Economic Papers* 4, no. 1 (2005): 1–39.

Auerswald, Philip, Lewis M. Branscomb, Todd M. La Porte, and Erwann Michel-Kerjan. "The Challenge of Protecting Critical Infrastructure." *Issues in Science and Technology* 22, no. 1 (2005): 77–83.

Author redacted. *Definitions of "Inherently Governmental Function" in Federal Procurement Law and Guidance*. Washington, D.C.: Congressional Research Service, 2014.

Baize, Sylvain, Delphine Pannetier, Lisa Oestereich, Toni Rieger, Lamine Koivogui, N'Faly Magassouba, Barrè Soropogui, et al. "Emergence of Zaire Ebola Virus Disease in Guinea." *New England Journal of Medicine* 371, no. 15 (2014): 1418–25. https://doi.org/10.1056/NEJMoa1404505.

Baker, Michael S. "Casualties of the Global War on Terror and Their Future Impact on Health Care and Society: A Looming Public Health Crisis." *Military Medicine* 179, no. 4 (2014): 348–55.

Balaraman, Kavya. "PG&E Foresees $600m or Greater Loss for Kincade Fire, Files to Securitize $7.5b in Fire Costs."*Utility Dive*, May 4, 2020. https://www.utilitydive .com/news/pge-foresees-600m-or-greater-loss-for-kincade-fire-files-to-securitize /577238/.

Ballesteros, L., T. Wry, and M. Useem. *Halos or Horns? Reputation and the Contingent Financial Returns to Non-Market Behavior.* Philadelphia: Wharton School, 2018.

Barnshaw, John, and Joseph Trainor. "Race, Class, and Capital Amidst the Hurricane Katrina Diaspora." In *The Sociology of Katrina: Perspectives on a Modern Catastrophe,* ed. David L. Brunsma, David Overfelt, and J. Steven Picou, 103–18. Lanham, Md.: Rowman & Littlefield, 2007.

BBC. "California Utility PG&E Pleads Guilty to 84 Wildfire Deaths." *BBC,* June 16, 2020. https://www.bbc.com/news/world-us-canada-53072946.

Bea, Keith. *Federal Emergency Management Policy Changes After Hurricane Katrina: A Summary of Statutory Provisions.* Washington, D.C.: Congressional Research Service, 2007. https://fas.org/sgp/crs/homesec/RL33729.pdf.

Becker-Olsen, Karen, and Sean Potucek. "Greenwashing." In *Encyclopedia of Corporate Social Responsibility,* ed. Samuel O. Idowu, Nicholas Capaldi, Liangrong Zu, and Ananda Das Gupta, 1318–23. Berlin: Springer, 2013.

Bell, B. P., I. K. Damon, D. B. Jernigan, T. A. Kenyon, S. T. Nichol, J. P. O'Connor, and J. W. Tappero. "Overview, Control Strategies, and Lessons Learned in the CDC Response to the 2014–2016 Ebola Epidemic." *MMWR Suppl* 65, no. 3 (July 8, 2016): 4–11. https://doi.org/10.15585/mmwr.su6503a2.

Benjamin, Georges C., Lisa Brown, and Ellen Carlin, eds. *Strengthening the Disaster Resilience of the Academic Biomedical Research Community: Protecting the Nation's Investment.* Washington, D.C.: National Academies Press, 2017. https://doi:10.17226 /24827.

Berkowitz, Michael, and Arnoldo Matus Kramer. "Helping Cities Drive Transformation: The 100 Resilient Cities Initiative. Interviews with Michael Berkowitz, President of 100 Resilient Cities, and Dr. Arnoldo Matus Kramer, Mexico City's Chief Resilience Officer." *Field Actions Science Reports,* Special issue 18 (2018): 52–57.

Berlin Social Science Center. "Interdisciplinarity and Research Creativity: New Ways of Generating Impact." 2019. https://www.wzb.eu/en/research/presidents-research -group/research-group/projects/generating-impact.

Beven II, John L., Robbie Berg, and Andrew Hagen. *National Hurricane Center Tropical Cyclone Report: Hurricane Michael (Al142018).* Washington, D.C.: National Oceanic and Atmospheric Administration, May 17, 2019.

Bhattacharjee, Abhijit, and Roberta Lossio. *Evaluation of OCHA Response to the Haiti Earthquake: Final Report.* OCHA: January 2011. https://www.unocha.org/sites

/unocha/files/dms/Documents/Evaluation%20of%20OCHA%20Response%20
to%20the%20Haiti%20Earthquake.pdf.

Bialik, Carl. "We Still Don't Know How Many People Died Because of Katrina."
FiveThirtyEight 26 (August 26, 2015). https://fivethirtyeight.com/features/we-still
-dont-know-how-many-people-died-because-of-katrina/.

Billings, Stephen B., Emily Gallagher, and Lowell Ricketts. "Let the Rich Be Flooded:
The Distribution of Financial Aid and Distress after Hurricane Harvey." *Journal
of Financial Economics* 146, no. 2 (November 2022). https://doi.org/10.1016/j.jfineco
.2021.11.006.

Bipartisan Commission on Biodefense. *Budget Reform for Biodefense: Integrated Budget Needed to Increase Return on Investment.* Washington, D.C.: Bipartisan Commission on Biodefense, February 2018. https://biodefensecommission.org/reports
/budget-reform-for-biodefense/.

Bipartisan Policy Center. *Positioning America's Public Health System for the Next Pandemic.* Washington, D.C.: Bipartisan Policy Center, June 2021. https://biparti
sanpolicy.org/download/?file=/wp-content/uploads/2021/06/Public-Health-Report
_RV2.pdf.

Birkland, Thomas A. *Lessons of Disaster: Policy Change After Catastrophic Events.*
Washington, D.C.: Georgetown University Press, 2006.

Blake, Adam, and M. Thea Sinclair. "Tourism Crisis Management: US Response to
September 11." *Annals of Tourism Research* 30, no. 4 (2003): 813–32.

Blake, Eric S., Todd B. Kimberlain, Robert J. Berg, John P. Cangialosi, and John L.
Beven II. *Tropical Cyclone Report: Hurricane Sandy (AL182012).* National Hurricane Center, February 12, 2013. https://www.nhc.noaa.gov/data/tcr/AL182012_Sandy
.pdf.

Bloodgood, Elizabeth A., and Joannie Tremblay-Boire. "International NGOs and
National Regulation in an Age of Terrorism." *VOLUNTAS: International Journal of
Voluntary and Nonprofit Organizations* 22, no. 1 (2011): 142–73.

Blue Ribbon Study Panel on Biodefense. *A National Blueprint for Biodefense: Leadership and Major Reform Needed to Optimize Efforts.* Washington, D.C.: Bipartisan
Commission on Biodefense, October 2015. https://biodefensecommission.org
/reports/a-national-blueprint-for-biodefense/.

——. "Transforming Medical Countermeasure Technology and Partnerships" (letter), May 4, 2018. https://biodefensecommission.org/wp-content/uploads/2019/07
/2018.05.04BRSPBMCMLetterEC.pdf.

Bogie, Justin. "Congress Must Stop the Abuse of Disaster and Emergency Spending."
Backgrounder, February 4, 2019. https://www.heritage.org/sites/default/files/2019
-02/BG3380.pdf.

Bolleyer, Nicole, and Anika Gauja. "Combating Terrorism by Constraining Charities?
Charity and Counter-Terrorism Legislation Before and After 9/11." *Public Administration* 95, no. 3 (2017): 654–69.

Borchers Arriagada, Nicolas, Andrew J. Palmer, David M. J. S. Bowman, Geoffrey G.
Morgan, Bin B. Jalaludin, and Fay H. Johnston. "Unprecedented Smoke-Related

Health Burden Associated with the 2019–20 Bushfires in Eastern Australia." *Medical Journal of Australia* 213, no. 6 (2020): 282–83. https://doi.org/10.5694/mja2.50545.

Borio, Luciana, and Scott Gottleib. "Patent Busting Won't Help Vaccinate the World Faster." *Wall Street Journal,* May 9 2021. https://www.wsj.com/articles/patent-busting-wont-help-vaccinate-the-world-faster-11620591133.

Bowman, David, Grant Williamson, Marta Yebra, Joshua Lizundia-Loiola, Maria Lucrecia Pettinari, Sami Shah, Ross Bradstock, and Emilio Chuvieco. *Wildfires: Australia Needs National Monitoring Agency.* Berlin: Nature Publishing Group, 2020.

Bram, Jason, James Orr, and Carol Rapaport. "Measuring the Effects of the September 11 Attack on New York City." *Economic Policy Review* 8, no. 2 (2002).

Brim, Bangin, and Clare Wenham. "Pandemic Emergency Financing Facility: Struggling to Deliver on Its Innovative Promise." *BMJ* 367 (2019).

Brown, Philip H., and Jessica H. Minty. "Media Coverage and Charitable Giving After the 2004 Tsunami." *Southern Economic Journal* 75, no. 1 (2008): 9–25.

Burci, Gian Luca, and Stefania Negri. "Governing the Global Fight Against Pandemics: The WHO, the International Health Regulations, and the Fragmentation of International Law." *New York University Journal of International Law and Politics* 53 (2020): 501–22.

Burns, Peter F., and Matthew O. Thomas. "A New New Orleans? Understanding the Role of History and the State-Local Relationship in the Recovery Process." *Journal of Urban Affairs* 30, no. 3 (2008): 259–71. https://doi.org/10.1111/j.1467-9906.2008.00395.x.

Cal Fire. *Top 20 Most Destructive California Wildfires,* April 28, 2021. https://www.fire.ca.gov/media/t1rdhizr/top20_destruction.pdf.

Candid and the Center for Disaster Philanthropy. *Philanthropy and COVID-19.* Washington, D.C., 2020.

——. *Philanthropy and COVID-19: Measuring One Year of Giving.* Washington, D.C., 2021.

Cangialosi, John P., Andrew S. Latto, and Robbie Berg. *National Hurricane Center Tropical Cyclone Report: Hurricane Irma (Al112017).* Washington, D.C.: National Oceanic and Atmospheric Administration, June 30, 2018.

Cannon, Terry. "Vulnerability Analysis and the Explanation of "Natural" Disasters." *Disasters, Development and Environment* 1 (January 1994): 13–30.

Carias, Cristina, Gabriel Rainisch, Manjunath Shankar, Bishwa B. Adhikari, David L. Swerdlow, William A. Bower, Satish K. Pillai, Martin I. Meltzer, and Lisa M. Koonin. "Potential Demand for Respirators and Surgical Masks During a Hypothetical Influenza Pandemic in the United States." *Clinical Infectious Diseases* 60, Suppl. 1 (2015): S42–S51. https://doi.org/10.1093/cid/civ141.

Carlin, Ellen P., and Jennifer B. Alton. "Now Is the Time to Resource the Public Health Emergency Fund." *The Hill,* February 28, 2020. https://thehill.com/blogs/congress-blog/healthcare/485163-now-is-the-time-to-resource-the-public-health-emergency-fund.

Carlin, Ellen P., M. S. Moore, E. Shambaugh, and W. B. Karesh. *Opportunities for Enhanced Defense, Military, and Security Sector Engagement in Global Health Security.* New York: EcoHealth Alliance, 2021. https://www.ecohealthalliance.org/wp-content/uploads/2021/02/Opportunities-for-Enhanced-Defense-Military-and-Security-Sector-Engagement-in-Global-Health-Security.pdf.

Carlin, Ellen P., and Ryan Remmel. "Assessing U.S. Congressional Exposure to the Issue of Emerging Infectious Disease Risk Prior to 2020." *Health Security* 20, no. 3 (May–June 2022): 212–21. https://doi.org/10.1089/hs.2021.0205.

Casamayou, Maureen Hogan. *Democracy in Crisis: Three Mile Island, the Shuttle Challenger, and Risk Assessment.* Boulder, Colo.: Westview Press, 1993.

Center for COVID-19 Response and Pandemic Preparedness, Rutgers University Foundation. 2022. https://support.rutgers.edu/signature-initiatives/center-for-covid-19-response-and-pandemic-preparedness/

Centers for Disease Control and Prevention. "Elimination of Malaria in the United States (1947–1951)." Updated July 23, 2018. https://www.cdc.gov/malaria/about/history/elimination_us.html.

——. "History of Ebola Virus Disease (EVDd) Outbreaks." Accessed May 24, 2021. https://www.cdc.gov/vhf/ebola/history/chronology.html.

——. "Public Health Preparedness and Response Research to Aid Recovery from Hurricane Sandy Publication Repository." Updated September 29, 2020. https://www.cdc.gov/cpr/science/sandy-publications.htm.

——. "2009 H1N1 Pandemic Timeline." Updated May 8, 2019. https://www.cdc.gov/flu/pandemic-resources/2009-pandemic-timeline.html.

Centre for Research on the Epidemiology of Disasters and UN Office for Disaster Risk Reduction. *Human Cost of Disasters: An Overview of the Last 20 Years (2000–2019).* Geneva: CRED and UNDRR, 2020.

Chan, Emily Ying Yang, and Wilson Li. "Role of Government and Ngos." In *Orthopedics in Disasters Orthopedic Injuries in Natural Disasters and Mass Casualty Events*, ed. Nikolaj Wolfson, Alexander Lerner, and Leonid Roshal, 47–59. Berlin: Springer, 2016.

Charbonneau, Mathieu, and Aaron Doyle. "The Contradictory Roles of the Insurance Industry in the Era of Climate Change." In *Criminology and Climate: Insurance, Finance, and the Regulation of Harmscapes*, ed. Cameron Holley, Liam Phelan, and Clifford Shearing, 76–92. London: Routledge, 2020.

Chen, H., G. J. D. Smith, K. S. Li, J. Wang, X. H. Fan, J. M. Rayner, D. Vijaykrishna, et al. "Establishment of Multiple Sublineages of H5N1 Influenza Virus in Asia: Implications for Pandemic Control." *Proceedings of the National Academy of Sciences of the United States of America* 103, no. 8 (2006): 2845–50. https://doi.org/10.1073/pnas.0511120103.

Cherry, Andrew L., and Mary Elizabeth Cherrys. "A Middle Class Response to Disaster: Fema's Policies and Problems." *Journal of Social Service Research* 23, no. 1 (1997): 71–87.

Chiacu, Doina. "Trump Disputes Puerto Rico Storm Death Toll, Draws Outcry." *Reuters*, September 13, 2018. https://www.reuters.com/article/us-usa-puertorico-tru mp/trump-disputes-puerto-rico-storm-death-toll-draws-outcry-idUSKCN1LT23H.

Chiglinsky, Katherine, and Elaine Chen. "Wildfire Risk Leaves Californians Without Homeowners Insurance." *Bloomberg*, December 4, 2020. https://www.bloomberg .com/news/features/2020-12-04/wildfire-risk-leaves-californians-without -homeowners-insurance.

Chmutina, K., J. Von Meding, J. C. Gaillard, and L. Bosher. "Why Natural Disasters Aren't All That Natural." *Open Democracy* 14 (2017). https://www.opendemocracy .net/en/why-natural-disasters-arent-all-that-natural/.

Choi, Jinbong, and Seohyeon Lee. "Managing a Crisis: A Framing Analysis of Press Releases Dealing with the Fukushima Nuclear Power Station Crisis." *Public Relations Review* 43, no. 5 (2017): 1016–24.

Christensen, Thomas J. *A Modern Tragedy? COVID-19 and US-China Relations*. Washington, D.C.: Brookings Institution, May 2020. https://www.brookings.edu /research/a-modern-tragedy-covid-19-and-us-china-relations/.

Claas, Eric C. J., Albert D. M. E. Osterhaus, Ruud van Beek, Jan C. De Jong, Guus F. Rimmelzwaan, Dennis A. Senne, Scott Krauss, Kennedy F. Shortridge, and Robert G. Webster. "Human Influenza A H5N1 Virus Related to a Highly Pathogenic Avian Influenza Virus." *Lancet* 351, no. 9101 (1998): 472–77. https://doi.org/10.1016 /S0140-6736(97)11212-0.

Cohen, Jon. "U.S. Officials Welcome New Zika Funding, but Say Delays Hurt." *Science*, October 3, 2016. https://www.sciencemag.org/news/2016/10/us-officials-welcome -new-zika-funding-say-delays-hurt.

Columbia University. "Columbia University Mailman School of Public Health to Lead New York City's Pandemic Response Institute." News release, September 29, 2021, https://icap.columbia.edu/news-events/columbia-university-mailman-school-of -public-health-to-lead-new-york-citys-pandemic-response-institute/.

Congressional Budget Office. *CBO Estimate for H.R. 6074, the Coronavirus Preparedness and Response Supplemental Appropriations Act, 2020, as Posted on March 4, 2020*. Washington, D.C.: Congressional Budget Office, March 4, 2020.

——. *Preliminary Estimate of the Effects of H.R. 748, the Cares Act, Public Law 116–136, Revised, with Corrections to the Revenue Effect of the Employee Retention Credit and to the Modification of a Limitation on Losses for Taxpayers Other than Corporations*. Washington, D.C.: Congressional Budget Office, April 27, 2020.

——. *Sequestration Update Report for Fiscal Year 2012*. Washington, D.C.: Congressional Budget Office, August 12, 2011. https://www.cbo.gov/sites/default/files/112th -congress-2011-2012/reports/08-12-2011_sequestration.pdf.

Congressional Research Service. *The 2009 H1N1 Influenza Pandemic: An Overview (R40554)*. Washington, D.C., November 16, 2009. https://crsreports.congress.gov /product/pdf/R/R40554.

——. *Stafford Act Assistance for Public Health Incidents (IN11229)*. March 22, 2021.

Cordes, Jack, and Marcia C. Castro. "Spatial Analysis of Covid-19 Clusters and Contextual Factors in New York City." *Spatial and Spatio-temporal Epidemiology* 34 (2020): 100355.

Coronavirus Aid, Relief, and Economic Security Act, Pub. L. 116-136, March 27, 2020. https://www.congress.gov/bill/116th-congress/house-bill/748.

Coronavirus Preparedness and Response Supplemental Appropriations Act, 2020, Pub. L. 116-123, March 6, 2020. https://www.congress.gov/bill/116th-congress/house-bill/6074.

Cowen, Amanda P., and Scott S. Cowen. "Rediscovering Communities: Lessons from the Hurricane Katrina Crisis." *Journal of Management Inquiry* 19, no. 2 (2010): 117–25.

Cozza, Stephen J., Joscelyn E. Fisher, Kathryn R. Hefner, Mary A. Fetchet, Shenglin Chen, Rafael F. Zuleta, Carol S. Fullerton, and Robert J. Ursano. "Human Remains Identification, Grief, and Posttraumatic Stress in Bereaved Family Members 14 Years After the September 11, 2001, Terrorist Attacks." *Journal of Traumatic Stress* 33, no. 6 (2020).

Croese, Sylvia, Cayley Green, and Gareth Morgan. "Localizing the Sustainable Development Goals Through the Lens of Urban Resilience: Lessons and Learnings from 100 Resilient Cities and Cape Town." *Sustainability* 12, no. 2 (2020): 550. https://doi.org/10.3390/su12020550

Dahl, Erik J. "The 9/11 Attacks: A New Explanation." In *Intelligence and Surprise Attack: Failure and Success from Pearl Harbor to 9/11 and Beyond*, 128–59. Washington, D.C.: Georgetown University Press, 2013.

David Swanson, R., and Ronn J. Smith. "A Path to a Public–Private Partnership: Commercial Logistics Concepts Applied to Disaster Response." *Journal of Business Logistics* 34, no. 4 (2013): 335–46.

de Jong, J. C., E. C. J. Claas, A. D. M. E. Osterhaus, R. G. Webster, and W. L. Lim. "A Pandemic Warning?" *Nature* 389, no. 6651 (1997): 554. https://doi.org/10.1038/39218.

Delany, Chelsey, "Bonds of Trust: Blockchain and Disaster Relief," *Blockchain Events*. IBM, 2020. https://www.ibm.com/blogs/blockchain/2020/01/bonds-of-trust-blockchain-and-disaster-relief/.

Department of Homeland Security Appropriations Act, Pub. L. 109-295 (2007), October 4, 2006.

Dixon, Lloyd, Flavia Tsang, and Gary Fitts. *California Wildfires: Can Insurance Markets Handle the Risk?* Santa Monica, Calif.: RAND Corporation, 2020. https://doi.org/10.7249/RBA635-1. https://www.rand.org/pubs/research_briefs/RBA635-1.html.

Donovan, Cynthia, Megan McGlinchy, John M Staatz, and David L Tschirley. "Emergency Needs Assessments and the Impact of Food Aid on Local Markets." MSU International Development Working Paper no. 87 (2006). https://www.canr.msu.edu/resources/emergency-needs-assessments-and-the-impact-of-food-aid-on-local-markets.

Dynes, Russell R. *Organized Behavior in Disaster.* Lexington, Mass.: Heath Lexington Books, 1970.

Dynes, Russell R., and Enrico Louis Quarantelli. "The Place of the 1917 Explosion in Halifax Harbor in the History of Disaster Research: The Work of Samuel H. Prince." 1993.

Earle, Timothy C. "Trust, Confidence, and the 2008 Global Financial Crisis." *Risk Analysis: An International Journal* 29, no. 6 (2009): 785–92.

Easterly, William. "How the Millennium Development Goals Are Unfair to Africa." *World Development* 37, no. 1 (2009): 26–35.

Eccleston-Turner, Mark, and Harry Upton. "International Collaboration to Ensure Equitable Access to Vaccines for COVID-19: The Act-Accelerator and the Covax Facility." *Milbank Quarterly* 99, no. 2 (2021): 426–49.

Economist. "Counting the Cost of Calamities," January 14, 2012. https://www .economist.com/briefing/2012/01/14/counting-the-cost-of-calamities.

Edelman. *Edelman Trust Barometer 2021.* https://www.edelman.com/sites/g/files /aatuss191/files/2021-03/2021%20Edelman%20Trust%20Barometer.pdf.

Eikenberry, Angela M., Verónica Arroyave, and Tracy Cooper. "Administrative Failure and the International Ngo Response to Hurricane Katrina." *Public Administration Review* 67 (2007): 160–70.

Eisinger, Peter. "Imperfect Federalism: The Intergovernmental Partnership for Homeland Security." *Public Administration Review* 66, no. 4 (2006): 537–45.

Elder, Keith, Sudha Xirasagar, Nancy Miller, Shelly Ann Bowen, Saundra Glover, and Crystal Piper. "African Americans' Decisions Not to Evacuate New Orleans Before Hurricane Katrina: A Qualitative Study." *American Journal of Public Health* 97, Supplement 1 (2007): S124–S29.

Elliott, Justin, and Laura Sullivan. "How the Red Cross Raised Half a Billion Dollars for Haiti and Built Six Homes." *Pro Publica*, June 3, 2015. https://www.propublica .org/article/how-the-red-cross-raised-half-a-billion-dollars-for-haiti-and-built-6 -homes.

Elliston, Jon. "A Disaster Waiting to Happen." *Illinois Times*, September 30, 2004. https://www.illinoistimes.com/springfield/a-disaster-waiting-to-happen /Content?oid=11439319.

"Emergence of a Novel Swine-Origin Influenza A(H1N1) Virus in Humans." *New England Journal of Medicine* 360, no. 25 (2009): 2605–15. https://doi.org/10.1056 /NEJMoa0903810.

Emergency Supplemental Appropriations Act for Defense, the Global War on Terror, and Hurricane Recovery, 2006, Pub. L. 109-234, June 15, 2006.

Epstein, David. *Range: Why Generalists Triumph in a Specilaized World.* New York: Riverhead Books, 2019.

Federal Emergency Management Agency. "History of FEMA." Washington, D.C.: FEMA, 2021. https://www.fema.gov/about/history.

——. *2018–2022 Strategic Plan.* Washington, D.C.: FEMA, 2018.

Fernandez, Glenn, and Iftekhar Ahmed. "'Build Back Better' Approach to Disaster Recovery: Research Trends Since 2006." *Progress in Disaster Science* 1 (2019): 100003. https://doi.org/10.1016/j.pdisas.2019.100003.

Fitzgibbons, Joanne, and Carrie L. Mitchell. "Just Urban Futures? Exploring Equity in '100 Resilient Cities.'" *World Development* 122 (2019): 648–59. https://doi.org/10 .1016/j.worlddev.2019.06.021.

Fleck, Robert K., and Christopher Kilby. "World Bank Independence: A Model and Statistical Analysis of US Influence." *Review of Development Economics* 10, no. 2 (2006): 224–40.

Frank, Sadie, Eric Gesick, and David Victor, "Are Federal Disaster Policies Making the Harmful Impacts of Climate Change Even Worse?" *Planet Policy.* Brookings Institution, March 26, 2021. https://www.brookings.edu/blog/planetpolicy/2021/03 /26/are-federal-disaster-policies-making-the-harmful-impacts-of-climate -change-even-worse/.

Fraser, Timothy, Daniel P. Aldrich, and Andrew Small. "Connecting Social Capital and Vulnerability: Citation Network Analysis of Disaster Studies." *Natural Hazards Review* 22, no. 3 (2021). https://doi.org/doi:10.1061/(ASCE)NH.1527-6996.000 0469.

Gaillard, Jean-Christophe, Catherine C. Liamzon, and Jessica D. Villanueva. "'Natural' Disaster? A Retrospect Into the Causes of the Late-2004 Typhoon Disaster in Eastern Luzon, Philippines." *Environmental Hazards* 7, no. 4 (2007): 257–70.

Gaillard, Jean-Christope, and Lori Peek. "Disaster-Zone Research Needs a Code of Conduct." *Nature*, November 20, 2019. https://www.nature.com/articles/d41586-019 -03534-z.

Gajewski, Stephanie, Holly Bell, Laura Lein, and Ronald J Angel. "Complexity and Instability: The Response of Nongovernmental Organizations to the Recovery of Hurricane Katrina Survivors in a Host Community." *Nonprofit and Voluntary Sector Quarterly* 40, no. 2 (2011): 389–403.

Gauthier-Clerc, M., C. Lebarbenchon, and F. Thomas. "Recent Expansion of Highly Pathogenic Avian Influenza H5N1: A Critical Review." *IBIS* 149, no. 2 (2007): 202– 14. https://doi.org/10.1111/j.1474-919X.2007.00699.x.

Gautier, Arthur, and Anne-Claire Pache. "Research on Corporate Philanthropy: A Review and Assessment." *Journal of Business Ethics* 126, no. 3 (2015): 343–69.

Georgetown University Center for Global Health Science and Security. "Health Security Net." Accessed January 21, 2021. http://healthsecuritynet.org.

Gerdin, Martin, Andreas Wladis, and Johan Von Schreeb. "Foreign Field Hospitals After the 2010 Haiti Earthquake: How Good Were We?" *Emergency Medicine Journal* 30, no. 1 (2013): e8.

Girard, M. P., J. S. Tam, O. M. Assossou, and M. P. Kieny. "The 2009 A (H1N1) Influenza Virus Pandemic: A Review." *Vaccine* 28, no. 31 (July 12, 2010): 4895–902. https:// doi.org/10.1016/j.vaccine.2010.05.031.

Giroux, Henry A. "The Militarization of Us Higher Education after 9/11." *Theory, Culture & Society* 25, no. 5 (2008): 56–82.

"Giving After Disasters." *Harvard Business Review* (January–February 2019): 17–20. https://hbr.org/2019/01/giving-after-disasters.

Glass, Andrew. "Bush Creates Office of Homeland Security, Oct. 8, 2001." *Politico*, October 8, 2016. https://www.politico.com/story/2016/10/bush-creates-office-of -homeland-security-oct-8-2001-229212.

Goel, Rajeev K. "Uncharitable Acts in Charity: Socioeconomic Drivers of Charity-Related Fraud." *Social Science Quarterly* 101, no. 4 (2020): 1397–412, https://doi.org /10.1111/ssqu.12794.

Goepner, Erik W. "Measuring the Effectiveness of America's War on Terror." *The US Army War College Quarterly: Parameters* 46, no. 1 (2016): 12.

Goldwater-Nichols Department of Defense Reorganization Act of 1986, Pub. L. 99-443, October 1, 1986.

González-Cabán, Armando. "The Economic Dimension of Wildland Fires." In *Vegetation Fires and Global Change–Challenges for Concerted International Action. A White Paper Directed to the United Nations and International Organizations*, ed. Johann Georg Goldammer, 229–37. Remagen-Oberwinter, Ger.: Kassel, 2013.

Goodwin, B. S., Jr., and J. C. Donaho. "Tropical Storm and Hurricane Recovery and Preparedness Strategies." *ILAR Journal* 51, no. 2 (2010): 104–19. https://doi.org/10 .1093/ilar.51.2.104.

Gordon, Avishag. "Terrorism as an Academic Subject After 9/11: Searching the Internet Reveals a Stockholm Syndrome Trend." *Studies in Conflict & Terrorism* 28, no. 1 (2005): 45–59. https://doi.org/10.1080/10576100590524339.

Gotham, Kevin Fox. "Disaster, Inc.: Privatization and Post-Katrina Rebuilding in New Orleans." *Perspectives on Politics* 10, no. 3 (2012): 633–46. https://doi.org/10.1017 /S153759271200165X.

Gould, Kevin A., M. Magdalena Garcia, and Jacob A.C. Remes. "Beyond 'Natural-Disasters-Are-Not-Natural': The Work of State and Nature After the 2010 Earthquake in Chile." *Journal of Political Ecology* 23, no. 1 (2016): 93–114.

Government Accountability Office. *Avian Influenza: USDA Has Taken Actions to Reduce Risks but Needs a Plan to Evaluate Its Efforts. GAO-17-360.* April 2017. https://www .gao.gov/assets/gao-17-360.pdf.

——. *COVID 19: HHS and DOD Transitioned Vaccine Responsibilities to HHS, but Need to Address Outstanding Issues.* January 2022. https://www.gao.gov/assets/gao-22 -104453.pdf.

Halverson, Jeffrey B., and Thomas Rabenhorst. "Hurricane Sandy: The Science and Impacts of a Superstorm." *Weatherwise* 66, no. 2 (2013): 14–23.

Hamby, Chris, and Sheryl Gay Stolberg. "How One Firm Put an 'Extraordinary Burden' on the U.S.'s Troubled Stockpile." *New York Times*, March 6, 2021. https://www .nytimes.com/2021/03/06/us/emergent-biosolutions-anthrax-coronavirus.html.

Hamel, Liz, Lunna Lopes, Grace Sparks, Mellisha Stokes, and Mollyann Brodie. "KFF COVID-19 Vaccine Monitor: April 2021." Kaiser Family Foundation, May 6, 2021. https://www.kff.org/coronavirus-covid-19/poll-finding/kff-covid-19-vaccine -monitor-april-2021/.

Hartocollis, A. "A Flooded Mess That Was a Medical Gem." *New York Times*, November 10, 2012.

Hartz, Marlena. "The Future of Disaster Philanthropy." Paper presented at the Conference Board, London/New York, July 2017.

Harvey, Daina Cheyenne, Yuki Kato, and Catarina Passidomo. "Rebuilding Others' Communities: A Critical Analysis of Race and Nativism in Non-Profits in the Aftermath of Hurricane Katrina." *Local Environment* 21, no. 8 (2016): 1029–46.

Healy, Andrew, and Neil Malhotra. "Myopic Voters and Natural Disaster Policy." *American Political Science Review* 103, no. 3 (2009): 387–406.

Helleiner, Eric. "Understanding the 2007–2008 Global Financial Crisis: Lessons for Scholars of International Political Economy." *Annual Review of Political Science* 14 (2011): 67–87.

Hemenway, Chad. "California Issues Moratorium on Insurers Non-Renewing or Cancelling Following Wildfires." *Insurance Journal*, November 5, 2020. https://www.insurancejournal.com/news/west/2020/11/05/589813.htm.

Henderson, Joan C. "Corporate Social Responsibility and Tourism: Hotel Companies in Phuket, Thailand, After the Indian Ocean Tsunami." *International Journal of Hospitality Management* 26, no. 1 (2007): 228–39.

Herring, Cedric. "Does Diversity Pay? Race, Gender, and the Business Case for Diversity." *American Sociological Review* 74, no. 2 (2009): 208–24, https://doi.org/10.1177/000312240907400203.

Horn, Diane P., and Baird Webel. *Introduction to the National Flood Insurance Program (NGIP)*. Washington, D.C.: Congressional Research Service, 2021.

Horwitz, Steven. "The Private Sector's Contribution to Natural Disaster Response." In *Bottom-Up Responses to Crisis*, ed. Stefanie Haeffele and Virgil Henry Storr, 57–70. Cham, Switz.: Springer, 2020.

Howell, Junia, and James R. Elliott. "As Disaster Costs Rise, So Does Inequality." *Socius* 4 (January 1, 2018). https://doi.org/10.1177/2378023118816795.

Hui, David Shu-Cheong, Poon-Chuen Wong, and Chen Wang. "SARS: Clinical Features and Siagnosis." *Respirology* 8 Suppl, Suppl 1 (2003): S20–S24. https://doi.org/10.1046/j.1440-1843.2003.00520.x.

Immerwahr, Daniel. "The Strange, Sad Death of America's Political Imagination." *New York Times*, July 2, 2021. https://www.nytimes.com/2021/07/02/opinion/us-politics-edward-bellamy.html.

Implementing Recommendations of the 9/11 Commission Act of 2007, Pub. L. 110-53, August 3, 2007.

Institute of Medicine. *Learning from SARS: Preparing for the Next Disease Outbreak: Workshop Summary*, ed. Knobler Stacey, Mahmoud Adel, Lemon Stanley, Mack Alison, Sivitz Laura, and Oberholtzer Katherine. Washington, D.C.: National Academies Press, 2004. https://doi.org/10.17226/10915.

Institute of Medicine Forum on Microbial Threats. "The National Academies Collection: Reports Funded by National Institutes of Health." In *The Domestic and International Impacts of the 2009-H1N1 Influenza a Pandemic: Global Challenges,*

Global Solutions: Workshop Summary. Washington, D.C.: National Academies Press, 2010.

Jenkins, Pamela, Tara Lambeth, Kim Mosby, and Bethany Van Brown. "Local Non-profit Organizations in a Post-Katrina Landscape: Help in a Context of Recovery." *American Behavioral Scientist* 59, no. 10 (2015): 1263–77.

Jessani, Nasreen S., Akshara Valmeekanathan, Carly M. Babcock, and Brenton Ling. "Academic Incentives for Enhancing Faculty Engagement with Decision-Makers—Considerations and Recommendations from One School of Public Health." *Humanities and Social Sciences Communications* 7, no. 1 (November 11, 2020): 148. https://doi.org/10.1057/s41599-020-00629-1.

Johnson, Glenn S. "Environmental Justice and Katrina: A Senseless Environmental Disaster." *Western Journal of Black Studies* 32, no. 1 (2008): 42–52.

Jones, K. E., N. G. Patel, M. A. Levy, A. Storeygard, D. Balk, J. L. Gittleman, and P. Daszak. "Global Trends in Emerging Infectious Diseases." *Nature* 451, no. 7181 (February 21, 2008): 990–93. https://doi.org/10.1038/nature06536.

Jorant, Caroline. "The Implications of Fukushima: The European Perspective." *Bulletin of the Atomic Scientists* 67, no. 4 (2011): 14–17.

Joseph, Samantha Rivera, Caroline Voyles, Kimberly D. Williams, Erica Smith, and Mariana Chilton. "Colonial Neglect and the Right to Health in Puerto Rico After Hurricane Maria." *American Journal of Public Health* 110, no. 10 (2020): 1512–18.

Kadlec, Robert P. *Written Testimony of Dr. Robert P. Kadlec, House Rules Subcommittee on Legislative and Budget Procedures of the House Rules Committee.* Washington, D.C.: United States Congress, January 19, 2021. https://www.congress.gov/117/meeting/house/114328/witnesses/HHRG-117-RU02-Wstate-KadlecR-20220119.pdf.

Kahneman, Daniel. "Maps of Bounded Rationality: Psychology for Behavioral Economics." *American Economic Review* 93, no. 5 (2003): 1449–75. https://doi.org/10.1257/000282803322655392.

Kaplan, Robert S., and David P. Norton. "The Balanced Scorecard: Measures That Drive Performance." *Harvard Business Review* (1992): 172.

Kapucu, Naim, E. Berman, and X. Wang. "Emergency Information Management and Public Disaster Preparedness: Lessons from the 2004 Florida Hurricane Season." *International Journal of Mass Emergencies and Disasters* 26, no. 3 (2008): 169–97.

Katz, Ingrid T., Rebecca Weintraub, Linda-Gail Bekker, and Allan M. Brandt. "From Vaccine Nationalism to Vaccine Equity—Finding a Path Forward." *New England Journal of Medicine* 384, no. 14 (2021): 1281–83.

Katz, Lily. "A Racist Past, a Flooded Future: Formerly Redlined Areas Have $107 Billion Worth of Homes Facing High Flood Risk—25% More than Non-Redlined Areas." *Redfin.com*, March 14, 2021. https://www.redfin.com/news/redlining-flood-risk/.

Katz, Rebecca, Aurelia Attal-Juncqua, and Julie E. Fischer. "Funding Public Health Emergency Preparedness in the United States." *American Journal of Public Health* 107, no. S2 (2017): S148–S52.

Kean, Thomas, and Lee Hamilton. *The 9/11 Commission Report: Final Report of the National Commission on Terrorist Attacks Upon the United States.* Vol. 3. Washington, D.C.: Government Printing Office, 2004.

Kerr, Steven. "An Academy Classic: On the Folly of Rewarding a, While Hoping for B." *Academy of Management Executive* 9, no. 1 (1995): 7–14.

Kettl, Donald F. "Performance and Accountability: The Challenge of Government by Proxy for Public Administration." *American Review of Public Administration* 18, no. 1 (1988): 9–28.

Kim, Jim Y. Millen, Joyce V. Irwin, and John Alec Gershman. *Dying for Growth: Global Inequality and the Health of the Poor.* Monroe, Maine: Common Courage Press, 2000.

Kirsch, Thomas D., and Mark Keim. "US Governmental Spending for Disaster-Related Research, 2011–2016: Characterizing the State of Science Funding Across 5 Professional Disciplines." *Disaster Medicine and Public Health Preparedness* 13, no. 5–6 (2019): 912–19. https://doi.org/10.1017/dmp.2019.14.

Kirsch, Thomas D., Lauren Sauer, and Debarati Guha Sapir. "Analysis of the International and US Response to the Haiti Earthquake: Recommendations for Change." *Disaster Medicine and Public Health Preparedness* 6, no. 3 (2012): 200–208.

Klein, Naomi. "Disaster Capitalism." *Harper's Magazine* 315 (2007): 47–58.

——. *The Shock Doctrine: The Rise of Disaster Capitalism.* New York: Macmillan, 2007.

Knabb, Richard D., Jamie R. Rhome, and Daniel P. Brown. "Tropical Cyclone Report: Hurricane Katrina, National Hurricane Center." *NOAA* (2011). https://www.nhc.noaa.gov/data/tcr/AL122005_Katrina.pdf.

Knezo, Genevieve J. *Homeland Security and Counterterrorism Research and Development: Funding, Organization, and Oversight (RS21270).* Washington, D.C.: Congressional Research Service, 2003.

Knox, Richard. "5 Years After Haiti's Earthquake, Where Did the $13.5 Billion Go?" *NPR*, January 12, 2015. https://www.npr.org/sections/goatsandsoda/2015/01/12/376138864/5-years-after-haiti-s-earthquake-why-aren-t-things-better.

Kochan, Thomas, Katerina Bezrukova, Robin Ely, Susan Jackson, Aparna Joshi, Karen Jehn, Jonathan Leonard, David Levine, and David Thomas. "The Effects of Diversity on Business Performance: Report of the Diversity Research Network." *Human Resource Management* 42, no. 1 (2003): 3–21.

Kolata, Gina. "Fauci Wants to Make Vaccines for the Next Pandemic Before It Hits." *New York Times*, July 26, 2021. https://www.nytimes.com/2021/07/25/health/fauci-prototype-vaccines.html.

Kremer, Michael, Jonathan D. Levin, and Christopher M. Snyder. *Designing Advance Market Commitments for New Vaccines.* Chicago: Becker Friedman Institute for Economics, December 2020. https://bfi.uchicago.edu/wp-content/uploads/2020/12/BFI_WP_2020175.pdf.

Kunz, M., B. Mühr, T. Kunz-Plapp, J. E. Daniell, B. Khazai, F. Wenzel, M. Vannieuwenhuyse, et al. "Investigation of Superstorm Sandy 2012 in a Multi-Disciplinary

Approach." *Natural Hazards and Earth System Sciences* 13, no. 10 (2013): 2579–98. https://doi.org/10.5194/nhess-13-2579-2013.

Kushner, Jacob. "Haiti and the Failed Promise of US Aid." *Guardian*, October 11, 2019. https://www.theguardian.com/world/2019/oct/11/haiti-and-the-failed-promise-of -us-aid.

Kweifio-Okai, Carla. "Where Did the Indian Ocean Tsunami Aid Money Go?" *Guardian*, December 25, 2014. https://www.theguardian.com/global-development/2014 /dec/25/where-did-indian-ocean-tsunami-aid-money-go.

LaFraniere, Sharon, Chris Hamby, and Rebecca Ruiz. "Vaccine Maker Earned Record Profits but Delivered Disappointment in Return." *New York Times*, June 16, 2021. https://www.nytimes.com/2021/06/16/us/emergent-biosolutions-covid-vaccine .html.

Lakdawalla, Darius, and George Zanjani. "Catastrophe Bonds, Reinsurance, and the Optimal Collateralization of Risk Transfer." *Journal of Risk and Insurance* 79, no. 2 (2012): 449–76.

Lam, Clarence, Crystal Franco, and Ari Schuler. "Billions for Biodefense: Federal Agency Biodefense Funding, FY2006–FY2007." *Biosecurity and Bioterrorism: Biodefense Strategy, Practice, and Science* 4, no. 2 (2006): 113–27.

Lay, Thorne, and Hiroo Kanamori. "Insights from the Great 2011 Japan Earthquake." *Physics Today* 64, no. 12 (2011): 33–39.

Le Guenno, B., P. Formenty, M. Wyers, P. Gounon, F. Walker, and C. Boesch. "Isolation and Partial Characterisation of a New Strain of Ebola Virus." *Lancet* 345, no. 8960 (1995): 1271–74. https://doi.org/10.1016/S0140-6736(95)90925-7.

Leiras, Adriana, Irineu de Brito Jr, Eduardo Queiroz Peres, Tábata Rejane Bertazzo, and Hugo Tsugunobu Yoshida Yoshizaki. "Literature Review of Humanitarian Logistics Research: Trends and Challenges." *Journal of Humanitarian Logistics and Supply Chain Management* 4, no. 1 (2014): 95–130. https://doi.org/10.1108/JHLSCM -04-2012-0008.

Liesen, Andrea, Frank Figge, and Tobias Hahn. "Net Present Sustainable Value: A New Approach to Sustainable Investment Appraisal." *Strategic Change* 22, no. 3–4 (2013): 175–89. https://doi.org/https://doi.org/10.1002/jsc.1931.

Lindsay, Bruce R. *FEMA's Disaster Relief Fund: Overview and Selected Issues.* Washington, D.C.: Congressional Research Service, May 7, 2014.

Lindsay, Bruce R., and Shawn Reese. *FEMA and SBA Disaster Assistance for Individuals and Households: Application Process, Determinations, and Appeals" (R45238).* Washington, D.C.: Congressional Research Service, June 22, 2018.

Lister, Sarah A., and C. Stephen Redhead. *The 2009 Influenza Pandemic: An Overview (R40554).* Washington, D.C.: Congressional Research Service, November 16, 2009.

Lizarralde, Gonzalo. "Unnatural Disasters." In *Unnatural Disasters*: Columbia University Press, 2021.

Loewenstein, Antony. *Disaster Capitalism: Making a Killing out of Catastrophe.* Verso Books, 2015.

Long, Brock. "Why Will Fema Spend as Much in Past 2 Years as the Previous 37? Here's How Disaster Aid Works." *The Hill*, June 3 2019, Contributors. https://thehill.com/opinion/energy-environment/446635-why-will-fema-spend-as-much-in-past-2-years-as-the-previous-37.

Lupkin, Sydney. "Pfizer's Coronavirus Vaccine Supply Contract Excludes Many Taxpayer Protections." *NPR.org*, November 24, 2020. https://www.npr.org/sections/health-shots/2020/11/24/938591815/pfizers-coronavirus-vaccine-supply-contract-excludes-many-taxpayer-protections.

Lynch, Megan S. *Lifting the Earmark Moratorium: Frequently Asked Questions (R45429).* Washington, D.C.: Congressional Research Service, December 3, 2020. https://crsreports.congress.gov/product/pdf/R/R45429.

Makinen, Gail E. *The Economic Effects of 9/11: A Retrospective Assessment (Rl31617).* Washington, D.C.: Congressional Research Service, September 27, 2002.

Mallapaty, S. "Where Did COVID Come From? Five Mysteries That Remain." *Nature* 591, no. 7849 (March 2021): 188–89. https://doi.org/10.1038/d41586-021-00502-4.

Marcozzi, David. "During Times of Crisis Our Health-Care Delivery Is Still Lagging." *Hill*, May 24, 2018. https://thehill.com/opinion/healthcare/389276-during-times-of-crisis-our-health-care-delivery-is-still-lagging.

Marmar, Charles R., Daniel S. Weiss, Thomas J. Metzler, Heidi M Ronfeldt, and Clay Foreman. "Stress Responses of Emergency Services Personnel to the Loma Prieta Earthquake Interstate 880 Freeway Collapse and Control Traumatic Incidents." *Journal of Traumatic Stress* 9, no. 1 (1996): 63–85.

Marx, Julian, Milad Mirbabaie, and Christian Ehnis. "Sense-Giving Strategies of Media Organisations in Social Media Disaster Communication: Findings from Hurricane Harvey," paper presented at Australasian Conference on Information Systems, Sydney, 2018. https://arxiv.org/pdf/2004.08567.pdf.

Maslow, Carey B., Stephen M. Friedman, Parul S. Pillai, Joan Reibman, Kenneth I. Berger, Roberta Goldring, Steven D. Stellman, and Mark Farfel. "Chronic and Acute Exposures to the World Trade Center Disaster and Lower Respiratory Symptoms: Area Residents and Workers." *American Journal of Public Health* 102, no. 6 (2012): 1186–94.

Massey, Nathanael. "Fukushima Disaster Blame Belongs with Top Leaders at Utilities, Government and Regulators." *Climatewire*, July 6, 2012. https://www.scientificamerican.com/article/fukushima-blame-utilities-goverment-leaders-regulators/.

May, Peter J., Joshua Sapotichne, and Samuel Workman. "Widespread Policy Disruption and Interest Mobilization." *Policy Studies Journal* 37, no. 4 (2009): 793–815. https://doi.org/https://doi.org/10.1111/j.1541-0072.2009.00335.x.

——. "Widespread Policy Disruption: Terrorism, Public Risks, and Homeland Security." *Policy Studies Journal* 37, no. 2 (2009): 171–94. https://doi.org/10.1111/j.1541-0072.2009.00309.x.

Mayer, Bradley W., Jimmy Moss, and Kathleen Dale. "Disaster and Preparedness: Lessons from Hurricane Rita." *Journal of Contingencies and Crisis Management* 16, no. 1 (2008): 14–23.

McAlister, Elizabeth. "Soundscapes of Disaster and Humanitarianism: Survival Singing, Relief Telethons, and the Haiti Earthquake." *Small Axe: A Caribbean Journal
of Criticism* 16, no. 3 39 (2012): 22–38.

McFall-Johnson, Morgan. "Over 1,500 California Fires in the Past 6 Years—Including
the Deadliest Ever—Were Caused by One Company: PG&E. Here's What It
Could Have Done but Didn't." *Business Insider*, November 3, 2019. https://www
.businessinsider.com/pge-caused-california-wildfires-safety-measures-2019-10.

Mena, I., M. I. Nelson, F. Quezada-Monroy, J. Dutta, R. Cortes-Fernández, J. H. Lara-
Puente, F. Castro-Peralta, et al. "Origins of the 2009 H1N1 Influenza Pandemic in
Swine in Mexico." *eLife* 5 (June 28, 2016). https://doi.org/10.7554/eLife.16777.

Merlot, Elizabeth S., and Helen De Cieri. "The Challenges of the 2004 Indian Ocean
Tsunami for Strategic International Human Resource Management in Multinational Nonprofit Enterprises." *International Journal of Human Resource Management* 23, no. 7 (2012): 1303–19.

Milken Institute School of Public Health. *Project Report: Ascertainment of the Excess
Mortality from Hurricane Maria in Puerto Rico.* Washington, D.C.: George Washington University, 2018.

Mills, Mark P. "On My Mind: The Security-Industrial Complex." *Forbes*, November 29,
2004. https://www.forbes.com/forbes/2004/1129/044.html.

Mitchell, Denis, René Tinawi, and Richard G. Redwood. "Damage to Buildings Due
to the 1989 Loma Prieta Earthquake—a Canadian Code Perspective." *Canadian
Journal of Civil Engineering* 17, no. 5 (1990): 813–34.

Morales-Burnett, Jorge, and Rebecca Marx. *The Rise of the Chief Resilience Officer.*
Washington, D.C.: Urban Institute, 2022.

Multi-Hazard Mitigation Council. *Short Natural Hazard Mitigation Saves: 2019 Report.*
Washington, D.C.: National Institute of Building Sciences, 2019.

National Academies of Sciences, Engineering, and Medicine. *Exploring the Translation
of the Results of Hurricane Sandy Research Grants Into Policy and Operations: Proceedings of a Workshop in Brief.* Washington, D.C.: National Academies Press, 2017.

National Center for Disaster Medicine and Public Health. *Disasters and Health: State
of Science Symposium 2019.* Washington, D.C., 2019.

National Centers for Environmental Information. "U.S. Billion-Dollar Weather and
Climate Disasters: Overview." Accessed January 11, 2022. https://www.ncdc.noaa
.gov/billions/.

National Oceanic and Atmospheric Administration. "4 Hurricanes in 6 Weeks? It
Happened to One State in 2004." 2019. https://www.noaa.gov/stories/4-hurricanes
-in-6-weeks-it-happened-to-one-state-in-2004.

National Research Council on Ocean Studies Board. *Tsunami Warning and Preparedness: An Assessment of the U.S. Tsunami Program and the Nation's Preparedness
Efforts.* Washington, D.C.: National Academies Press, 2011.

National Science Foundation. "Federal R&D Obligations Increased 10% in 2019; Largest Year-to-Year Change Since 2009." Accessed December 2, 2021. https://ncses
.nsf.gov/pubs/nsf21328.

——. "NSF's Response to the Hurricanes." 2005. https://www.nsf.gov/news/news_summ.jsp?cntn_id=104474.

National Weather Service. "Hurricane Florence: September 14, 2018." Updated March 29, 2019. https://www.weather.gov/ilm/HurricaneFlorence.

——. "Hurricane Harvey & Its Impacts on Southeast Texas." National Oceanic and Atmospheric Administration. Accessed June 9, 2021. https://www.weather.gov/hgx/hurricaneharvey.

——. "Major Hurricane Maria—September 20, 2017." National Oceanic and Atmospheric Administration. Accessed June 23, 2021, https://www.weather.gov/sju/maria2017.

New York City Emergency Management. *NYC's Risk Landscape: A Guide to Hazard Mitigation. Chapter 4.1: Coastal Storms.* November 2014. https://www1.nyc.gov/assets/em/downloads/pdf/hazard_mitigation/nycs_risk_landscape_a_guide_to_hazard_mitigation_final.pdf.

Nguyen, D. K., and S. F. Slater. "Hitting the Sustainability Sweet Spot: Having It All." *Journal of Business Strategy* 31, no. 3 (2010): 5–11. https://doi.org/10.1108/02756661011036655.

Nian, Victor, and S. K. Chou. "The State of Nuclear Power Two Years After Fukushima—the ASEAN Perspective." *Applied Energy* 136 (2014): 838–48.

North American Alliance of Hazards and Disaster Research Institutes. "Institutes, Centers and Laboratories." Accessed December 30, 2021. https://www.naahdri.org/membership/institutes-centers-and-laboratories/.

Office of the Director of National Intelligence. "Background and Authorities—ISE." 2020. https://www.dni.gov/index.php/who-we-are/organizations/national-security-partnerships/ise/about-the-ise/ise-background-and-authorities.

Oklahoma City National Memorial and Museum. "Recovery: The Financial Impact of the Oklahoma City Bombing." Accessed February 23, 2022. https://memorialmuseum.com/wp-content/uploads/2019/09/okcnm-recovery-the-financial-impact.pdf.

Oulahen, Greg, Brennan Vogel, and Chris Gouett-Hanna. "Quick Response Disaster Research: Opportunities and Challenges for a New Funding Program." *International Journal of Disaster Risk Science* (2020): 1–10.

"Outbreak of Swine-Origin Influenza A (H1N1) Virus Infection—Mexico, March–April 2009." *Morbidity and Mortality Weekly Report* 58, no. 17 (May 8, 2009): 467–70.

Painter, William L., and Jared T. Brown. *FY2013 Supplemental Funding for Disaster Relief* (R42869). Washington, D.C.: Congressional Research Service, February 19, 2013.

Pandemic and All-Hazards Preparedness Act, Pub. L. 109-417, December 19, 2006.

Pandemic and All-Hazards Preparedness Act, S. Rept. 109-319, August 3, 2006.

Pappas, G., I. J. Kiriaze, P. Giannakis, and M. E. Falagas. "Psychosocial Consequences of Infectious Diseases." *Clinical Microbiology and Infection* 15, no. 8 (August 1, 2009): 743–47. https://doi.org/10.1111/j.1469-0691.2009.02947.x.

Pasch, Richard J., Andrew B. Penny, and Robbie Berg. *National Hurricane Center Tropical Cyclone Report: Hurricane Maria (Al152017)*. Washington, D.C.: National Oceanic and Atmospheric Administration, February 14, 2019.

Patel, Anita, Maryann M. D'Alessandro, Karen J. Ireland, W. Greg Burel, Elaine B. Wencil, and Sonja A. Rasmussen. "Personal Protective Equipment Supply Chain: Lessons Learned from Recent Public Health Emergency Responses." *Health Security* 15, no. 3 (2017): 244–52. https://doi.org/10.1089/hs.2016.0129.

Patrick, Jonathan. "Evaluation Insights Haiti Earthquake Response Emerging Evaluation Lessons." *Evaluation Insights*, no. 1 (2011). https://www.oecd.org/dac/evaluation/48432995.pdf.

Pearson, Lucy, and Mark Pelling. "The UN Sendai Framework for Disaster Risk Reduction 2015–2030: Negotiation Process and Prospects for Science and Practice." *Journal of Extreme Events* 2, no. 1 (2015): 1571001. https://doi.org/10.1142/S2345737615710013.

Pennsylvania State University, Smeal College of Business. "Net Present Sustainable Value." Accessed October 6, 2021. https://majorsustainability.smeal.psu.edu/finance/concepts/net-present-sustainable-value/.

Perrow, Charles. "The Disaster After 9/11: The Department of Homeland Security and the Intelligence Reorganization." *Homeland Security Affairs* 2, no. 1 (April 2006), art. 3. https://www.hsaj.org/articles/174.

Peterson, Joann, and Alan Treat. "The Post-9/11 Global Framework for Cargo Security." *Journal of International Commerce and Economics* 2 (2009): 1.

Pew. "What We Don't Know About State Spending on Natural Disasters Could Cost Us." Fiscal Federalism. *Pew Charitable Trusts*, June 19, 2018, https://www.pewtrusts.org/en/research-and-analysis/reports/2018/06/19/what-we-dont-know-about-state-spending-on-natural-disasters-could-cost-us.

Philippe, Cécile, and Nicolas Marques. *The Zero Covid Strategy Protects People and Economies More Effectively*. Paris: Institut Économique Molinari, 2021.

Picard, Pierre. "Natural Disaster Insurance and the Equity-Efficiency Trade-Off." *Journal of Risk and Insurance* 75, no. 1 (2008): 17–38.

Pickrell, John. "Facts and Figures: Asian Tsunami Disaster." *New Scientist*, January 20, 2005. https://www.newscientist.com/article/dn9931-facts-and-figures-asian-tsunami-disaster/.

Porter, K., N. Dash, C. Huyck, J. Santos, and C. Scawthorn, eds. *Natural Hazard Mitigation Saves: 2019 Report*. Washington, D.C.: National Institute of Building Sciences, Multi-Hazard Mitigation Council, 2019.

Porter, Michael E., and Mark R. Kramer. "Creating Shared Value: How to Reinvent Capitalism—and Unleash a Wave of Innovation and Growth." *Harvard Business Review*. 2011. https://hbr.org/2011/01/the-big-idea-creating-shared-value.

Public Health Security and Bioterrorism Preparedness and Response Act of 2002, Pub. L. 107-188, June 12, 2002.

Pullium, J. K. *Disaster Response and Recovery. Presentation to the Committee on Strengthening the Disaster Resilience of Academic Research Communities of the*

National Academies of Science. Washington, D.C.: National Academies' Public Access Records Office, March 2, 2016.

Quarantelli, Enrico L. *Disasters: Theory and Research.* London: Sage, 1978.

——. "The Early History of the Disaster Research Center." *History in the Making.* University of Delaware, Disaster Research Center. Accessed March 6, 2022. https:// www.drc.udel.edu/drc-vision-history/.

Quarantelli, Enrico L., and Russell R. Dynes. "Response to Social Crisis and Disaster." *Annual Review of Sociology* 3, no. 1 (1977): 23–49.

Rabener, Nicolas. "Avoiding Disaster with Catastrophe Bonds?" *Enterprising Investor.* CFA Institute, January 21, 2021, https://blogs.cfainstitute.org/investor/2021/06 /21/avoiding-disaster-with-catastrophe-bonds/.

Ramachandran, Vijaya, and Julie Walz. "Haiti: Where Has All the Money Gone?" *Journal of Haitian Studies* 21, no. 1 (2015): 26–65.

Ratner, Jackie, and Jeff Schlegelmilch. "We Can't Afford to Ignore Climate Risk." *Government Finance Review* (June 2020): 63–69.

Redhead, C. Stephen, and Mary Tiemann. *Public Health Security and Bioterrorism Preparedness and Response Act (PL 107–188): Provisions and Changes to Preexisting Law (Rl31263).* Washington, D.C.: Congressional Research Service, August 21, 2002.

Reese, Shawn. *Fiscal Year 2005 Homeland Security Grant Program: State Allocations and Issues for Congressional Oversight (Rl32696).* Washington, D.C.: Congressional Research Service, February 16, 2005.

Reeves, Andrew. "Political Disaster: Unilateral Powers, Electoral Incentives, and Presidential Disaster Declarations." *Journal of Politics* 73, no. 4 (2011): 1142–51.

Reich, E. S. "Science After 9/11: How Research Was Changed by the September 11 Terrorist Attacks." *Scientific American*, September 1, 2011. https://www.scientificamerican .com/article/how-research-was-changed-by-september-11-terrorist-attacks.

Reinsberg, Bernhard, Katharina Michaelowa, and Stephen Knack. "Which Donors, Which Funds? Bilateral Donors' Choice of Multilateral Funds at the World Bank." *International Organization* 71, no. 4 (2017): 767–802.

"Report: Industry Earned Over $3 Billion on H1N1 Vaccine." *Pharmaceutical Processing World*, May 11, 2010. https://www.pharmaceuticalprocessingworld.com/report -industry-earned-over-3-billion-on-h1n1-vaccine/.

Reppy, Judith. "A Biomedical Military-Industrial Complex?" *Technovation* 28, no. 12 (2008): 802–11.

Roemer, Tim. "Why Do Congressmen Spend Only Half Their Time Serving Us?" *Newsweek*, July 29, 2015. https://www.newsweek.com/why-do-congressmen-spend-only -half-their-time-serving-us-357995.

Rogers, Tiana N., Charles R. Rogers, Elizabeth VanSant-Webb, Lily Y. Gu, Bin Yan, and Fares Qeadan. "Racial Disparities in Covid-19 Mortality Among Essential Workers in the United States." *World Medical & Health Policy* 12, no. 3 (2020): 311–27.

Rosling, Lesley, and Mark Rosling. "Pneumonia Causes Panic in Guangdong Province." *British Medical Journal (Clinical Research Edition)* 326, no. 7386 (2003): 416–16. https://doi.org/10.1136/bmj.326.7386.416.

Ruane, Michael E. "Yellow Fever Led Half of Philadelphians to Flee the City. Ten Percent of the Residents Still Died." *Washington Post*, April 4, 2020. https://www.washingtonpost.com/history/2020/04/04/yellow-fever-led-half-philadelphians-flee-city-ten-percent-residents-still-died/.

Rutkow, Lainie, Holly A. Taylor, and Lance Gable. "Emergency Preparedness and Response for Disabled Individuals: Implications of Recent Litigation." *Journal of Law, Medicine & Ethics* 43, no. s1 (2015): 91–94.

Sadasivam, Naveena. "How Homeowners of Color Are Threatened by Climate Change—and Climate Policy." *Grist*, June 23, 2021. https://grist.org/housing/fhfa-fannie-mae-freddie-mac-mortgages-climate-risk/.

Sageman, Marc. "The Stagnation in Terrorism Research." *Terrorism and Political Violence* 26, no. 4 (2014): 565–80.

Santiago, Leyla. "Puerto Rico's New Hurricane Maria Death Toll Is 46 Times Higher than the Government's Previous Count." *CNN.com*, August 28, 2018. https://www.cnn.com/2018/08/28/health/puerto-rico-gw-report-excess-deaths/index.html.

Sapir, André. "Why Has COVID-19 Hit Different European Union Economies So Differently?" *Policy Contribution*, no. 18 (September 2020). https://www.bruegel.org/wp-content/uploads/2020/09/PC-18-2020-22092020-final.pdf.

Savitz, Andrew W., with Karl Weber. *The Triple Bottom Line: How Today's Best-Run Companies Are Achieving Economic, Social and Environmental Success—and How You Can Too.* San Francisco: Jossey-Bass, 2013.

Scanlon, T. Joseph. "Disaster's Little Known Pioneer: Canada's Samuel Henry Prince." *International Journal of Mass Emergencies and Disasters* 6, no. 3 (1988): 213–32.

Schlegelmilch, Jeff. "The Biggest Test Trump Faces with Hurricane Harvey." *Fortune*, August 28, 2017. https://fortune.com/2017/08/28/hurricane-harvey-houston-trump-response/.

——. *Rethinking Readiness: A Brief Guide to Twenty-First-Century Megadisasters.* New York: Columbia University Press, 2020.

——. "3 Reasons Trump Is Wrong About California's Deadly Fires, and One Reason He May Be Right." *Hill*, November 13, 2018. https://thehill.com/opinion/energy-environment/416523-3-reasons-trump-is-wrong-about-californias-deadly-fires-and-one.

——. *Written Testimony of Jeff Schlegelmilch, Subcommittee on Legislative and Budget Process of the House Rules Committee.* Washington, D.C., January 16, 2022.

Schlegelmilch, Jeffrey, and Joseph Albanese. "Applying Business Intelligence Innovations to Emergency Management." *Journal of Business Continuity & Emergency Planning* 8, no. 1 (2014): 31–40.

Schlegelmilch, Jeff, and Irwin Redlener. "California Blackouts Are a Planned Disaster." *Hill*, October 11, 2019. https://thehill.com/opinion/energy-environment/465362-california-blackouts-are-a-planned-disaster.

Schlegelmilch, Jeffrey, Jonathan Sury, Jeremy Brooks, and Thomas Chandler. "A Philanthropic Approach to Supporting Emergent Disaster Response and Recovery." *Disaster Medicine and Public Health Preparedness* 14, no. 1 (2020): 158–60. https://doi.org/10.1017/dmp.2019.97.

Schneier, Bruce. "Why the Human Brain Is a Poor Judge of Risk." *WIRED*, March 22, 2007. https://www.wired.com/2007/03/security-matters0322/.

Schuurman, Bart. "Research on Terrorism, 2007–2016: A Review of Data, Methods, and Authorship." *Terrorism and Political Violence* 32, no. 5 (January 3, 2018): 1011–26. https://doi.org/10.1080/09546553.2018.1439023.

Shen, Shi, Changxiu Cheng, Jing Yang, and Shanli Yang. "Visualized Analysis of Developing Trends and Hot Topics in Natural Sisaster Research." *PLOS ONE* 13, no. 1 (2018): e0191250. https://doi.org/10.1371/journal.pone.0191250.

Shimura, Tsutomu, Ichiro Yamaguchi, Hiroshi Terada, Erik Robert Svendsen, and Naoki Kunugita. "Public Health Activities for Mitigation of Radiation Exposures and Risk Communication Challenges After the Fukushima Nuclear Accident." *Journal of Radiation Research* 56, no. 3 (2015): 422–29.

"A Short History of FEMA." *Frontline*, 2005. https://www.pbs.org/wgbh/pages/frontline/storm/etc/femahist.html.

Shrestha, S. S., D. L. Swerdlow, R. H. Borse, V. S. Prabhu, L. Finelli, C. Y. Atkins, K. Owusu-Edusei, et al. "Estimating the Burden of 2009 Pandemic Influenza A(H1N1) in the United States (April 2009–April 2010)." *Clinical Infectious Disease* 52 Suppl 1 (January 1, 2011): S75–S82. https://doi.org/10.1093/cid/ciq012.

Simpson, Andrew G. "FEMA Renews $1.3 Billion Reinsurance for Flood Program with 27 Carriers." *Insurance Journal*, January 6, 2020. https://www.insurancejournal.com/news/national/2020/01/06/553631.htm.

Sisco, Hilary Fussell, Erik L. Collins, and Lynn M. Zoch. "Through the Looking Glass: A Decade of Red Cross Crisis Response and Situational Crisis Communication Theory." *Public Relations Review* 36, no. 1 (2010): 21–27.

Smith, Adam B. "2020 U.S. Billion-Dollar Weather and Climate Disasters in Historical Context." *Climate.gov*, January 8, 2021. https://www.climate.gov/disasters2020.

Smith, Allan. "Trump Threatens to Pull Federal Aid for California Wildfires." *NBC News*, November 3, 2019. https://www.nbcnews.com/politics/donald-trump/trump-threatens-pull-federal-aid-california-wildfires-n1075866.

Smith, Neil, "There's No Such Thing as a Natural Disaster." *Insights from the Social Sciences: Understanding Katrina*, June 11, 2006. https://items.ssrc.org/understanding-katrina/theres-no-such-thing-as-a-natural-disaster/.

Snyder, Samantha. "A Philadelphia Story." *Mount Vernon*, Fall 2020. https://magazine.mountvernon.org/2020/Fall/a-philadelphia-story.html.

Spencer, Saranac Hale. "Contrary to Viral Claim, Trump OK'd Aid for California Fires." Debunking Viral Claims. *FactCheck.org*, updated October 16, 2020.

https://www.factcheck.org/2020/09/contrary-to-viral-claim-trump-okd-aid-for
-california-fires/.

Spiro, Topher, and Zeke Emanuel. *A Comprehensive COVID-19 Vaccine Plan.* CAP,
July 28, 2020.

Stanley-Becker, Isaac. "How the U.S. Vaccination Drive Came to Rely on an Army of
Consultants." *Washington Post*, August 22, 2021. https://www.washingtonpost.com
/health/2021/08/22/private-consultants-vaccination-drive-outsourced/.

Stewart, Stacy R., and Robbie Berg. *National Hurricane Center Tropical Cyclone Report:
Hurricane Florence (Al062018).* Washington, D.C.: National Oceanic and Atmospheric Administration, May 30, 2019.

Stine, Deborah D. *The Manhattan Project, the Apollo Program, and Federal Energy Technology R&D Programs: A Comparative Analysis (Rl34645).* Washington, D.C.: Congressional Research Service, June 30, 2009.

Stoddard, Abby, Adele Harmer, Katherine Haver, Dirk Salomons, and Victoria
Wheeler. "Cluster Approach Evaluation: Final Draft." Humanitarian Policy Group,
OCHA Evaluation and Studies Section. https://www.humanitarianresponse.info/
sites/www.humanitarianresponse.info/files/2019/08/ClusterEvaluationFinal.pdf.

Strohecker, Karin. "Coronavirus Spread Triggers World Bank Pandemic Bond Payout." *Reuters*, April 20, 2020. https://www.reuters.com/article/health-coronavirus
-pandemic-bonds/coronavirus-spread-triggers-world-bank-pandemic-bond
-payout-idUSL8N2C861O.

Suarez, Ray. "Red Cross Woes," vol. 19. Transcript. *News Hour with Jim Lehrer.* 2001.

Suppasri, Anawat, Kazuhisa Goto, Abdul Muhari, Prasanthi Ranasinghe, Mahmood
Riyaz, Muzailin Affan, Erick Mas, Mari Yasuda, and Fumihiko Imamura. "A
Decade After the 2004 Indian Ocean Tsunami: The Progress in Disaster Preparedness and Future Challenges in Indonesia, Sri Lanka, Thailand and the Maldives." *Pure and Applied Geophysics* 172, no. 12 (2015): 3313–41. https://doi.org/10.1007
/s00024-015-1134-6.

Thorvaldsdottir, Svanhildur. "How to Win Friends and Influence the UN: Donor
Influence on the United Nations' Bureaucracy." Paper presented at the 9th Annual
Conference on the Political Economy of International Organizations (PEIO), 2016.

Torres-Spelliscy, Ciara. "Time Suck: How the Fundraising Treadmill Diminishes
Effective Governance." *Seton Hall Legislative Journal* 42, no. 2 (2018): 271–310.
https://scholarship.shu.edu/cgi/viewcontent.cgi?article=1136&context=shlj.

Trust for America's Health. *The Impact of Chronic Underfunding on America's Public
Health System: Trends, Risks, and Recommendations, 2020.* (2020). https://www.tfah
.org/report-details/publichealthfunding2020/.

Tsunami Warning and Education Act, Pub. L. 109-424, December 20, 2006.

Tudor, Grant, and Justin Warner. *The Congressional Futures Office: A Modern Model
for Science and Technology Expertise in Congress.* Cambridge, Mass.: Harvard Kennedy School Belfer Center for Science and International Affairs, May 2019.

Union of Concerned Scientists. *The Minerals Management Service: Bad Science in the
Name of Private Interests.* Cambridge, Mass.: Union of Concerned Scientists,

August 5, 2010. https://www.ucsusa.org/resources/attacks-on-science/minerals-management-service-bad-science-name-private-interests.

United Nations Office for Coodination of Humanitarian Affairs. "What Is the Cluster Approach?" Accessed March 14, 2021. https://www.humanitarianresponse.info/en/coordination/clusters/what-cluster-approach.

United Nations Office for Disaster Risk Reduction. "History." Accessed August 10, 2021. https://www.undrr.org/about-undrr/history.

——. "What Is the Sendai Framework for Disaster Risk Reduction?" Accessed January 2, 2022. https://www.undrr.org/implementing-sendai-framework/what-sendai-framework.

United Nations Security Council. "UN Security Council Resolution 1308 (2000) on the Responsibility of the Security Council in the Maintenance of International Peace and Security: HIV/AIDS and International Peace-Keeping Operations." New York: United Nations Security Council, 2000.

United States Congress. "Actions Overview H.R.3162—107th Congress (2001–2002)." Accessed October 15, 2020. https://www.congress.gov/bill/107th-congress/house-bill/3162/actions.

——. *A Failure of Initiative: Final Report of the Select Bipartisan Committee to Investigate the Preparation for and Response to Hurricane Katrina*. Vol. 109. Washington, D.C.: Government Printing Office, 2006.

——. Senate Committee on Governmental Affairs. *Homeland Security Grant Enhancement Act of 2003: Report of the Committee on Governmental Affairs, United States Senate, to Accompany S. 1245 to Provide for Homeland Security Grant Coordination and Simplification, and for Other Purposes, Together with Additional Views*. Washington. D.C.: Government Printing Office, 2004. https://www.govinfo.gov/content/pkg/CRPT-108srpt225/html/CRPT-108srpt225.htm.

United States Department of Health and Human Services. "Hurricane Sandy Research Grants." Updated December 21, 2017. https://www.phe.gov/Preparedness/planning/SandyResearch/Pages/default.aspx.

——. "Scientific Research." Updated January 5, 2016. https://www.phe.gov/Preparedness/planning/science/Pages/research.aspx.

United States Department of Health and Human Services, Public Health Emergency Medical Countermeasures Enterprise. *Multiyear Budget Fiscal Years 2015–2019*.

United States Department of Health and Human Services and National Institutes of Health. *NIAID Strategic Plan for Biodefense Research*. Bethesda, Md., 2002.

United States Department of Homeland Security. "Who Joined DHS." Washington, D.C., 2015. https://www.dhs.gov/who-joined-dhs.

United States Department of Justice. *Amerithrax Investigative Summary*. Washington, D.C., February 19, 2010.

United States Department of State, Bureau of Diplomatic Security. "1993 World Trade Center Bombing." Washington, D.C., February 21, 2019. https://www.state.gov/1993-world-trade-center-bombing/.

United States General Accounting Office. *September 11: More Effective Collaboration Could Enhance Charitable Organizations' Contributions in Disasters: Report to the Ranking Minority Member, Committee on Finance, U.S. Senate.* Washington, D.C.: GAO, 2002.

Uniting and Strengthening America by Providing Appropriate Tools Required to Intercept and Obstruct Terrorism (USA PATRIOT ACT) Act of 2001, Pub. L. 107-56, October 26, 2001.

University at Albany. "Higher Education in a Post-9/11 World: Q&a with UAlbany Assistant Professor of Educational Administration and Policy Studies Jason Lane." News release, 2011. https://www.albany.edu/news/16124.php.

University of Liverpool. "Liverpool Announces World Leading 'End-to-End' Pandemic Institute." News release, September 13, 2021. https://news.liverpool.ac.uk/2021/09/13/liverpool-announces-world-leading-end-to-end-pandemic-institute/.

University of Michigan. "New $13.8m Center at U-M Will Study Infectious Disease, Pandemic Preparedness." News release, October 19, 2021. https://news.umich.edu/new-13-8m-center-at-u-m-will-study-infectious-disease-pandemic-preparedness/.

"Update: Novel Influenza A(H1N1) Virus Infections—Worldwide, May 6, 2009." *Morbidity and Mortality Weekly Report* 58, no. 17 (May 8, 2009): 453–58.

Van der Hoeven, Rolph. *MDGS Post 2015: Beacons in Turbulent Times or False Lights?* New York: UN System Task Team, 2012.

Van Kerkhove, M. D., S. Hirve, A. Koukounari, and A. W. Mounts. "Estimating Age-Specific Cumulative Incidence for the 2009 Influenza Pandemic: A Meta-Analysis of a(H1N1)PDM09 Serological Studies from 19 Countries." *Influenza and Other Respiratory Viruses* 7, no. 5 (September 2013): 872–86. https://doi.org/10.1111/irv.12074.

Wainscott, Joe. "Navigating National Incident Management System Training Requirements." *Citeseer*, 2008. https://citeseerx.ist.psu.edu/viewdoc/download?doi=10.1.1.176.5379&rep=rep1&type=pdf.

Wang, Cailin, Jidong Wu, Xin He, Mengqi Ye, Wenhui Liu, and Rumei Tang. "Emerging Trends and New Developments in Disaster Research After the 2008 Wenchuan Earthquake." *International Journal of Environmental Research and Public Health* 16, no. 1 (2019): 29. https://www.mdpi.com/1660-4601/16/1/29.

Webster, Robert G., Yi Guan, Malik Peiris, David Walker, Scott Krauss, Nan Nan Zhou, Elena A. Govorkova, et al. "Characterization of H5N1 Influenza Viruses That Continue to Circulate in Geese in Southeastern China." *Journal of Virology* 76, no. 1 (2002): 118–26. https://doi.org/10.1128/jvi.76.1.118-126.2002.

Wenham, Clare. "What We Have Learnt About the World Health Organization from the Ebola Outbreak." *Philosophical Transactions of the Royal Society of London. Series B, Biological Sciences* 372, no. 1721 (2017): 20160307. https://doi.org/10.1098/rstb.2016.0307.

White House. "Executive Orders Issued by President George W. Bush." 2009. https://georgewbush-whitehouse.archives.gov/news/orders/.

——. "Fact Sheet: Emergency Funding Request to Enhance the U.S. Government's Response to Ebola at Home and Abroad." News release, November 5, 2014, https://obamawhitehouse.archives.gov/the-press-office/2014/11/05/fact-sheet-emergency-funding-request-enhance-us-government-s-response-eb.

Willison, Charley E., Phillip M. Singer, Melissa S. Creary, and Scott L. Greer. "Quantifying Inequities in US Federal Response to Hurricane Disaster in Texas and Florida Compared with Puerto Rico." *BMJ Global Health* 4, no. 1 (2019): e001191.

Wilson, Jennifer, and Arthur Oyola-Yemaiel. "The Evolution of Emergency Management and the Advancement Towards a Profession in the United States and Florida." *Safety Science* 39, no. 1–2 (2001): 117–31.

Wilson, Kumanan, Sam Halabi, and Lawrence O. Gostin. "The International Health Regulations (2005), the Threat of Populism and the Covid-19 Pandemic." *Globalization and Health* 16, no. 1 (July 28, 2020): 70. https://doi.org/10.1186/s12992-020-00600-4.

Woiwode, Hendrik, and Anna Froese. "Two Hearts Beating in a Research Centers' Chest: How Scholars in Interdisciplinary Research Settings Cope with Monodisciplinary Deep Structures." *Studies in Higher Education* 46, no. 11 (2021): 2230–44. https://doi.org/10.1080/03075079.2020.1716321.

Woods, Robert. "Ancient and Early Modern Mortality: Experience and Understanding." *Economic History Review* 60, no. 2 (2007): 373–99. https://doi.org/10.1111/j.1468-0289.2006.00367.x.

World Bank. *2014–2015 West Africa Ebola Crisis: Impact Update.* (2016). https://www.worldbank.org/en/topic/macroeconomics/publication/2014-2015-west-africa-ebola-crisis-impact-update.

World Health Assembly. *Resolution WHA58.3: Revision of the International Health Regulations* Geneva: World Health Assembly, May 23, 2005.

——. *Resolution WHA58.5: Strengthening Pandemic-Influenza Preparedness and Response.* Geneva: World Health Assembly, May 23, 2005.

World Health Organization. "Cumulative Number of Confirmed Human Cases for Avian Influenza A(H5N1) Reported to WHO, 2003–2023, 24 April 2023." Accessed April 24, 2023. https://www.who.int/publications/m/item/cumulative-number-of-confirmed-human-cases-for-avian-influenza-a(h5n1)-reported-to-who-2003-2023-24-april-2023.

——. "Cumulative Number of Reported Probable Cases of SARS." Emergencies Preparedness, Response. Accessed February 3, 2021. https://www.who.int/csr/sars/country/2003_07_11/en/.

——. *Pandemic Influenza Preparedness Framework for the Sharing of Influenza Viruses and Access to Vaccines and Other Benefits.* 2nd ed. Geneva: WHO, 2021.

——. *Revision of the International Health Regulations: Report by the Secretariat.* Geneva: WHO, May 16, 2003.

——. *WHO Inter-Country Consultation: Influenza A/H5N1 in Humans in Asia.* Geneva: WHO, 2005.

——. "World Bank to Work Together with WHO to Set up Secretariat at the World Bank, with WHO as Lead Technical Partner." News release, June 30, 2022.

https://www.who.int/news/item/30-06-2022-world-bank-board-approves-new -fund-for-pandemic-prevention—preparedness-and-response-(ppr).

Wright, Richard N. *Building and Fire Research at NBS/NIST 1975–2000.* Gaithersburg, Md.: National Institute of Standards and Technology, December 2003. https:// www.nist.gov/publications/building-and-fire-research-nbsnist-1975-2000.

WWF Australia. "Australia's 2019–2020 Bushfires: The Wildlife Toll," June 1, 2020.

Ye, Min. "The COVID-19 Effect: US-China Narratives and Realities." *Washington Quarterly* 44, no. 1 (2021): 89–105.

Yi, Honglei, and Jay Yang. "Research Trends of Post Disaster Reconstruction: The Past and the Future." *Habitat International* 42 (2014): 21–29. https://doi.org/10.1016/j .habitatint.2013.10.005.

Zandi, Mark. "The Economic Impact of Sandy." *Moody's Analytics*, November 1, 2012.

Zimmermann, Doron. "The European Union and Post-9/11 Counterterrorism: A Reappraisal." *Studies in Conflict & Terrorism* 29, no. 2 (2006): 123–45.

INDEX

GPSR Authorized Representative: Easy Access System Europe, Mustamäe tee
50, 10621 Tallinn, Estonia, gpsr.requests@easproject.com

www.ingramcontent.com/pod-product-compliance
Lightning Source LLC
Chambersburg PA
CBHW021857020426
42334CB00013B/371